International Normalcy

THE OPEN DOOR PEACE
WITH THE FORMER
CENTRAL POWERS, 1921–29

International Normalcy

THE OPEN DOOR PEACE WITH THE FORMER CENTRAL POWERS, 1921–29

by
Peter H. Buckingham

SR *Scholarly Resources Inc.*
Wilmington, Delaware

Scholarly Resources Inc.
104 Greenhill Avenue
Wilmington, Delaware 19805

Library of Congress Cataloging in Publication Data

Buckingham, Peter H., 1948–
   International normalcy.

   Bibliography: p.
   Includes index.
   1. World War, 1914–1918—Peace. 2. World War,
1914–1918—Reparations. 3. Europe—Foreign relations—
United States. 4. United States—Foreign Relations—
Europe. 5. United States—Foreign relations—Turkey.
6. Turkey—Foreign relations—United States. I. Title.
D644.B85   1983   327.7304   83-18935
ISBN 0-8420-2215-5

ACKNOWLEDGMENTS

In the process of researching and writing this book, I have accumulated debts that cannot be repaid and friendships which will last a lifetime. A grant from the Herbert Hoover Presidential Library in West Branch, Iowa, provided the funds which allowed me to complete the research. In addition to the most excellent staff at the Hoover Library, I wish to thank the librarians and archivists at the Bancroft Library, University of California at Berkeley; the Hoover Institution on War, Revolution and Peace, Stanford University; the Library of Congress; the National Archives; and the Houghton Library, Harvard University.

I would also like to express my deep appreciation to several outstanding educators for giving me the benefit of their wise and spirited counsel through the years: Norman O. Forness and Charles H. Glatfelter of Gettysburg College; LeRoy Ashby, Patrick Morgan, Howard Payne, and David Stratton of Washington State University; and Richard Dean Burns of California State University, Los Angeles. Most of all, my thanks go to Edward M. Bennett, who believed in this project when it was just an idea and helped to shape it from the beginning. This book is dedicated to my parents, Jean and Henry Buckingham, for all their love and support.

CONTENTS

INTRODUCTION

On 14 May 1920, a month before his nomination to the presidency, Warren Gamaliel Harding told an audience in Boston that "America's present need is not heroics, but healing; not nostrums but normalcy."[1] The spurious hybrid "normalcy" caught on during the campaign because it seemed to capture a public yearning. Journalist Mark Sullivan believed that most people in 1920 did not long for a return to any particular time or place. Rather, normalcy expressed the common man's general discontent with the uncertainties of the postwar period; it was a desire for settled ways, for a set routine, and for a world made comprehensible again.[2] "By 'normalcy,'" Harding explained, "I do not mean the old order, but a regular, steady order of things. I mean normal procedure, the natural way, without excess."[3] In no area was the yearning for a return to "normal procedure" greater than in foreign affairs.

Charles Evans Hughes became Harding's secretary of state at a time when American foreign policy had been in limbo for over two years following a bitter disagreement between President Woodrow Wilson and Congress over how to make peace with the former Central Powers. On 4 March 1921 Wilson left the White House for retirement a broken man. His face, twisted with pain and emotion, and his frail figure embodied the paralyzed state of American foreign affairs. Yet the day was not a sad one for the United States; the inauguration of a healthy, buoyant new president seemed to hold the implicit promise of a break in the foreign policy deadlock. In time the new administration ended the stalemate, but the diplomatic and economic "normalcy" of Harding, Hughes, and their successors had much more in common with Wilsonian internationalism than either side would have cared to admit.

On the surface the Wilson and Harding administrations had totally different conceptions of American foreign policy. Harding and Hughes took

---

[1]Speech before the Home Market Club, Boston, 14 May 1920, Warren G. Harding Papers, microfilm, reel 238, Ohio Historical Society, Columbus, OH (hereafter cited as Harding Papers).

[2]Mark Sullivan, *Our Times, 1900–1925,* vol. 2, *The Twenties* (New York: Charles Scribner's Sons, 1946), p. 1. See also John F. Wilson, "Harding's Rhetoric of Normalcy, 1920–1923," *Quarterly Journal of Speech* 48 (December 1962): 406–11.

[3]*New York Times*, 21 July 1920, p. 7.

credit for the return of the traditional American policy of freedom from entangling alliances. Nevertheless, during his last eighteen months in office, President Wilson began the return to political isolation from Europe even before the Senate's final rejection of the Treaty of Versailles. Wilson refused to send representatives to the Brussels Conference on reparations. Shortly thereafter the president ordered the ambassador to France to withdraw from the Council of Ambassadors. He also told the unofficial American observer on the Reparation Commission not to sit in on further meetings. Wilson even refused to make arrangements for American participation in a forthcoming International Road Congress.[4]

To be sure, Wilson's bitter political defeats in the Senate and in the 1920 election had much to do with his retreat from involvement in European affairs. William R. Castle, Jr., chief of the European Division in the Department of State, charged privately that the president withdrew American representation on the Reparation Commission in "a deliberate effort to sabotage useful activities . . . to make it harder for the incoming Administration."[5] Wilson's reversion to isolation was also motivated by a growing suspicion of Britain and France and by disenchantment with the great crusade to make the world safe for democracy—and its aftermath—feelings he shared with millions of disillusioned voters who turned to the man promising normalcy.[6] As a leading scholar of Wilsonian diplomacy has noted, it was Wilson who pointed the way toward the limited internationalism of the 1920s.[7]

Wilsonians and moderate Republicans such as Hughes and Herbert Clark Hoover, the two most prominent members of the Harding cabinet, and even Wilson's great enemy, Henry Cabot Lodge, shared far more than disillusionment with European affairs. They wanted the United States to take the lead in promoting disarmament and the Open Door policy to assure future American prosperity. The quarrel between Democrats and Republicans arose over how to achieve these ends. Wilson and his followers advocated a strong League of Nations armed with the power to punish aggressor states through collective security. The Republicans would only endorse a League without the enforcement provisions out of fear that a strong international body might drag the nation into future foreign wars while placing possible limitations on American freedom of action. After the Treaty of Versailles failed to pass the Senate,

---

    [4]Keith L. Nelson, *Victors Divided: America and the Allies in Germany, 1918–1923* (Berkeley: University of California Press, 1975), p. 179; Daniel M. Smith, *Aftermath of War: Bainbridge Colby and Wilsonian Diplomacy, 1920–1921* (Philadelphia: American Philosophical Society, 1970), pp. 53–54.
    [5]Ellis Loring Dresel to William R. Castle, Jr., 4 February 1921, Ellis Loring Dresel Papers, box 68, folder 4, Houghton Library, Harvard University, Cambridge, MA (hereafter cited as Dresel Papers).
    [6]Joseph Brandes, *Herbert Hoover and Economic Diplomacy* (Pittsburgh: University of Pittsburgh Press, 1962), p. 27; William E. Leuchtenburg, *The Perils of Prosperity, 1914–32* (Chicago: University of Chicago Press, 1970), p. 87; Smith, *Aftermath of War*, pp. 54–55.
    [7]Smith, *Aftermath of War*, p. 55.

Republicans took up the idea that peace and prosperity could be achieved through a series of limited piecemeal American-led initiatives including conferences on the reduction of arms, a world court system, and the codification of international law.[8]

Republicans may have opposed Wilson's vision of a League of Nations covenant, but most of them shared his belief in America as the moral and economic leader of the world. They also approved of the Wilsonian revival of the Open Door policy as the chosen instrument of American economic expansion. The Great War accelerated the nation's economic growth, with the United States becoming a net creditor for the first time. After the war, the search for raw materials, new markets, and investment opportunities for surplus capital had to be intensified.[9] Collision with the more advanced empires of Europe seemed certain, especially after the 1916 Paris Economic Conference, when the Entente powers agreed to scrap their unconditional most-favored-nation commercial policy in favor of a system of trade preferences.[10] State Department officials feared that the Allies might extend their military alliance into the economic field. "Should such an economic alliance be formed," Henry P. Fletcher warned, "it would, from the very nature of things, be able to force preferential tariff treatment in the great consuming markets of South America, not only as against present enemies, but also as against ourselves and the rest of the world."[11] After the war, President Wilson resurrected the concept of the Open Door as a peaceful alternative to the commercial imperialism of the Allies. The Harding administration merely had to elaborate on the Open Door framework inherited from the Wilsonians.[12]

[8]John A. Garraty, *Henry Cabot Lodge: A Biography* (New York: Alfred A. Knopf, 1953), p. 399; Carl Parrini, *Heir to Empire: United States Economic Diplomacy 1916–1923* (Pittsburgh: University of Pittsburgh Press, 1969), pp. 13–14; Frank H. Simonds, *American Foreign Policy in the Post-War Years* (Baltimore: Johns Hopkins University Press, 1935), p. 117; Robert Freeman Smith, "American Foreign Relations, 1920–1942," in *Towards A New Past: Dissenting Essays in American History*, ed. Barton J. Bernstein (New York: Random House, 1968), p. 240; Eugene P. Trani and David L. Wilson, *The Presidency of Warren G. Harding* (Lawrence: Regents of Kansas, American Presidency Series, 1977), p. 165; William A. Williams, *The Tragedy of American Diplomacy* (Cleveland: World Press, 1959), pp. 110–11; Joan Hoff Wilson, *American Business and Foreign Policy, 1920–1933* (Lexington: University of Kentucky Press, 1971), p. 25.

[9]Herbert Feis, *The Diplomacy of the Dollar: First Era, 1919–1932* (Baltimore: Johns Hopkins University Press, 1950), pp. 3–10; Smith, "American Foreign Relations," p. 238; Williams, *The Tragedy of American Diplomacy*, pp. 57–60; Wilson, *American Business*, pp. 8–9.

[10]Michael J. Hogan, *Informal Entente: The Private Structure of Cooperation in Anglo-American Diplomacy, 1918–1928* (Columbia: University of Missouri Press, 1977), p. 14; Parrini, *Heir to Empire*, pp. 15–16 and 37–39.

[11]Henry P. Fletcher to Robert Lansing, 13 November 1916, Trade Relations, Tariff Treaties, Arrangements, etc. Between the United States and Foreign Countries, general records of the Department of State, RG 59, 611.0031/138, Decimal Files, Department of State, National Archives, Washington (hereafter cited as DSNA).

[12]Hogan, *Informal Entente*, pp. 16–17; Cordell Hull, *The Memoirs of Cordell Hull*, 2 vols. (New York: Macmillan, 1948), pp. 81–85; Parrini, *Heir to Empire*, p. 142; Williams, *The Tragedy of American Diplomacy*, pp. 80–84; Wilson, *American Business*, p. 187.

4	INTERNATIONAL NORMALCY

In the 1920s American leaders applied the Open Door principle of equal economic opportunity in regions where European investments had been domi-nant. At the same time the United States did not choose to open vast areas of the world—including Central and South America, the Caribbean, and the Philippines—where American businessmen were well entrenched. Republicans offered the Open Door as a means for peaceful and equitable economic expansion for all nations. In reality the rules of the Open Door game benefited the strongest competitor, that is, the country with the most capital surplus, which in the 1920s was the United States.[13]

During the era of normalcy, Republican policymakers pursued American economic expansion through the Open Door, but they could not afford to become involved directly in European politics for domestic political reasons. Wilson had tried to transform the 1920 election into a "solemn referendum" on the Treaty of Versailles.[14] Although Harding defeated his Democratic opponent, James M. Cox, by over seven million votes, historians have been nearly unanimous in echoing Samuel Flagg Bemis's judgment that "the election was not a referendum, nor was it even solemn."[15] Cox ran on an ambiguous platform designed to placate the isolationist wing of the Democratic party, while the Republican candidate found himself caught between such prestigious party elders as Hughes, Elihu Root, and William Howard Taft, who favored American participation in the League of Nations, and "bitter-enders" led by Senators William E. Borah and Hiram Johnson, who were absolutely against it.[16] Harding and two of his speech writers, George Harvey and Richard Washburn Child, worked up a careful formula on the treaty and the League ambiguous enough to be acceptable to all factions.[17] The importance of the 1920 election lay in its psychological impact. Though the reasons for the

[13]Betty Glad, *Charles Evans Hughes and the Illusions of Innocence: A Study in American Diplomacy* (Urbana: University of Illinois Press, 1966), p. 317; Scott Nearing and Joseph Freeman, *Dollar Diplomacy: A Study in American Imperialism* (New York: Monthly Review Press, 1966), p. 274; Mira Wilkens, *The Maturing of Multinational Enterprise: American Business Abroad From 1914–1970* (Cambridge, MA: Harvard University Press, 1974), p. 156; Wilson, *American Business*, pp. 9–10 and 18.
[14]Thomas A. Bailey, *Woodrow Wilson and the Great Betrayal* (Chicago: Quadrangle, 1963), p. 294; Jean-Baptiste Duroselle, *From Wilson to Roosevelt: Foreign Policy of the United States, 1913–1945*, trans. Nancy Lyman Roelker (Cambridge, MA: Harvard University Press, 1963), p. 125.
[15]Samuel Flagg Bemis, *The United States as a World Power: A Diplomatic History, 1900–1955* (New York: Henry Holt, 1955), p. 187. See also Wesley M. Bagby, *The Road to Normalcy: The Presidential Campaign and Election of 1920*, Johns Hopkins University Studies in Historical and Political Science (Baltimore: Johns Hopkins University Press, 1962), 80:160–61.
[16]Selig Adler, *The Isolationist Impulse: Its Twentieth Century Reaction* (New York: Collier, 1961), pp. 105–9; Duroselle, *From Wilson to Roosevelt*, p. 126; Leuchtenburg, *The Perils of Prosperity*, p. 87; Ralph Stone, *The Irreconcilables: The Fight Against the League of Nations* (Lexington: University of Kentucky Press, 1970), p. 176; Sullivan, *The Twenties*, pp. 109–10.
[17]Sullivan, *The Twenties*, pp. 120–23.

landslide were complex, popular opinion pinned the Democratic defeat on Wilson's peace policy. The lesson seemed clear to both Democrats and Republicans: Wilsonian internationalism was out.[18]

The irreconcilables of the Senate who had opposed the entire Treaty of Versailles remained a powerful force after the 1920 election. Ideologically and geographically, the fourteen Republicans and two Democrats were a very diverse group. A prominent student of the irreconcilable movement has divided them into three factions: the peace progressives, the realists, and the supernationalists. Robert La Follette and his fellow peace progressives opposed the League as too devoted to an unjust world status quo. Philander C. Knox, leader of the realist faction, objected to the moral foundation of Wilson's New Diplomacy, preferring traditional military alliances as the surest base for national security. The supernationalists, including Borah, Johnson, and James Reed, shared La Follette's disgust with a league of the victors and Knox's chauvinism, but they also advocated strict adherence to the Founding Fathers' dictum of no entangling alliances. Even though eighty of the ninety-six senators approved of the Treaty of Versailles in some form, the irreconcilables managed to defeat it through hard work, clever parliamentary maneuvers, and a rather one-sided alliance with the chairman of the Foreign Relations Committee, Henry Cabot Lodge.[19]

The widespread print coverage of the treaty debate caused the public to view the Senate in general and the irreconcilables in particular as the most dynamic force in national politics.[20] When the Harding administration took office, the Senate Foreign Relations Committee, which Lodge and the irreconcilables still dominated, stood ready to guard against State Department gestures in the direction of international cooperation. Some senators even favored a congressional takeover of traditional executive powers in the field of foreign policy.

Personally Harding seemed inclined toward a rather weak and docile presidency and, after Wilson, that was just the way many members of Congress wanted it.[21] In spite of his years on the Foreign Relations Committee, the new president had a very limited knowledge of foreign affairs. He once told correspondent Arthur S. Draper, "I don't know anything about this European stuff," and his understanding of the complicated Eastern Question was equally unsophisticated.[22] Harding was a smart political operator, but utterly incapable of being his own secretary of state. His old friends in the Senate, especially Borah, tried to steer him toward Knox as secretary of state. When Harding

---

[18] Adler, *Isolationist Impulse*, pp. 104–10; Stone, *The Irreconcilables*, p. 176.

[19] Stone, *The Irreconcilables*, pp. 178–88.

[20] Robert K. Murray, *The Politics of Normalcy: Governmental Theory and Practice in the Harding–Coolidge Era* (New York: W. W. Norton, 1973), p. 41.

[21] Ibid., pp. 42–43; Trani and Wilson, *Harding*, p. 115.

[22] Quoted in Francis Russell, *The Shadow of Blooming Grove: Warren G. Harding in His Times* (New York: McGraw-Hill, 1968), p. 452.

named Hughes to the post instead, Senator Boies Penrose professed noncha-
lance. "I do not think that it matters much who is Secretary of State," the
Pennsylvanian told reporters, "Congress—especially the Senate—will blaze
the way in connection with our foreign policies."[23] Privately, however, Harding's choice infuriated Penrose and several of his colleagues.

In contrast to Harding, Hughes had a brilliant legal mind and a good
general background in international affairs, although he was, as Theodore
Roosevelt once remarked, "a bearded iceberg," with little feeling for the
public mood.[24] Roosevelt, who had been something of a political mentor to
Hughes, told William Allen White in 1916, "I think Hughes is a man of the
Wilson type; I think he is little better than Wilson."[25] Many of the irreconcilables, including Borah and Johnson, and other Republicans, such as Penrose
and Lodge, shared Roosevelt's antipathy toward the "whiskered Wilson."[26]
Not only was Hughes an internationalist, but he promised to be a stubborn
and strong opponent in the impending tug-of-war over control of foreign
policy. Harding and Hughes would have something of a symbiotic relationship,
with the president gladly leaving management of foreign affairs to Hughes
while the secretary of state counted on Harding for political savoir faire.[27]

Although the dominant mood in the Senate and the country at large
seemed to demand a policy of limited political internationalism, Wilsonianism
did not die out in the 1920s. The influential *Independent* magazine, the *New
York Times*, and many other newspapers and periodicals continued to advocate
bits and pieces of Wilson's New Diplomacy. Democrats inside and outside
of Congress still looked to Wilson and his former floor managers for leadership
and advice. Many important Republicans, among them Hughes and Hoover,
sympathized with conservative eastern banking interests which had found
Wilsonian internationalism to be quite compatible with their growing overseas
investments.[28]

The Republicans came into office determined to avoid repeating Wilson's
misguided entry into the vortex of international politics. Instead, they hoped

---

[23]Quoted in Trani and Wilson, *Harding*, p. 110

[24]Robert K. Murray, *The Harding Era: Warren G. Harding and His Administration*
(Minneapolis: University of Minnesota Press, 1969), p. 132; Russell, *Shadow of Blooming Grove*,
p. 271.

[25]"T. R. on the Telephone," in *A Treasury of American Heritage: A Selection From the
First Five Years of the Magazine of History*, ed. John A. Garraty (New York: Simon and Schuster,
1960), p. 357.

[26]Robert J. Maddox, *William E. Borah and American Foreign Policy* (Baton Rouge:
Louisiana State University Press, 1969), p. 84; Russell, *Shadow of Blooming Grove*, p. 433;
William Allen White, *The Autobiography of William Allen White* (New York: Macmillan, 1946),
p. 531.

[27]Glad, *Illusions of Innocence*, p. 141; Murray, *The Harding Era*, p. 133; Bertram D.
Hulen, *Inside the Department of State* (York: Maple Press, 1939), pp. 49–51.

[28]Adler, *Isolationist Impulse*, p. 139; Selig Adler, *The Uncertain Giant, 1921–1941*
(London: Collier, 1965), p. 49.

to focus on a conservative domestic program of tax cuts, a balanced budget, reduced government expenditures, and protection of home industries designed to return the nation to pre-Wilsonian normalcy. The new policymakers also realized that there could be no real economic normalcy at home without a concomitant revival in trade with Europe, which was running well below prewar figures.[29] "The stabilization of the European economic situation," Herbert Hoover wrote, "should result in a revival in the volume of world trade, in which our country is bound to have its share."[30] Shattered Europe seemed incapable of rehabilitating itself; so, a compelling argument could be made that it was in America's own best interest to help the Europeans to straighten out their affairs. But how to do this without becoming involved in the nether world of international power politics? This was the central dilemma facing the Republicans in the 1920s.

Wilson bequeathed a mountain of problems to his successors. In foreign affairs the most serious questions facing Hughes grew out of American participation in the late war. Because the Senate had declined to ratify the Treaty of Versailles and the president and his secretary of state, Bainbridge Colby, had rejected German offers of "a separate treaty following a declared peace," the new administration found the United States still technically at war with the Central Powers nearly two and one half years after the armistice.[31] Some sort of arrangements would have to be made as a prelude to a claims settlement and renewed commercial intercourse—and to safeguard America's fruits of victory as one of the Allies. Personally Hughes favored ratification of the Treaty of Versailles with reservations as the most practical way of making peace, but there was some question as to how much, if any, of that treaty the Senate would accept.[32]

Hughes and Harding also had to reckon with five areas of serious disagreement between the United States and its erstwhile wartime friends: disposition of former German overseas territories, Near Eastern policy, the Open Door, reparations, and war debts. In one of the many secret treaties made among the Allies during the war, Japan and Great Britain had agreed to divide Germany's Pacific island outposts between them. Japan took everything north of the equator, while the British took German possessions to the south. At the Paris Peace Conference, the Allies sanctioned this arrangement

[29]Melvyn P. Leffler, *The Elusive Quest: America's Pursuit of European Stability and French Security, 1913–1933* (Chapel Hill: University of North Carolina Press, 1978), pp. ix and 41–42.
[30]Herbert Hoover, "The Effect Upon the United States of a Settlement of Europe's Economic Problems," Box 11, Herbert Hoover Papers, Hoover Institution on War, Revolution and Peace, Stanford University, Stanford, CA (hereafter cited as Hoover Papers, Hoover Institution).
[31]The commissioner at Berlin (Dresel) to secretary of state, 15 January 1921, RG59, 711.62119/–DSNA. For Colby's reply, see secretary of state to the high commissioner at Berlin (Dresel), 16 January 1921, ibid.
[32]Merlo J. Pusey, *Charles Evans Hughes*, 2 vols. (New York: Macmillan, 1951), p. 431.

in spite of American protests, assigning the islands to Japan and Britain as mandates. The Japanese mandate over Yap in the Carolines had vexed Wilson especially because of the island's importance as a cable center. Subsequently the United States refused to recognize the Yap mandate. Hughes, like Wilson before him, pressed for recognition of American rights as one of the five Principal Allied and Associated Powers.[33]

Although they fought on opposite sides during the Great War, the United States and Turkey never declared war on each other. The Near Eastern peace settlement still interested Americans for economic and humanitarian reasons. The war had demonstrated the importance of petroleum to any modern military machine; after the armistice, as the automobile came of age, public demands grew for inexpensive fuel in great quantities. The U.S. Geological Survey estimated domestic oil reserves at only twelve years with new discoveries declining, so that increasing American petroleum holdings abroad seemed a matter of national security.[34] "We must go into foreign fields," Herbert Hoover warned, "and in a big way."[35] Exploitation in the American closed-door regions of the New World was a fairly easy task, but most of the world's known oil reserves lay in the Near East, and the Allies had shut the economic door to that area by virtue of the San Remo Agreement.

France and Great Britain partitioned the remnants of the Ottoman Empire between them at San Remo in 1920, with the British awarding themselves mandates over Palestine and Mesopotamia, while acquiescing in French mandates for Lebanon and Syria. This dividing of the spoils marked a triumph for the Turkish Petroleum Company, an international cartel of state and private British, French, and Dutch oil interests which had been granted a monopoly in Mesopotamia by the Turkish sultan just before the war. Convinced that this was part of a British plot to monopolize the world oil supply, Secretary of State Colby protested that the San Remo sphere-grabbing violated the principle of equal treatment reached at Versailles.[36] British Secretary of State

[33]Thomas H. Buckley, *The United States and the Washington Conference, 1921–1922* (Knoxville: University of Tennessee Press, 1970), p. 142; Arthur S. Link, *Wilson the Diplomatist: A Look at His Major Foreign Policies* (Chicago: Quadrangle, 1965), pp. 112–13; Smith, *Aftermath of War*, pp. 89–92; John Chalmers Vinson, *The Parchment Peace: The United States and the Washington Conference, 1921–1922* (Athens: University of Georgia Press, 1955), p. 44.

[34]Raymond L. Buell, "Oil Interests in the Fight for Mosul," *Current History* (March 1923): 933–35; Feis, *Diplomacy of the Dollar*, pp. 48–55; John D. Hicks, *Republican Ascendency, 1921–1933* (New York: Harper and Row, 1963), pp. 27–28; Herbert Hoover, *The Memoirs of Herbert Hoover*, vol. 2, *The Cabinet and the Presidency* (New York: Macmillan, 1952), p. 69; Leonard Mosley, *Power Play: Oil In the Middle East* (New York: Random House, 1973), p. 115; Murray, *Harding Era*, p. 356; Benjamin Shwadran, *The Middle East, Oil and the Great Powers* (New York: Frederick A. Praeger, 1955), p. 216; Wilkens, *Multinational Enterprise*, pp. 50 and 113.

[35]Quoted in Edward M. Earle, "Oil and American Foreign Policy," *New Republic*, 20 August 1924, p. 355.

[36]George S. Gibb and Evelyn H. Knowlton, *History of Standard Oil Company (New Jersey)*, vol. 2, *The Resurgent Years, 1911–1927* (New York: Harper and Brothers, 1956), pp.

for Foreign Affairs George Nathaniel, the Earl (later Marquess) Curzon of Kedleston, expressed outrage that the Americans, who already controlled 80 percent of the world's oil, should complain about European attempts to solve their own petroleum shortage.[37] The controversy over Allied imperialism in the Levant continued into 1921, with incoming Secretary of State Hughes "convinced of the soundness of our position."[38]

Americans had become very interested in the fate of the Armenians, a small Christian minority within the Ottoman Empire. The Turks allowed the Armenians to practice their religion freely during the nineteenth century until 1895 when, with the encouragement of American missionaries, they revolted unsuccessfully against their overlords. In 1915 the Armenians rebelled again; this time, Turkey, preoccupied with the war and fearful of an Allied fifth column within its borders, massacred thousands of Christians. American missionary groups began a propaganda campaign against Turkey and for Armenian relief and independence.[39] The "Terrible Turk" became as hated in wartime America as "the Boche," even though the Americans and the Turks never fired a shot at one another on the battlefield.

"I have set my heart," President Wilson wrote in 1920, "on seeing this Government accept the mandate for Armenia."[40] After an intensive lobbying effort by missionary and philanthropic groups, the Senate rejected Wilson's scheme out of a belief that the mandate might drag the United States into another war.[41] Armenia played a prominent part in the 1920 presidential campaign, with the Republicans against accepting the mandate and the Democrats in favor of "every possible and proper aid for Armenian autonomy."[42]

282–89; John Isle, *The United States Oil Policy* (New Haven, CT: Yale University Press, 1926), pp. 473–75; Stephen H. Longrigg, *Oil in the Middle East: Its Discovery and Development* (London: Oxford University Press, 1968), pp. 42–44; Shwadran, *Middle East, Oil*, pp. 215–16; Smith, *Aftermath of War*, pp. 46–48.

[37]Smith, *Aftermath of War*, p. 49.

[38]Charles Evans Hughes, *The Autobiographical Notes of Charles Evans Hughes*, eds. David J. Danelski and Joseph S. Tulchin (Cambridge, MA: Harvard University Press, 1973), p. 255.

[39]Robert L. Daniel, *American Philanthropy in the Near East, 1820–1960* (Athens: Ohio State University Press, 1970), pp. 157–61; Robert L. Daniel, "The Armenian Question and Turkish-American Relations, 1914–1927," *Mississippi Valley Historical Review* 46 (June 1959): 252–56; John A. DeNovo, *American Interests and Policies in the Middle East, 1900–1939* (Minneapolis: University of Minnesota Press, 1963), pp. 98–105; Laurence Evans, *United States Policy and the Partition of Turkey, 1914–1924* (Baltimore: Johns Hopkins University Press, 1950), pp. 73–74; Joseph L. Grabill, *Protestant Diplomacy in the Near East* (Minneapolis: University of Minnesota Press, 1971), pp. 155–85; Roger R. Trask, *The United States Response to Turkish Nationalism and Reform, 1914–1939* (Minneapolis: University of Minnesota Press, 1971), pp. 26–27.

[40]Quoted in Smith, *Aftermath of War*, p. 41.

[41]Daniel, "The Armenian Question," p. 264; Grabill, *Protestant Diplomacy*, p. 246.

[42]Kirk H. Porter and Donald Bruce Johnson, eds., *National Party Platforms, 1840–1960* (Urbana: University of Illinois Press, 1961), pp. 222 and 230–31.

Church groups bombarded President-elect Harding with petitions on behalf of emancipation, a pressure campaign which Hughes found especially embarrassing since he had once headed the American Committee for the Independence of Armenia.[43] The American concern for Armenia—and for future access to oil—forced the new administration to turn its attention to the Near East in spite of the trend toward political isolation.

Great Britain, France, and the United States had fundamental differences over reparations. In the Treaty of Versailles, the French compromised on their desire to put Germany into a permanent position of artificial inferiority.[44] The resulting peace left Germany far stronger than the French had wished, but American and British leaders promised automatic assistance in case of German attack. Unfortunately for France, the Americans never ratified the Treaty of Guarantee, a situation which automatically released "perfidious Albion" from its part in the pact. France then felt forced to use reparations unilaterally as the major bulwark against a resurgent Germany, while they attempted to negotiate a substitute for the Treaty of Guarantee with the new nations of Eastern Europe.[45]

American leaders opposed high German indemnities for the same reason that France insisted upon them: Reparations would retard German economic recovery. Because Germany was the industrial heart of the continent, American economists feared that German stagnation would spread to Eastern Europe, thus spoiling a vital area for trade with the United States. Furthermore, such a narrowed world market might produce a war among the big powers as it had in 1914. The artificial inferiority of Germany, the Americans believed, could lead to a xenophobic nationalism among the German people, and that too could lead to another great conflict.[46]

Wilson fought long and hard at Paris for the establishment of a Reparation Commission with the power to set up a payment schedule for a fixed period based on Germany's capacity to pay. As the conference dragged on, with Wilson ill and his chief adviser, Colonel Edward M. House, weary of the endless haggling over details, the Americans finally gave in to the French demands that the commission merely compute the amount of damages and enforce its payment in full.[47] When Hughes and Harding came into office in

---

[43]Pusey, *Charles Evans Hughes*, p. 574.

[44]Howard C. Payne, Raymond Callahan, and Edward M. Bennett, *As the Storm Clouds Gathered: European Perceptions of American Foreign Policy in the 1930's* (Durham, NC: Moore, 1979), pp. 4–5.

[45]Ibid., pp. 4–7; Stephan A. Schuker, *The End of French Predominance in Europe: The Financial Crisis of 1924 and the Adoption of the Dawes Plan* (Chapel Hill: University of North Carolina Press, 1976), pp. 4–6. See also Nelson, *Victors Divided*, pp. 67, 80–87, and 128.

[46]Carl Parrini, "Reparations," in *Encyclopedia of American Foreign Policy, Studies of the Principal Movements and Ideas*, ed. Alexander DeConde, 3 vols. (New York: Charles Scribner's Sons, 1978), p. 895; Schuker, *End of French Predominance*, p. 5.

[47]Duroselle, *From Wilson to Roosevelt*, pp. 98–101; Link, *Wilson the Diplomatist*, pp. 111–12; Charles Seymour, *The Intimate Papers of Colonel House*, 4 vols. (Boston: Houghton Mifflin, 1926), 4:402–5.

March 1921, the Allies still had not settled on the total amounts due the victors. Americans were united on the question of Allied indebtedness resulting from the war; Wilsonians and Republicans alike contended that moral nations, like moral men, should pay their debts in full.[48] The problem, of course, was not that simple. Seventy-five percent of the American loans went to financially solvent France and Britain, countries which had in turn lent their Entente partner, Imperial Russia, billions which the czar's Bolshevik successors refused to repay. The Europeans could remunerate the United States with goods and services, but the Americans were in the process of erecting high tariff barriers to protect industry at home. When France and Britain suggested, quite logically, recognition of a direct connection between the reduction in reparations, which the United States favored, and a downward revision of interallied debts, the Americans declined consistently to link the two problems despite the fact that the Europeans could pay their debts only through the collection of reparations.[49]

Policymakers such as Colonel House and Secretary Hughes advocated privately a realistic package settlement of reparations and debts, but the public and many congressional leaders were not ready to face that solution.[50] The irreconcilables went a step further, refusing even to see that full collection of the billions Britain and France owed meant inevitable American involvement in European political and economic affairs.[51] As a result, mutual indignation built up between the United States and its former partners, especially France, and American leaders could not act until disaster struck, even though men like Hughes saw it coming.

The most vexing of the war-related problems confronting the new administration concerned trade. From his post in Berlin, the American commissioner, Ellis Loring Dresel, wrote to Hoover, "I believe we should at the earliest moment make plans to develop intensively our trade with Germany, as otherwise we run the risk of losing one of our best markets."[52] Hughes and Hoover shared Dresel's sense of urgency; however, the restoration of diplomatic relations with former enemies and the clearing up of significant differences with former allies would have to be accomplished before embarking on any serious program aimed at the development of commercial intercourse with Central Europe.[53] Furthermore, the majority of America's commercial treaties,

---

[48]Duroselle, *From Wilson to Roosevelt*, p. 148; Glad, *Illusions of Innocence*, p. 218; Leuchtenburg, *Perils of Prosperity*, p. 110; Wilson, *American Business*, p. 125.

[49]Leuchtenburg, *Perils of Prosperity*, pp. 110–11; Payne, Callahan, and Bennett, *Storm Clouds*, pp. 6–7; Schuker, *End of French Predominance*, pp. 9–10.

[50]Glad, *Illusions of Innocence*, p. 218; Seymour, *Colonel House*, 4:500–503.

[51]Glad, *Illusions of Innocence*, p. 218.

[52]Dresel to Hoover, 28 May 1921, Herbert Hoover Department of Commerce Papers, box 184, Herbert Hoover Presidential Library, West Branch, IA (hereafter cited as Hoover Papers, HHL).

[53]Hoover to Dresel, 17 June 1921, ibid.

as products of the nineteenth century, had long since outlived time and circumstances. Wilson laid the foundation for a modern international economic policy through his advocacy of freer trade and the Open Door, ideas which made sense to moderate Republicans and their friends in the business community. But a majority in Congress and the newly elected president seemed bent on protecting home industries, regardless of the cost to long-range American interests. Internationalist Republicans, then, faced a seemingly insurmountable task: They had to return the nation to diplomatic and economic "normalcy" while updating commercial policy to safeguard the future.

This study will analyze the attitudes and actions of the United States, both official and unofficial, with regard to peacemaking efforts with the former Central Powers. Several factors dictated Hughes's course in the separate peace settlements. First, he had to renew diplomatic ties with Germany, Austria, Hungary, and Turkey. Second, the secretary of state maneuvered for the impending showdown with the Allies over postwar economic dominance. Finally, this political and economic activity in Europe and the Near East, which many viewed as essential for future American prosperity, had significant domestic ramifications as well. Thus, notable attention is given both to American relations with France, Great Britain, and Japan and internal American political and economic developments in this analysis of United States policy toward the former Central Powers. These considerations interacted upon one another in such a fashion to limit the effectiveness of American foreign policy in spite of the laborious and often resourceful efforts of Hughes and other Republicans to continue Wilson's search for a stable world order.

1

PEACEMAKING, 1921
The Separate American Peace With
Germany, Austria, and Hungary

Secretary of State-designate Hughes, like President Wilson before him, advocated ratification of the Treaty of Versailles and American entrance into the League of Nations. Hughes believed that Wilson had blundered in his insistence upon linking the League with the treaty, a mistake which made the League not an impartial international organization dedicated to world peace, but a mechanism for maintaining the status quo as defined by the Allies at the Paris Peace Conference. The League covenant, Hughes had written in 1919, "ascribes a prescience and soundness of judgment to the present Peace Conference in erecting States and defining boundaries which no body in the history of the world has ever possessed." The linkage between the treaty and the League made the covenant too inflexible. "It gives no fair opportunity for adjustments," he concluded. "It is in the teeth of experience."[1] Yet if the League could be divorced from the Treaty of Versailles, it might be transformed into a true international forum for the promotion of peace and prosperity. Hughes set out to put his idea into practice even before assuming control of the Department of State.

In February of 1921, the secretary-designate invited the French ambassador in Washington, Jean Jules Jusserand, to his New York apartment. Ostensibly it was to be just a friendly chat between two old acquaintances, but Hughes used the occasion to launch a diplomatic trial balloon. How would the French government react to the possibility of separating the League from the Versailles Treaty in order to make it an independent peace organization rather than an engine to enforce the treaty? Hughes discussed the idea cautiously without making any firm commitments. During the course of their

---

[1]Beerits's memorandum, "The Separate Peace with Germany, the League of Nations, and the Permanent Court of International Justice," in Charles Evans Hughes Papers, box 172, folder 25, pp. 6–7, Library of Congress, Manuscript Division, Washington (hereafter cited as Hughes Papers). In 1933 Hughes hired Henry Beerits, a young Princeton graduate, to arrange his papers and write a series of essays on his public career, anticipating the day when he might write his memoirs. See Hughes, *Autobiographical Notes*, pp. xi and 2.

conversation the French ambassador made it very clear that the scheme did not interest the Third Republic. For France, as Hughes had suspected, the League existed primarily to safeguard the harsh peace of the victors.[2] There would be no help from the only remaining great power on the continent of Europe in Hughes's quest to make the impending peace settlement between the United States and the former Central Powers more palatable to the Republicans.

In spite of the French rebuff, Secretary Hughes continued to advocate ratification of the Versailles Treaty with reservations designed to minimize the American commitment to collective security and maximize American freedom of action. When the irreconcilables indicated that they would not accept the treaty under any circumstances, the secretary created a new pact, one which included a congressional resolution ending the state of war and numbered references to the Treaty of Versailles confirming American rights as a victorious power. This strategy avoided the endless diplomatic problems surrounding the negotiation of an entirely new basis for peace and a political confrontation with the bitter-enders and their many friends over the acceptance of the inevitable obligations that went along with the advantages in the Versailles pact. Hughes made a one-sided peace with Germany, and then Austria and Hungary, but found the whole process to be distasteful from a philosophical viewpoint. He persevered in order to break the domestic deadlock between the executive and congressional branches of government over foreign affairs, a stalemate which had proven very harmful to American economic interests overseas. Circumstances forced the secretary of state to make a most un-Wilsonian peace in order to salvage at least part of the former president's efforts at Paris and to tie the nation, albeit loosely, to the Versailles superstructure.

THE POLITICS OF PEACE

The internationalist and isolationist wings of the Republican party put great pressures on President-elect Harding to come to a decision regarding his peace policy. For a time Harding leaned toward the internationalist position that the Treaty of Versailles—complete with the League covenant—should be resubmitted to the Senate with revised reservations.[3] But by the time of the inauguration, the new president had begun to waver. In his inaugural address, Harding announced that "we do not mean to be entangled." But he

[2]See Beerits's memorandum, "The League of Nations and the World Court," box 172, folder 24, Hughes Papers.

[3]"The Separate Peace with Germany," box 172, folder 24, p. 15, Hughes Papers; Hughes, *Autobiographical Notes*, pp. 212–13; Pusey, *Charles Evans Hughes*, p. 431.

also declared, "We are ready to associate ourselves with the nations of the world, great and small, for conference, for counsel. . . ."[4] The president's vacillation continued through his first month in office as both party factions stepped up their pressure campaigns.

Senate Republican leaders gathered at the White House on 2 April to inform the president that they planned to renew the effort to make peace with the Central Powers through a congressional resolution similar to one which President Wilson had vetoed in 1920.[5] Senator Knox, the author of the original peace bill, had been giving the matter a great deal of thought. He prepared a carefully worded amendment to his separate peace plan which pledged the United States, in case of a menace to peace in Europe, to "consult with other powers affected with the view to devising means for the removal of such menace, and will, the necessity arising in the future, cooperate with the friends of civilization for its defense." The United States need not join the League, for the resolution provided a kind of instantaneous collective security in the case of trouble. The resolution, Knox noted immodestly, would "serve with the Monroe Doctrine, as a fundamental doctrine of American diplomacy."[6] For Knox, Hiram Johnson wrote, this was to be "the crowning incident, in his view, of a long career of brilliant statesmanship."[7] Many of his fellow irreconcilables liked the idea well enough to endorse it as the centerpiece of congressional foreign policy.[8] However the irreconcilables also felt increasingly edgy over the internationalist pretensions of Harding's key advisers.

Hughes, Hoover, and other members of the business-oriented internationalist wing of the Republican party remained convinced that the administration should push the Treaty of Versailles with reservations through the Senate for the sake of national interests. Hoover asked John Foster Dulles, a prominent Wall Street attorney who had served on the American Peace Commission, to write a brief on the importance of the economic provisions of the treaty to the United States. In a subsequent memorandum, Dulles argued that a Germany "so tied and bound by the Treaty of Versailles" was in no position to secure American rights as one of the victors. If the Senate chose to make a separate peace, then the government would have to undertake lengthy negotiations with the Allies confirming American treaty rights. Therefore, Dulles

---

[4]Fred L. Israel, ed. *The Chief Executive: Inaugural Addresses of the Presidents of the United States from George Washington to Lyndon B. Johnson* (New York: Crown, 1965), pp. 232–33.

[5]*New York Times*, 3 April 1921, p. 2.

[6]Speech of Senator Philander C. Knox, 30 December 1920, Philander C. Knox Papers, book 23, pp. 3810–12, Library of Congress, Manuscript Division, Washington (hereafter cited as Knox Papers).

[7]Hiram Johnson to Maj. Archibald M. Johnson and Hiram Johnson, Jr., 18 June 1921, Hiram Johnson Papers, part 6, box 3, Bancroft Library, University of California, Berkeley (hereafter cited as Johnson Papers).

[8]*New York Times*, 5 April 1921, pp. 1–2; and 6 April 1921, pp. 1–2.

concluded, "instead of hastening a return to normal conditions we will be perpetuating and accentuating uncertainty, which is the element the effect of which is most deadly to a revival of trade and commerce."⁹ Hoover, finding himself in wholehearted agreement with Dulles's conclusions, sent the memorandum to Secretary Hughes in case the State Department needed more ammunition for the imminent confrontation with the Senate.[10]

Senator Frank B. Brandegee, the acid-tongued and often indolent irreconcilable Republican from Connecticut, called on Secretary Hughes in early April to offer advice on how to avoid "European entanglements." When the senator returned to Capitol Hill, he told his colleagues that Hughes wanted to press for early passage of the Versailles Treaty and American entrance into the League.[11] The bitter-enders came to the conclusion that there would be no point in trying to win Hughes over to their position, for as J. Reuben Clark, Jr. told his friend Senator Knox, "I doubt if the Infinite himself could change the views of the Methodist."[12] President Harding was a different case altogether. A few days later, a delegation of irreconcilables, including Brandegee, Borah, and Johnson, told the president bluntly that they would block the administration's domestic economic program if Hughes persisted. That threat forced the president into a qualified surrender.[13]

On 12 April, just before addressing the opening session of the Sixty-seventh Congress, Harding called members of the Senate Foreign Relations Committee to the White House to hear portions of the message dealing with foreign affairs. "It was so much better upon the League and the Peace Resolution than I expected," Johnson wrote to his sons, "that I was delighted with it."[14] President Harding said that he would not ask the Senate for American entrance into the League of Nations; he merely hinted that the Versailles Treaty might be returned to the Senate at some unspecified future date. In the meantime the president would support the Knox Resolution—provided that Congress cut the bill back to its original function of merely declaring the war to be over—news which pleased all of the irreconcilables with the exception of Knox.[15] "The League is dead," Johnson wrote gleefully, "a state of peace will be declared, and the present moment, therefore, is to our liking."[16]

Secretary Hughes was powerless to protest against the president's action, for it seemed that Harding had taken the only practical way out of a difficult

---

⁹Memorandum, John Foster Dulles, 7 April 1921, box 571, Hoover Papers, HHL.
[10]Hoover to Dulles, 6 April 1921, Dulles to Hoover, 7 April 1921, and Hoover to Hughes, 8 April 1921, ibid.
[11]Pusey, *Charles Evans Hughes*, p. 432; [Clinton Wallace Gilbert], *The Mirrors of Washington* (New York: G. P. Putnam's Sons, 1921), pp. 67–69.
[12]J. Reuben Clark, Jr. to Knox, 9 April 1921, book 23, p. 3851, Knox Papers.
[13]Pusey, *Charles Evans Hughes*, p. 432.
[14]Johnson to A. Johnson, 13 April 1921, part 6, box 2, Johnson Papers.
[15]*New York Times*, 13 April 1921, p. 1.
[16]Johnson to A. Johnson, 13 April 1921, part 6, box 2, Johnson Papers.

situation. Senator Frank B. Kellogg and other pro-League Republicans met with Hughes and convinced him that the League covenant would fall far short of the necessary two-thirds majority. Still, Hughes found the administration's abandonment of one of its chief foreign policy objectives to be extremely embarrassing, as he had committed himself the previous year to work for ratification of the covenant "until the declared object is attained."[17] Pro-League forces charged that the secretary had betrayed his promise. For a time he even considered resignation, but soon decided against it. "I accepted office to do the best that I could for the country," he later wrote, "and I have remained in office for the same reason."[18] In his first personal crisis as secretary of state, Hughes rationalized what was to be his guiding principle in dealing with a recalcitrant Congress: a policy of flexibility.

Hughes did not acknowledge easily that he had put political interests ahead of the general welfare. Many years after the fact, in his *Autobiographical Notes*, while conceding that American entrance into the League would have been "valuable training," Hughes refused to accept any part of the accountability for rejection of the covenant; Wilson and the irreconcilables were entirely to blame for that.[19] He had merely acquiesced in the exorcism of the League because the situation was hopeless politically. In a perceptive essay on Hughes, Clinton Wallace Gilbert noted, "His head, like a book of etiquette, is full of 'Don'ts,' diplomatic 'Don'ts,' all deduced from the experience of Wilson."[20] The experience of Wilson showed Hughes that further efforts on behalf of the League might well have wrecked the administration.[21] After Harding made his decision, the secretary turned to the problem of how much of the Versailles Treaty he could salvage, a task he pondered while the Senate made its own peace-by-resolution.

THE KNOX-PORTER RESOLUTION

Dutifully Senator Knox introduced a revised version of his peace resolution on 13 April. As agreed, the pretentious definition of American foreign policy had been excised. Senate Joint Resolution 16 repealed the congressional

---

[17]Pusey, *Charles Evans Hughes*, p. 432.

[18]"The Separate Peace with Germany," box 172, folder 25, p. 18a, Hughes Papers. See also William R. Castle, Jr., "The U.S. and the League," unpublished manuscript, William R. Castle, Jr. Papers, Box 34, Herbert Hoover Presidential Library, West Branch, IA (hereafter cited as Castle Papers).

[19]Glad, *Illusions of Innocence*, pp. 180–84; Hughes, *Autobiographical Notes*, pp. 215–22.

[20][Gilbert], *The Mirrors of Washington*, p. 82.

[21]"The Separate Peace with Germany," box 172, folder 25, p. 18, Hughes Papers; Denna Frank Fleming, *The United States and World Organization, 1920–1933* (New York: Columbia University Press, 1938), p. 46.

declarations of war against Germany and Austria-Hungary and called for the retention of all seized enemy alien properties until claims adjustments could be negotiated. Finally, the Knox resolution provided that the United States "although it has not ratified the Treaty of Versailles, reserves all of the rights, powers, claims, privileges, indemnities, reparations, or advantages to which it and its nationals have become entitled. . . ."[22] In essence the resolution claimed for the United States all the benefits of the victors while avoiding the considerable responsibilities connected with the wartime alliance, the armistice, and the Versailles Treaty. It seemed to be the very antithesis of Wilsonian idealism.

Senator Lodge guided the Knox resolution through the Foreign Relations Committee quickly—in marked contrast to the slow and tortuous path he had charted for Wilson's peace treaty two years earlier—with debate beginning on the measure just two weeks after Knox first introduced it. Nevertheless, loyal Wilsonian Democrats were ready: Senator Atlee Pomerene wrote the minority report of the Foreign Relations Committee on behalf of Democratic Senators Gilbert M. Hitchcock, John Sharp Williams, and Claude A. Swanson. Pomerene, arguing that the resolution represented an attempt to usurp presidential treaty-making powers, called on President Harding either to resubmit the Versailles pact with reservations to the Senate or negotiate new treaties with the former Central Powers which would then be sent to Congress for ratification.[23]

Democratic Minority Leader Oscar W. Underwood of Alabama opened the debate, observing that passage of the resolution implied that the United States had made a mistake in declaring war on Germany and Austria-Hungary.[24] Hitchcock of Nebraska, who had been the floor manager of the Versailles Treaty, picked up on Pomerene's point that the resolution infringed on presidential prerogatives. The irreconcilable Reed replied sarcastically that although it was surprising that Hitchcock should be defending the prerogatives of a Republican president, he was pleased that the senator had discovered the concept of three independent branches of government. "It has seemed to me for a number of years," Reed continued, "that there were some gentlemen in the Senate of the United States who were inclined to doubt that there was such a thing as a division of power. They seemed to think that all power had been conferred upon the Executive."[25] Reed's irony had little effect on the Wilsonians, who continued to argue that the Knox bill should be defeated on constitutional grounds and that the Versailles Treaty should be resubmitted.

[22]U.S., Congress, Senate, *Congressional Record*, Senate Joint Resolution 16, 67th Cong., 1st sess., pp. 188–89. See also *New York Times*, 14 April 1921, p. 1.

[23]U.S., Congress, Senate, Committee on Foreign Relations, Senate Report 2, 67th Cong., 1st sess., pt.2:1–5.

[24]*Congressional Record*, 67th Cong., 1st sess., p. 750.

[25]Ibid., pp. 783–88.

On 30 April, the third and final day of debate, Majority Leader Lodge began his defense of the resolution. He emphasized the practical advantages of ending "the totally abnormal and anomalous situation in which we now are."[26] Borah also took the floor to argue for the Knox bill as a positive alternative to the horrors of the Versailles Treaty, that "simoon of misery and ruin" which was "forcing all Europe into helpless barbarism."[27] Democratic Senator A. Owsley Stanley ended the debate with an impassioned speech against the resolution. "This scene, this act is tragic," he said, "it is pathetic." Then, turning to face the Republican side of the aisle, Stanley stated pointedly, "You are drunk with power."[28] Senate Joint Resolution 16 passed easily by a vote of forty-nine to twenty-three; twenty-four senators, including Knox, did not vote.[29] Immediately Lodge sent the resolution over to the House where he expected equally swift action.

Stephen G. Porter, the powerful Republican chairman of the House Committee on Foreign Affairs, did not favor the Knox resolution. Like Senator Underwood, Porter contended that peace through repeal of the war declarations could be interpreted as a disavowal of the entire war effort.[30] On 30 April 1921, Porter introduced resolutions which simply declared that the war between the United States and Germany and its ally Austria-Hungary was officially at an end. Congressman Porter also included clauses reserving American rights without the responsibilities of the victors and freezing enemy assets pending a claims settlement.[31]

The separate peace resolutions did not sail through the House as the irreconcilables had anticipated, for in early May President Harding asked House leaders to pigeonhole them, pending the outcome of a political crisis in Europe. The Reparation Commission had agreed to set the German indemnity at 132 billion marks, while Allied political leaders, demanding German acquiescence, threatened occupation of the Ruhr. Upon the recommendation of Secretary Hughes, Harding resumed informal American diplomatic observation at both the Reparation Commission and the Council of Allied Ambassadors as gestures of solidarity with the Allies. The administration also pressured the House to shelve the separate peace proposals temporarily so as not to hold out hope to the Germans that the United States was abandoning its friends at a time of heightened tensions.[32]

To the irreconcilables, it seemed that the president was deserting his

---

[26]Ibid., pp. 836–37.
[27]Ibid., p. 855.
[28]Ibid., p. 861.
[29]Ibid., p. 865.
[30]Kurt and Sarah Wimer, "The Harding Administration, the League of Nations, and the Separate Peace Treaty," *The Review of Politics* 29 (January 1967): 16.
[31]*Congressional Record*, House Joint Resolutions 74 and 75, 67th Cong., 1st sess., p. 630. See also Murray, *Harding Era*, p. 130.
[32]Nelson, *Victors Divided*, pp. 182–83; *New York Times*, 8 May 1921, p. 1.

former colleagues in the Senate. Within a week after Harding's action, the bitter-enders were in a state of "near rebellion." Majority Leader Lodge averted attacks on administration policy in open session by Republicans only after negotiation of what one newspaper described as "a two-day armistice."[33] Johnson found Knox to be "extremely bitter." "I heard more harsh things said by him of the Administration," he wrote, "than I have ever dared utter."[34]

Knox grew even angrier when the president gave his blessing to the Porter resolution, which the House Foreign Affairs Committee finally approved on 7 June. The *New York Times* praised Harding for siding with the House and Porter for standing up to the irreconcilables. Where did the House leader get the notion, the *Times* asked rhetorically, that the Knox resolution was a stain on American honor? The newspaper speculated that Wilson's message vetoing the original Knox bill might have been the source. "Today," the *Times* concluded, "the Republican majority in the House is tacitly siding with Wilson and against Knox."[35] In its eagerness to vindicate the fallen Democratic president, the *Times* missed the major significance of the episode: Harding, the man who was supposed to be the captive of the Senate, had defied the irreconcilables for the first time and no one in the upper house could do anything about it.

The House assured passage of Porter's version of the peace resolution on 11 June, enacting a special rule that the bill would be voted on without amendments within two days.[36] Representative Tom Connally of Texas led the forces opposed to the separate peace; still, the Wilsonians did little more than to put themselves on record against "this scrap of paper covered with surrender."[37] The Porter resolution passed 304 to 61.[38] Although a conference committee composed of Lodge, Knox, and Hitchcock from the Senate, and Porter, John J. Rogers, and Henry D. Flood from the House deadlocked for a time, the president's endorsement of Porter's resolution made Senate surrender virtually certain. Johnson was disgusted that Knox let Harding destroy "the fondest creation of all his career" without a fight. "He has crawled, and crawled, and crawled," Johnson sneered, "and feels that he has been sufficiently rewarded for the destruction of his fondest hope in being permitted to entertain the President week-ends at his country home."[39]

---

[33]*Milwaukee Journal*, 12 May 1921, box 241, Hughes Papers.
[34]Johnson to A. Johnson and H. Johnson, Jr., 18 June 1921, part 6, box 3, Johnson Papers.
[35]"Admirable Consistency," *New York Times*, 9 June 1921, p. 14.
[36]Ibid., 12 June 1921, p. 1; Frederic L. Paxson, *American Democracy and the World War*, vol. 3; *Postwar Year: Normalcy, 1918–1923* (Berkeley: University of California Press, 1948), p. 208.
[37]*Congressional Record*, 67th Cong., 1st sess., p. 2513.
[38]Ibid., p. 2547.
[39]Johnson to A. Johnson and H. Johnson, Jr., 18 June 1921, part 6, box 3, Johnson Papers.

Both houses held only brief final debates on the conference report. On 30 June the Knox-Porter resolution passed the House 263 to 59, with 108 not voting.[40] In the Senate Knox, once again swallowing his pride, made an uninspired defense of the joint bill in which he claimed that the dissimilarities between his resolution and Porter's were "purely the difference between tweedledum and tweedledee, which the Senate conferees did not care to take up and argue."[41] In reality the president and the House had forced the Senate to change Knox's bill from an isolationist blueprint to a mere declaration of peace. On 1 July 1921 the Senate voted thirty-eight to nineteen to accept the conference report.[42] By that time Senator Knox had already left town for the holiday weekend. The resolution which he had once hoped would be the crowning achievement of his long career passed Congress, but it underwent such a metamorphosis that Knox seemed to lose interest. Nevertheless, the irreconcilables had their separate peace resolution, and it appeared to signify the triumph of the bitter-enders over Wilsonianism.

On 2 July 1921 a White House aide rushed the Knox-Porter resolution to the home of Senator Joseph S. Frelinghuysen in Raritan, New Jersey where President Harding planned to spend the Fourth of July. The aide waited almost two hours while the president finished a round of golf. When Harding finally arrived, he glanced at the document, quickly signed it and declared, "That's all," as an ink blot the size of a nickel splashed over his signature. A few minutes later, he was back on the golf course.[43]

The rest of the nation showed about as much interest as President Harding did in the signing of the resolution which ended America's part in the Great War. The *New York Times* devoted six full-length front-page columns and a banner headline to coverage of Jack Dempsey's fourth-round knockout of French challenger Georges Carpentier. A modest one-column story entitled "Harding Ends War" sufficed to relate details of what some already disparaged as "the Peace of Raritan."[44] "Wholly overshadowed by the accounts of the prizefight," the *Nation* reported, "there appeared on Sunday, July 3, the momentous news that at last a state of peace with Germany had been legally restored."[45] The American champion Jack Dempsey defeated the European challenger in a few furious minutes of action. Most people were more interested in the easy vicarious victory over Europe offered by this sporting event than in the seemingly endless domestic political quarrel over how to make peace.

---

[40]*Congressional Record*, 67th Cong., 1st sess., p. 3261.
[41]Ibid., p. 3248.
[42]Ibid., p. 3299.
[43]*New York Times*, 3 July 1921, p. 1; Russell, *Shadow of Blooming Grove*, p. 461.
[44]*New York Times*, 3 July 1921, p. 1
[45]"Peace At Last," *The Nation*, 13 July 1921, p. 34.

HUGHES'S DILEMMA

In an editorial of 7 July, the *New York Times* commented that the passage and signing of the Knox-Porter resolution "fell flat in this country. There was not the slightest sign of public enthusiasm or even interest." If American leaders were really interested in securing the advantages of the victors mentioned in the peace resolution, then they had to make treaties with the former Central Powers. The *Times* went on to endorse the Versailles pact as "better than any new one that could be negotiated." If Secretary of State Hughes resubmitted the treaty to the Senate, the editorial concluded, he would have the backing of the country.[46] Such sentiments, coming from a bastion of Wilsonian internationalism, the *New York Times*, probably did not disturb the irreconcilables, but they might have been unsettled if they had known that Hughes already had plans for a final attempt to push Wilson's treaty through the Senate.

Hughes realized that Congress's unilateral declaration of peace did not guarantee American rights under the peace treaties and the armistice agreements. For legal purposes formal acceptance by the former Central Powers of the cession of interests and rights to the United States as one of the victors had to be confirmed directly through bilateral treaties. Therefore, Secretary Hughes wanted to retain key rights granted to the United States at Versailles, including a voice in the disposition of former German colonial possessions, arrangements for repayment of occupation costs, and use of the machinery for claims settlements. The State Department looked with dread upon the task of negotiating comprehensive treaties satisfactory to the administration, the former Central Powers, and the Senate. Even if such a job could be accomplished, immense complications with the Allies might result because the whole postwar European political system rested upon the foundation of the Versailles Treaty. Hughes saw no practical alternative to the resubmission of the Versailles pact to the Senate.[47]

In a series of conferences with the president during the first week in July, Hughes suggested that the Senate might approve the Treaty of Versailles with a new set of reservations and without any references to the League of Nations. Impressed, Harding called a key group of senators to the White House to hear the secretary's argument. Although Hughes gained support among some moderates, he could not win over either the irreconcilables, who opposed the entire treaty, or a majority of regular Republicans, who saw no

---

[46]"No Escaping a Treaty," *New York Times*, 7 July 1921, p. 10.
[47]"The Separate Peace with Germany," box 172, folder 25, pp. 20–21, Hughes Papers; L. Ethan Ellis, *Republican Foreign Policy, 1921–1923* (New Brunswick, NJ: Rutgers University Press, 1968), p. 61; Glad, *Illusions of Innocence*, p. 215; Hughes, *Autobiographical Notes*, p. 225; Murray, *Harding Era*, p. 139; Pusey, *Charles Evans Hughes*, p. 440.

partisan advantage to be gained. Some of the bitter-enders had seen the Hughes plan coming. Two weeks earlier Johnson wrote to his sons that "a few of us have determined upon our course" if the administration chose to resubmit the hated treaty. "The instant that the thing begins," Johnson pledged, "I shall open in New York City, and Borah probably in the middle West, and we'll go to the bat, just exactly as we did in the old league struggle."[48] At the White House conference, the consensus was that most senators would not vote for the treaty even with new reservations.[49] As Lodge explained to his friend Dresel, "We feel very strongly here in the Senate that it would be a great mistake to undertake to make the Peace of Versailles a foundation for anything and that we ought to have a fresh start."[50]

Once again defeated behind the scenes, the secretary of state had no choice but to file away the certified copy of the Versailles Treaty which the Department of State, ironically, had just located after a frantic search a few days before in a "private fireproof file" at the home of Wilson.[51] Hughes now faced the prospect of having to negotiate new treaties with Germany, Austria, and Hungary, treaties which would have to be nearly as voluminous as the original accords in order to protect American rights and privileges adequately. The negotiations alone could take years and, after all that, the Senate might not accept the finished project, especially if it included diplomatic compromises. Hughes found an ingeniously simple solution to this difficult problem, one he later claimed came to him in his sleep. For the German-American treaty the secretary performed a union between the Knox-Porter resolution and those parts of the Versailles Treaty which specified American rights and privileges. He used portions of the Treaty of St. Germain-en-Laye with Austria and the Treaty of Trianon with Hungary to construct similar new pacts with the other wartime enemies. The former Central Powers could hardly refuse the terms because they had already granted them to the other Allies. The Knox-Porter resolution made up the heart of the treaties, so the scheme seemed to comply with the will of Congress.[52] Still, there was always the chance that the Central European diplomats whom the department would be facing across the negotiating tables might seize the opportunity to gain some advantage—and that could cause trouble for the administration.

---

[48]Johnson to A. Johnson and H. Johnson, Jr., 25 June 1921, part 6, box 3, Johnson Papers.

[49]Hughes, *Autobiographical Notes*, p. 226.

[50]Lodge to Dresel, 19 July 1921, box 263, folder 5, Dresel Papers.

[51]Woodrow Wilson to Charles Evans Hughes, 15 July 1921, Public Papers of the Presidents of the United States, microfilm, Woodrow Wilson, reel 113, National Archives, Washington (hereafter cited as Wilson Papers).

[52]"The Separate Peace with Germany," box 172, folder 25, pp. 21b–21c, Hughes Papers; Hughes, *Autobiographical Notes*, p. 226; Charles C. Hyde, "Charles Evans Hughes," in *The American Secretaries of State and Their Diplomacy*, ed. Samuel Flagg Bemis (New York: Pageant, 1958), 10:227; Pusey, *Charles Evans Hughes*, p. 441.

THE TREATY OF BERLIN

Hughes wasted no time in pressing Germany to open discussions on the separate peace. He cabled the text of the Knox-Porter resolution to Commissioner Dresel, asking him to inquire informally whether the Germans intended to raise questions about any of the rights and privileges accruing to the United States under the Versailles Treaty. The American government would not agree to any treaty which failed to secure these rights. "Have it clearly understood," Hughes continued, "that resumption of diplomatic relations which is in discretion of President and further steps with respect to relations between the United States and Germany, will largely depend on attitude of German Government in this matter."[53]

In his opening instructions, Hughes played upon the German desire to make a peace separate from the Versailles settlement. Germany, as Dresel explained to Dulles, favored a separate peace "as her consistent policy has been to get herself loose from all the Versailles obligations without absolutely repudiating the Treaty, and I think a great many people here believe that it must fall into discredit if we refuse to ratify it."[54] The secretary of state seemed to be saying that if the Germans wanted a separate peace, it would have to be on American terms. Only then, with diplomatic ties renewed, would "further steps"—including possible American intercession on the reparations question and negotiation of a lucrative commercial treaty—be within the realm of possibilities.

Dresel made informal inquiries at the German Foreign Office on 6 July and became "rather annoyed" when he received no reply after five days. "I had hoped that Germany would have the sense to meet us more than half way on the subject," he wrote to William R. Castle, Jr., "but this is not in accordance with their mentality . . . and I expect that they are capable of doing some further fencing in the hopes of getting concessions."[55] On 22 July German Foreign Minister Dr. Friedrich Rosen replied unofficially to the American queries through a note expressing the wish that the United States would assume its responsibilities under the Versailles Treaty as well as its rights and advantages, a reference to possible American participation in the work of such bodies as the Reparation Commission, which the Germans hoped would have a moderating influence on the Allies.[56] A memorandum enclosed with Rosen's

---

[53]The secretary of state to the commissioner at Berlin (Dresel), 5 July 1921, 711.62119/9A-10A, DSNA.

[54]Dresel to Dulles, 30 April 1921, box 114, folder 5, Dresel Papers.

[55]Dresel to Castle, 13 July 1921, box 68, folder 6, ibid.

[56]The commissioner at Berlin (Dresel) to the secretary of state, 22 July 1921, 711.62119/16, DSNA.

note indicated the German willingness to confirm a protocol acknowledging American rights and privileges.[57] However, in return for making a peace treaty completely on American terms, the Germans expected some favors.

Rosen asked Dresel if it would be possible for the American government to issue a statement announcing the forthcoming restoration of German property seized in the United States by the Alien Property Custodian. This act, the German foreign minister explained, would have a favorable effect on his people and give a boost to his government.[58] Dresel sympathized with Rosen's delicate political position as a minister in Dr. Josef Wirth's "cabinet of surrender," formed two months earlier during the reparations crisis. The *Reichskabinett* had an avowed policy of German economic recovery through cooperation with the Allies, but extreme nationalists kept the government under great pressure. "The position of the Cabinet is so precarious," Dresel wrote Lodge, "that they are exceedingly anxious to point to some success in discussions with America."[59]

Hughes had his own domestic problems to worry about: The secretary did not want to make any statements regarding German property "as Congress alone has the power to deal with that matter." He feigned puzzlement over the American responsibilities which Rosen mentioned.[60] Dresel telegraphed that the foreign minister had in mind a treaty which would spell out American rights and privileges and their limitations.[61] Hughes regarded this idea as "wholly inadvisable" because "it would amount to an attempt to insert in the Treaty a commentary upon the Treaty of Versailles, which is not our intention." Dresel's approach would also bog the negotiations down while limiting the administration's latitude for interpretation of the treaty. All the department needed at this point was a brief agreement granting the rights specified in the Knox-Porter resolution to the United States and a series of cross references, by the numbers, to parts of the Versailles Treaty which dealt with American privileges as one of the victors. These included special trade and transportation rights, claims, reparations, and army occupation cost reimbursements, as well

---

[57]The commissioner at Berlin (Dresel) to the secretary of state, 22 July 1921, 711.62119/17, ibid.

[58]The commissioner at Berlin (Dresel) to the secretary of state, 22 and 23 July 1921, 711.62119/18 and 15, ibid.

[59]Dresel to Henry Cabot Lodge, 26 July 1921, box 263, file 2, Dresel Papers. See also Dresel to Castle, 26 July 1921, box 68, file 6, ibid.; and Erich Eyck, *A History of the Weimar Republic*, 2 vols. (New York: Atheneum, 1970), p. 183.

[60]The secretary of state to the commissioner at Berlin (Dresel), 23 July 1921, 711.62119/18, DSNA.

[61]The commissioner at Berlin (Dresel) to the secretary of state, 27 July 1921, 711.62119/19, ibid.

as the right to take part in the disposition of German colonies and the repatria-
tion of war prisoners. Further negotiations could be taken up later. "Present
object," Hughes concluded, "is to avoid controversy over portions of Treaty
of Versailles unacceptable here."[62] The secretary had indeed learned his diplomatic etiquette from Wilson's example, for he negotiated with the Germans
while keeping one eye on the Senate.

On 1 August 1921, the American commissioner at Berlin presented a
treaty draft to the German foreign minister. Rosen, seeing that the Americans
had failed to include a declaration of German rights in the pact, commented
that the "cabinet would not dare to come before [the] German people with
an instrument which in no wise alluded to these rights."[63] But the State
Department would not dare to come before the Senate with a treaty containing
such a declaration of German rights.[64]

Dresel continued to urge various members of the *Reichskabinett* informally that it would be best for Germany to sign the agreement immediately.
On 6 August he reported that the German cabinet was "very anxious to arrange
slight modifications partly of substance and partly of form so as to make the
treaty acceptable to Parliament and to the people generally." The Germans
had five reservations. First, Rosen continued to demand that the United States
recognize German rights. He asked for insertion of part thirteen of the Versailles Treaty into the pact which dealt with the International Labor Office.
The Germans desired clarification of several Versailles articles referred to in
the separate peace only by number. Rosen also wanted articles dealing
explicitly with the renewal of diplomatic relations and areas which would be
the subject of future negotiations. Finally, because some acts in the Versailles
Treaty had already expired and others had fixed periods of time, the foreign
minister argued that German agreement to them now would give the Americans
a two-year advantage over the rest of the Allies, a stipulation he regarded as
"impracticable and unreasonable."[65] When Dresel pressed him, Rosen admitted
that the first and last points provided the only real obstacles to German
ratification.[66]

Two days later Hughes rejected four out of the five objections raised
by the Germans, although he did offer to add a sentence to Article 2, as a
sop to German nationalism, reading, "The United States, in availing itself of

---

[62]The secretary of state to the commissioner at Berlin (Dresel), 28 July 1921, 711.62119/19,
ibid. See also Castle to Dresel, 2 August 1921, box 6, Castle Papers.
[63]The commissioner at Berlin (Dresel) to the secretary of state, 1 August 1921, 711.62119/
22, DSNA.
[64]Castle to Dresel, 2 August 1921, box 68, file 16, Dresel Papers.
[65]The commissioner at Berlin (Dresel) to the secretary of state, 4 and 6 August 1921,
711.62119/25 and 26, DSNA; Dresel to Castle, 8 August 1921, box 6, Castle Papers.
[66]The commissioner at Berlin (Dresel) to the secretary of state, 6 August 1921, 711.62119/
27, DSNA.

the rights and advantages stipulated in the provisions of that Treaty [of Versailles] . . . will do so in a manner consistent with rights accorded to Germany under such provisions."[67] This did not satisfy the German cabinet, which continued to press for a stronger declaration on German rights as well as a statement on the release of alien property held in the United States. "On the whole," Dresel wrote, "I am rather encouraged than other–wise, though I fear very much, in spite of all my efforts, I shall not be able to get Rosen to the point of signing until a decision has been made as to Upper Silesia."[68] Once again domestic politics, this time on the German side, threatened to delay the peacemaking process further.

The situation in Upper Silesia had nothing whatsoever to do with the German-American treaty, but it did complicate Dresel's task. A plebiscite of March 1921, held to determine the Polish-German border along the lines of national self-determination, resulted in a majority voting to remain in Germany. Polish volunteers began arming for war; German volunteers soon opposed them in a series of pitched battles. Tension between Britain and France prevented the Allies from imposing a solution on Germany and Poland. By the time of the German-American peace talks in August, the Allied Supreme Council had not yet decided on the fate of Upper Silesia.[69] The *Reichskabinett* feared that the Allies would hand down an adverse decision at any time, a ruling which might precipitate yet another political crisis. Therefore Rosen and his colleagues hesitated to sign an agreement with the United States which could in itself weaken their political position. On the other hand, a separate peace treaty might be potentially profitable politically if Germany handled the negotiations correctly. Dresel believed that the Germans would sign eventually, provided that the State Department agreed to a few more modifications.[70]

Several members of the United States Senate, meanwhile, grew restless over the prolonged German-American talks. Hughes was negotiating the treaty with the Senate in mind, but he did not brief individual senators on the progress of the discussions. On 10 August Democrats denounced Majority Leader Lodge as a hypocrite because he had criticized Wilson for keeping the Senate in the dark throughout the Paris Peace Conference and said nothing when the Republican administration followed a similar policy during the Berlin negotiations.[71] Determined to avoid further attacks on administration

[67]The secretary of state to the commissioner at Berlin (Dresel), 8 August 1921, 711.62119/26, ibid.
[68]Dresel to Castle, 8 August 1921, box 68, file 6, Dresel Papers.
[69]Eyck, *Weimar Republic*, pp. 180–82 and 191. See also the commissioner at Berlin (Dresel) to the secretary of state, 10 August 1921, 711.62119/30, DSNA.
[70]Dresel to Castle, 8 August 1921, box 68, file 6, Dresel Papers; the commissioner at Berlin (Dresel) to the secretary of state, 8 August 1921, 711.62119/28, DSNA.
[71]*New York Times*, 11 August 1921, p. 1.

policy, Hughes telegraphed new instructions to Dresel on 11 August authorizing him to clarify the American recognition of German rights under the
Versailles Treaty. Hughes remained firm on the point that "Congress alone
can determine disposition of property held by Alien Property Custodian." He
also told the commissioner to make it very clear that further delays would
not be beneficial to the Germans.[72] The next day Dresel reported optimistically
that the minor changes now satisfied Dr. Rosen personally, although the
foreign minister could not vouch for the entire cabinet.[73]

The *Reichskabinett* continued to stall in spite of Hughes's minor concessions. The German leaders informed Dresel that they were conceding even
more to the Americans than they had to the Allies at Paris because the separate
peace treaty also referred to rights acquired by participation in the Great War
and under the armistice.[74] Hughes could do nothing to meet this complaint
without tampering with the Knox-Porter resolution.[75] For his part, Dresel, in
a series of meetings with German cabinet members, alternated between bul-
lying ("sometimes it is of use in dealing with the German mentality to blow
up occasionally . . . .")[76] and gentle prodding ("unless specifically instructed
by the Department I shall avoid anything in the nature of peremptory
language . . . .").[77]

Unmoved by American explanations, the German cabinet asked again
for a redrafting of the article containing the Knox-Porter resolution. Hughes
would not assent to any changes in this part of the treaty no matter how much
the Germans objected. "On account of conditions here," he wrote on 20 August,
"no opportunity should be offered for contention that terms of Peace Resolution
are not observed. This is a practical situation which the German Government
should not fail to consider." The secretary did offer two small concessions
and a rather large incentive for concluding the pact. He consented to the
earlier German request that periods of time referred to in the Versailles Treaty
should run from the time the separate peace came into force. Hughes also
authorized a small and rather meaningless change in the preamble. He decided
to try a different tack regarding German property: Dresel was to express his
profound sympathy with the Germans on the issue, explaining that prompt
signature of the treaty "will pave the way for consideration of the questions
relating to property sequestered here which the President desires to be dealt

---

[72]The secretary of state to the commissioner at Berlin (Dresel), 11 August 1921, 711.62119/
29, DSNA.
[73]The commissioner at Berlin (Dresel) to the secretary of state, 12 August 1921, 711.62119/
33, ibid.
[74]The commissioner at Berlin (Dresel) to the secretary of state, 18 August 1921, 711.62119/
37, ibid.
[75]The secretary of state to the commissioner at Berlin (Dresel), 19 August 1921, 711.62119/
37, ibid.
[76]Dresel to Castle, 23 August 1921, box 68, file 6, Dresel Papers.
[77]The commissioner at Berlin (Dresel) to the secretary of state, 18 August 1921,
711.62119/37, DSNA.

with upon the most fair and righteous basis."[78] These sweeteners, which cost the administration nothing, made the treaty acceptable enough for the *Reichskabinett* to live with.

Hughes grew annoyed when minor matters threatened to postpone the signing ceremony for several days.[79] "It is important that [the] signing of [the] Treaty should not be further postponed," he wrote, anticipating the final phase of the treaty making process, "[the] matter has been taken up today with [the] Senate Foreign Relations Committee, and inasmuch as public interest is very keen, desire to have [the] Treaty signed tomorrow."[80] German and American diplomats signed the Treaty of Berlin on 25 August 1921 with Commissioner Dresel reporting that the signing took place without ceremony. "There was an evident desire," he wrote, "on the part of the Germans to have it as little like Versailles as possible," a sentiment they undoubtedly shared with Secretary Hughes, who was already looking ahead to ratification in the Senate.[81] First, separate treaty talks with the other wartime enemies would have to be wrapped up.

ONE-SIDED NEGOTIATIONS WITH AUSTRIA

"However much one may condemn the Austro-Hungarian Empire," a G-2 report from the U.S. Army War College noted, "it has become clear that it was an economic necessity."[82] The Austria of 1921 was a mere torso of the venerable multinational empire which had gone to war seven years earlier. The Allied decision to make the new Austrian republic the direct successor of the Hapsburg dominion made it liable for a crushing burden of reparations, a situation Winston Churchill, among others, found to be "pure nonsense."[83] Nevertheless, the Allies did not move to remedy Austria's plight until the republic verged on economic collapse and, even then, aid proved to be slow and inadequate. The ruling Social Democrats created a short-term sham prosperity

---

[78]The secretary of state to the commissioner at Berlin (Dresel), 20 August 1921, 711.62119/39, ibid.
[79]The commissioner at Berlin (Dresel) to the secretary of state, 22 August 1921, 711.62119/43, ibid.
[80]The secretary of state to the commissioner at Berlin (Dresel), 24 August 1921, 711.62119/48, ibid.
[81]Dresel to Castle, 6 September 1921, box 68, file 2, Dresel Papers.
[82]U.S., Army War College, G-2, "Summary of the Estimate on Succession States, Austria–Hungary," box 35, Hoover Papers, HHL.
[83]Winston S. Churchill, *The Aftermath, 1918–1928* (New York: Charles Scribner's Sons, 1929), p. 237. See also Elisabeth Barker, *Austria, 1918–1972* (Coral Gables, FL: University of Miami Press, 1973), p. 41; C. Groves Haines and Ross J. S. Hoffman, *The Origins and Background of the Second World War* (New York: Oxford University Press, 1947), pp. 98–99.

through massive government spending financed by deliberate inflation. In the summer of 1921, the boom came to an end as foreign nations moved to protect themselves against Austrian currency dumping.[84] Faced with a deteriorating economy and a restless work force, Austrian leaders were in no position to dicker with the powerful Americans over terms of a separate peace.[85]

During the first week of August, Secretary Hughes instructed the American commissioner at Vienna, Arthur Hugh Frazier, to inquire if the Austrian government would sign a protocol confirming American rights and privileges under the Treaty of St. Germain-en-Laye.[86] On 10 August Frazier cabled that, after a cabinet meeting, Chancellor Johannes Schober had decided on "unconditional acceptance of [the] demands."[87] Schober coupled this announcement with a plea to Frazier for financial assistance so that his government might purchase foodstuffs abroad.[88] The American commissioner replied that "no nation has ever lost anything by throwing itself upon the generosity of the United States."[89]

Having dutifully reported the Austrian request for aid, Frazier advised the department that the chancellor seemed to favor the United States over the other victorious powers. "The field is thus admirably prepared," he continued, "for the reception of American enterprise in Austria." Frazier seemed certain that Austria would be an excellent market for American surplus copper and machinery.[90] The two nations worked quickly to conclude their peace talks for different reasons. The desperate Austrians wanted to treat on any terms out of a desire for American aid; the United States wanted peace to open up markets which American industry needed badly. Although the two sides signed the peace treaty within a matter of days, both parties would be disappointed in the new relationship.[91]

---

[84]Barker, *Austria, 1918–1972*, pp. 48–50; Charles A. Gulick, *Austria From Habsburg to Hitler*, vol 2, *Labor's Workshop of Democracy* (Berkeley: University of California Press, 1948), pp. 144–57.

[85]Lindley to Curzon, 17 December 1920, Great Britain, Foreign Office, *Documents on British Foreign Policy, 1919–1939*, Rohan Butler, J. P. T. Bury, and M. E. Lambert, eds., 1st ser., 21 vols. (London: Her Majesty's Stationery Office, 1947–78), 12:355–56 (hereafter cited as DBFP). See also Curzon to Lindley, 31 December 1920, 12:361, ibid.

[86]The secretary of state to the commissioner at Vienna (Frazier), 5 August 1921, RG 59, 711.63119/-, DSNA.

[87]The commissioner at Vienna (Frazier) to the secretary of state, 10 August 1921, 711.63119/1, ibid.

[88]The commissioner at Vienna (Frazier) to the secretary of state, 10 August 1921, 711.63119/2, ibid.

[89]The commissioner at Vienna (Frazier) to the secretary of state, 11 August 1921, 711.63119/7, ibid.

[90]Ibid.

[91]The commissioner at Vienna (Frazier) to the secretary of state, 24 August 1921, 711.63119/4, ibid.

INSTABILITY AND STALLING IN HUNGARY

The situation in postwar Hungary combined the political instability of Germany with the financial plight of Austria. Since 1920 the landlocked nation had been a monarchy without a king ruled by *Reichsverweser* (Regent) Vice Admiral Miklós Horthy, although he let the National Assembly and a cabinet council handle the day-to-day affairs of state. The Allies dealt harshly with Hungary in the Treaty of Trianon, giving large tracts of territory to Rumania, Yugoslavia, and Czechoslovakia. In spite of a fierce irredentism, Hungary's feeble economic condition dictated that Foreign Minister Nicholas Bánffy pursue a policy of peaceful collaboration with the hated neighboring states created at Hungarian expense.[92] The time seemed to be especially propitious as well for Hungary to make a peace settlement with the United States.

Hughes began the peace process on 9 July, when he met with an unofficial representative of the Hungarian regime to ask for a guarantee to the United States of all rights and privileges to which it was entitled under the Trianon Treaty. The secretary telegraphed Ulysses Grant-Smith, the American commissioner at Budapest, that the United States would reject any agreement which did not conform to the Knox-Porter resolution. As in the case of Germany, Hughes warned that if Hungary wanted to take "further steps" in the process of normalization—that is, restoration of diplomatic and commercial relations—Hungarian diplomats would have to agree promptly to the separate peace.[93] Nine days later the commissioner reported that while the Hungarian government would make a treaty confirming American rights as stipulated in the Knox-Porter resolution, it wished to avoid specific mention of the Trianon Treaty, a proposition Hughes found acceptable since formal Hungarian recognition of the joint resolution meant tacit acceptance of American rights under the Trianon pact.[94]

On 27 July Grant-Smith explained that Foreign Minister Bánffy had consented to make mention of the Trianon Treaty in connection with a reservation designed to recognize Hungarian as well as American rights.[95] Hughes responded immediately and unequivocally that there must be no Hungarian

---

[92]Malbone W. Graham, *New Governments of Central Europe* (New York: Henry Holt, 1924), pp. 248–67; Hugh Seton-Watson, *Eastern Europe Between the Wars, 1918–1941* (Cambridge: Cambridge University Press, 1945), pp. 189–92.

[93]The secretary of state to the commissioner at Budapest (Grant-Smith), 9 July 1921, RG 59, 711.64119/-, DSNA.

[94]The commissioner at Budapest (Grant-Smith) to the secretary of state, 18 July 1921, and the secretary of state to the commissioner at Budapest (Grant-Smith), 23 July 1921, 711.64119/1, ibid.

[95]The commissioner at Budapest (Grant-Smith) to the secretary of state, 27 July 1921, 711.64119/2, ibid.

reservations. "Make it clear," he wired to Grant-Smith, "that insistence upon reservations would be prejudicial to the continuance of negotiations."[96] Bánffy refused to retreat, but "he also plead for some argument to use before the National Assembly, which was evidently a question of face saving." On 3 August Grant-Smith wrote that Bánffy had agreed to recommend to the National Assembly that the reservation be dropped, although the commissioner was "on the outlook for the next squirm." The American diplomat assured Hughes that continued "firm but gentle pressure" on the Hungarians would bring about excellent results.[97]

Castle contributed to the pressure campaign by meeting at the Harvard Club with the influential former premier, Count Paul Teleki, who had helped Horthy to orchestrate the "White Terror" against leftists and Jews the previous year. The Western European division chief told Teleki bluntly that the peace treaty was a take-it-or-leave-it proposition and that, if the Hungarians accepted it promptly without reservations, they would be "in a very advantageous position."[98] Shortly thereafter the National Assembly agreed to accept the Knox-Porter resolution as originally presented to them.[99] Hughes telegraphed a copy of the proposed treaty to Budapest for immediate signature by Bánffy and Grant-Smith.[100]

The Hungarian foreign minister did not see any reason to hurry; for two weeks Bánffy and his colleagues continued to raise minor points, until 30 August, when the American commissioner "went to the telephone and 'burnt the wires'" in a fit of rage. The Hungarians finally signed the treaty a few hours later. "How it reminds one of Latin America," Grant-Smith commented condescendingly to a friend, adding that "in Vienna, they were always willing to sign anything so long as they have the prospect of getting another loan. Here we have at the Foreign Office a portion of the old band from the Ballplatz, with whom delay and finesse is as the breath in their nostrils."[101] The commissioner really had very little to complain about, for, as was so often the case in Latin America, the United States had virtually dictated terms and, after a face-saving interim, the Hungarians had agreed to them.

---

[96]The secretary of state to the commissioner at Budapest (Grant-Smith), 28 July 1921, 711.64119/2, ibid.

[97]The commissioner at Budapest (Grant-Smith) to the secretary of state, 3 August 1921, 711.64119/15, ibid.

[98]Memorandum, Castle to Hughes, 9 August 1921, 711.64119/49, ibid.

[99]The commissioner at Budapest (Grant-Smith) to the secretary of state, 12 August 1921, 711.64119/8, ibid.

[100]The secretary of state to the commissioner at Budapest (Grant-Smith), 17 August 1921, 711.64119/8, ibid.

[101]Grant-Smith to Henry P. Fletcher, 30 August 1921, 711.64119/41, ibid.

NEW TREATIES, NEW TIMES

With the signing of the Hungarian-American peace, the State Department concluded the diplomatic phase of ending the state of war with the former Central Powers. The Harding administration now had three treaties, more or less uniform in nature, which reserved to the United States "all rights, privileges, indemnities, reparations, or advantages" accruing to it as one of the principal victors and under the armistices and original treaties of peace without any of the corresponding military or political responsibilities which accompanied them, although the nation had the option of participating in any or all of the burdens of victory if it so chose. Additionally Washington had mortgaged enemy property against the pending financial claims settlements.[102]

In early 1921 Hughes accepted the defeat of his first peace plan—a mere modification of Wilson's grand design—with good grace, substituting a pragmatic plan combining the formal expression of congressional will with references to the Versailles, St. Germain-en-Laye, and Trianon treaties. The resulting documents seemed to give the Senate and the nation what they wanted, namely, the opportunity to participate in European affairs, but not the obligation. The separate peace set the stage for the United States to take part in the disposition of former German colonies; to preside over the disarmament of wartime enemies; to receive claims, reparations, and occupation costs as well as special shipping, aerial, rail, and navigation rights. However, the treaties did not give the nation the responsibility of accepting the burden of enforcing the peace either diplomatically or militarily, nor did they require any dealings with the League of Nations. Hughes not only designed, but negotiated, his treaties with the Senate in mind. He constantly urged his negotiators to proceed with all due speed because the political climate seemed right for Senate approval. The secretary of state understood the lesson of Wilson's disastrous clash with Lodge and the irreconcilables very well.

Despite their position of weakness, the former Central Powers could have caused trouble for Hughes. Dresel believed that negotiation of the German-American treaty "was indeed a tougher job than appeared on the surface," but he took no great part of the credit for it himself. "It was indeed an object lesson," he wrote to Castle, "to follow the way in which the Secretary handled the exceedingly difficult subject, and I especially admired the manner in which he gave way on minor matters, while firmly insisting on the essentials."[103] Hughes handled his weaker opponents skillfully through a combination of patient explanations and small concessions which cost the United States nothing, while making the unequal treaties slightly more acceptable to the

---

[102]*The Treaties of Peace, 1919–1923*, 2 vols. (New York: Carnegie Endowment for International Peace, 1924), pp. 945–56.

[103]Dresel to Castle, 26 September 1921, box 68, file 7, Dresel Papers.

other side. In the discussions with Germany, he used the alien property issue to advantage, intimating that prompt ratification would accelerate solution of the problem. Similarly, hints about food programs and trade agreements made the Austrians and the Hungarians almost eager to treat with the administration.

As a moderate internationalist, Hughes's diplomatic handiwork did not make him particularly proud. As he wrote to his son, "while it may be swallowed with a wry face, it is privately recognized by all those who have sense enough to appreciate the facts that it is the best that could be done."[104] He had at least saved part of Wilson's work at the peace conference, enough to reconstruct the peace within the Republican internationalist framework. The treaties reflected the American mood: Five years after the United States embarked on a crusade to make the world safe for democracy, the domestic political deadlock over the course of future foreign policy had so poisoned the atmosphere that advantage without accountability seemed to be the only peace settlement acceptable to the Senate.

---

[104]Quoted in Pusey, *Charles Evans Hughes*, p. 442.

2

WILSON'S LAST STAND
Advice and Consent of the Senate on the Separate Peace

Castle believed that Hughes had handled the separate peace problem well. "It was from the American point of view," he wrote to Commissioner Dresel, "an extremely clever move on the part of the Secretary because it will be almost impossible for the Senate to refuse to ratify it."[1] President Harding was not so sure; in July the Senate had agreed to accept the conference report on the Knox-Porter resolution by a bare two-thirds majority with only fifty-seven of the ninety-six senators troubling themselves to vote. The attitudes and actions of three key senators concerned Harding especially: Majority Leader Lodge, Minority Leader Underwood, and the spiritual leader of the irreconcilables, Borah.

Harding realized that any one of the three Senate leaders could block consent to ratification of the treaties. As leader of the president's party in the Senate and as a close personal friend of Commissioner Dresel, Lodge could be counted on to lead the fight for the separate peace, but age had eroded his once considerable parliamentary skills. In order to insure ratification, Lodge needed the support of Borah's bitter-enders, just as he had needed them two years earlier during the fight against the Versailles Treaty. The thirty-seven Democrats in the Senate also had enough votes to block the treaties if Underwood and his allies chose to avenge Wilson's bitter defeat.

As it turned out, Harding had every right to be concerned about the fate of the separate peace. The treaties passed only because a majority of the irreconcilables and a significant minority of Democrats voted with the Lodge forces. The two major opponents of the peace pacts were Senator Borah and, from his sickbed across town, Wilson. It was ironic that these two men should find themselves waging a common battle, but not altogether inappropriate; for just as Hughes and Wilson held similar views of America's expanding world role as an economic power, so Wilson and Borah shared a Utopian vision of America as moral leader among nations.

---

[1]Castle to Dresel, 30 August 1921, box 68, file 16, Dresel Papers.

THE SENATE FOREIGN RELATIONS COMMITTEE—
AND SENATOR BORAH

In mid-August President Harding began to woo the irreconcilables as Secretary Hughes wrapped up the separate peace talks. The president telephoned Johnson, emphasizing "that the Versailles Treaty would be, of course, a thing of the past if he could accomplish what he was striving to do." Then the president turned his attention to Senator Borah. According to Johnson, Harding told Borah quite candidly that "there was no real leadership in the Senate now, that what leadership there was there was afraid of Johnson and Borah, and because of this fact, he was most anxious to have us come along with the administration." Borah would have none of it; to him principles meant more than parties and "there were men who in one contingency or another must follow the line they believed to be right."[2] The "Lion of Idaho" put the president on notice that "they," meaning, presumably, a significant number of the irreconcilables, opposed his separate peace because the treaties would tie the nation indirectly to the heinous Versailles settlement.

On 21 September 1921 President Harding submitted the treaties of peace with Germany, Austria, and Hungary to the Senate with the hope that there would be an "early expression of approval and ratification."[3] The previous day the *New York Times* reported that Borah planned to fight the peace pacts since "they would involve the United States in European problems and diplomacy."[4] However, news that all six Democrats on the Senate Foreign Relations Committee favored the treaties more than offset the defection of Borah. Immediately Chairman Lodge decided to dispense with hearings as well as the appearance of a long succession of witnesses.[5] With regular Republicans and all of the Democrats behind the treaties, Lodge had a clear majority of the committee on the administration's side.

Five irreconcilables served on the Foreign Relations Committee, not including Knox, who, by late 1921, was too ill to attend his duties. Three of them, Brandegee, Joseph Medill McCormick, and George H. Moses, part of Knox's realist faction of the bitter-enders, would probably not put up too much resistance against the treaties out of loyalty to President Harding.[6] That left only Borah and Johnson to provide hard-core opposition, and even Johnson did not want to oppose the administration; he liked the president personally and wanted to work with him. Johnson perceived the president to be "so indolent intellectually that in matters of mere policy, he becomes in his own

²Johnson to A. Johnson and H. Johnson, Jr., 13 August 1921, part 4, box 2, Johnson Papers.
³Harding to Lodge, 21 September 1921, reel 187, Harding Papers.
⁴*New York Times*, 21 September 1921, p. 3.
⁵Ibid., 22 September 1921, p. 1.
⁶Stone, *The Irreconcilables*, pp. 183–86.

Administration a negligible quantity. Mr. Hughes and Mr. Hoover are practically in command of our international relations."[7] Johnson would support Harding's peace if he could be sure that Hughes and Hoover did not plan to use it for their internationalist ends. Borah appeared to be the only member of the Foreign Relations Committee who opposed the treaties unconditionally. Still, the senator from Idaho could be very persuasive.

The Senate Foreign Relations Committee spent several hours of 22 September 1921 in bitter debate behind closed doors. Most of the arguments centered around the clause in the Berlin Treaty which gave the United States authorization to take part in the various peacemaking commissions. As expected, Borah led the fight against American participation, with Johnson's support, while Chairman Lodge and Senator Kellogg emerged as the main defenders of the pacts. Johnson wrote to his sons that "we had quite a spirited and somewhat bitter exchange."[8] Borah charged that whereas the German treaty only reserved to America the right to representation on the Versailles-created commissions, Harding and Hughes had every intention of appointing representatives to these organizations as soon as possible. It would be impossible, he continued, for the United States to participate in the Versailles economic commissions without becoming entangled in European politics. The irreconcilables resurrected Chairman Lodge's reservation seven to the Versailles Treaty as the basis for a new resolution which would circumscribe the president's power to make appointments to the Reparation Commission.[9]

Borah also objected to the first paragraph of Article 2, the section referring to American rights and privileges in the Versailles Treaty by number. Acceptance of these privileges, especially under Part 14 (Occupation of Germany), the senator argued, made the nation liable morally to maintain American troops on the Rhine indefinitely. Senator Harry S. New, a loyal Harding supporter, assured the committee that the president had every intention of withdrawing all of the fifteen thousand troops upon ratification of the Berlin Treaty, but Borah and the other bitter-enders asserted that Harding ought to tell the committee that himself. On that note Lodge adjourned the session in order to report the committee's objections to the secretary of state.[10]

The *New York Times* found much to admire in Borah's performance. After all, the paper noted, he wanted merely to show his fellow Republicans that the treaty with Germany "does not, as promised and represented, take the United States out of the affairs of Europe. It leaves us much entangled . . . . Republicans may not like to be reminded of the fact, but fact it is."[11] The *Times* editorial writer had a valid point; the Berlin Treaty tied the United

---

[7]Johnson to A. Johnson and H. Johnson, Jr., 23 September 1921, part 4, box 2, Johnson Papers. See also Johnson to H. Johnson, Jr., 22 September 1921, part 6, box 3, ibid.

[8]Johnson to A. Johnson and H. Johnson, Jr., 23 September 1921, part 4, box 2, ibid.

[9]*New York Times*, 23 September 1921, pp. 1–2.

[10]Ibid.

[11]"Those Awful Entanglements," *New York Times*, 23 September 1921, p. 14.

States directly into the Versailles Treaty system, including the Reparation Commission and all of the other enforcement agencies, except for the League. The administration had drawn up a separate peace which did not effect a separation from European politics since Hughes had designed it to preserve the fruits of common victory with the Allies. Borah objected to Lodge's billing the peace as one of disengagement when it was bound to engage the United States "into the whole militaristic scheme and system which is again being built up in Europe."[12]

Lodge informed Hughes that his committee had strong feelings favoring some sort of reservation to prevent American participation in the work of the Reparation Commission without congressional approval. Seeing no other alternative, the secretary of state acquiesced in the chairman's judgment. Lodge presented a reservation to the committee the next day, but the irreconcilables found it too mild. Johnson and Brandegee rewrote the resolution to make clear that the nation would not take part in any commission or body connected with the Versailles Treaty until Congress approved.[13] The committee accepted this resolution, as well as similar ones for the Austrian and Hungarian treaties, by votes of eight to two. New and Kellogg, the administration's two strongest supporters on the committee, voted against the reservations when they could not communicate with the White House for instructions.[14]

The chairman headed off another possible reservation with the announcement that, according to the secretary of state, the administration planned a phased withdrawal of American troops from the Rhine.[15] Then Senator Brandegee offered, and the committee approved, a reservation designed to make certain that American citizens could press for claims against the former Central Powers.[16]

The two reservations, combined with Hughes's assurances about troop withdrawals from Germany, made the treaty acceptable to every committee member present except Senator Borah. "I don't see," Johnson wrote, "that more could be done, or that more could be asked." The treaties gave the United States the benefits of the European pacts without the obligations. Hughes had promised the committee to bring home the last remaining doughboys in Europe. The "whiskered Wilson" could not entangle the country in any European body, board, or commission without congressional approval. "Having done this much," Johnson concluded, "the victory for the 'irreconcilables' is about complete, and I am unable to see why we should not ratify

---

[12]Borah to Reverend Chauncey T. Edwards, 28 September 1921, William E. Borah Papers, box 94, Library of Congress, Manuscript Division, Washington (hereafter cited as Borah Papers).
[13]*New York Times*, 24 September 1921, p. 1. See also Johnson to A. Johnson and H. Johnson, Jr., 23 September 1921, part 4, box 2, Johnson Papers.
[14]*New York Times*, 24 September 1921, pp. 1 and 3; Wimer and Wimer, "The Separate Peace," p. 18n.
[15]*New York Times*, 24 September 1921, pp. 1 and 3.
[16]Ibid.

WILSON'S LAST STAND

THE
UNIVERSITY OF WINNIPEG
PORTAGE & BALMORAL
WINNIPEG, MAN.   R3B 2E9
CANADA

39

the German Treaty."[17] On 23 September, after only two days of consideration, the Foreign Relations Committee voted nine to one to report the treaties to the floor with two reservations each.[18] The lopsided bipartisan vote in committee and the known support in the full Senate augured well for the separate peace. Behind the scenes, though, two old foes prepared to do battle against the treaties, quite independently from one another, but on similar philosophical grounds.

OPPOSITION GATHERS

Wilson had not changed his mind about the immorality of a separate peace in the sixteen months since his veto of Knox's original resolution. The former president worked himself into a rage when he heard that Lodge had pushed the bilateral treaties through the Foreign Relations Committee in just two days. He wrote to his faithful friend and former treasury secretary, Senator Carter Glass, that the Treaty of Berlin was "based upon the old Prussian principle of sacrificing the interests of every other nation, whether friend or foe, in order to gain your own object. We now figure as the pupils of Prussia."[19] Following his retirement, the ailing Wilson had stayed out of politics, but he resolved that in this case he would do what he could to prevent the separate peace from passing the Senate.

Wasting little time, Lodge presented the treaties to the full Senate on 24 September. In a brief opening statement, the majority leader congratulated Secretary Hughes for securing such treaties "under which it seems to me that we secure every advantage that the United States desired to secure and have not been asked to make any concessions that will be embarrassing."[20] Senator William H. King of Utah, an ardent Wilsonian, interrupted Lodge's explanation of the reservations to ask, "Does the Senator think that, claiming so many of the advantages of that treaty [of Versailles], we ought not to assume some of the responsibilities?"[21] Wilsonians asked Lodge this question many times and in many forms over the next month.

The harshest criticism of the treaties during the first day of discussion came from the irreconcilables. Tom Watson of Georgia, who had been elected in 1920 as an "anti-Wilson, anti-league, and anti-war measures Democrat"

---

[17]Johnson to A. Johnson and H. Johnson, Jr., 23 September 1921, part 4, box 2, Johnson Papers.
[18]Fleming, World Organization, p. 50; Murray, Harding Era, p. 139; New York Times, 24 September 1921, p. 1.
[19]Quoted in Wimer and Wimer, "The Separate Peace," p. 19.
[20]Congressional Record, 67th Cong., 1st sess., p. 5770.
[21]Ibid., p. 5772.

and quickly established himself as a fourth supernationalist bitter-ender (along with Borah, Johnson, and Reed), charged that the reservations would not keep the nation out of the Reparation Commission.[22] "If we plead to the jurisdiction of the Reparation Commission," he continued, "we have hit the tar baby the first blow, and the others will follow in due, logical course until every limb of our body will be stuck to the tar baby, and we will be backed into the League."[23] According to the logic of this "tar baby" theory, any economic involvement with Europe would lead straight toward membership in the League of Nations and future wars.

Picking up where he had left off in the Foreign Relations Committee, Borah denounced the German treaty's index references to the Versailles pact as a Trojan horse which would embroil the nation inevitably in the politics of Europe. Then the Idaho senator switched tracks to make a distinctly Wilsonian argument. He asked his colleagues to consider the moral aspect of ratifying treaties which claimed privileges without the corresponding responsibilities and then answered:

> I say that to go into Europe for the purpose of securing some moiety of trade, some advantage in business, some material compensation, some right or privilege under that treaty, and to refuse to stay to perform any obligations connected with the realization of that is a position that is indefensible in morals, and we will not long stand to it before the world.[24]

The only way the United States could claim the fruits of victory from a moral viewpoint, Borah concluded, was to duly execute provisions of the Treaty of Versailles, a policy he certainly did not favor. In a brilliant piece of oratory, Senator Borah linked the arguments of the most rabid irreconcilable isolationist with the Wilsonian case against the peace. Potentially his argument offered something to all of the moralists in the Senate, and there were more than enough of them to block ratification.

After one day of floor debate, the *New York Times* reported, at least twenty senators opposed the treaties, more than enough to prevent prompt action.[25] On 26 September when argument resumed, Borah took the floor once again, this time to announce his regret in being at odds with most of his Republican colleagues. The Idaho senator took pains to show that he was the consistent one in the fight against the surrender of traditional principles of American foreign policy. Borah did not speak in terms of *if* the United States joined the Reparation Commission; the senator claimed to have proof that Harding and Hughes planned to plunge the country into the reparations controversy as soon as the Senate ratified the treaties—and this was not even

---

[22]U.S., Congress, *Congressional Directory*, Joint Committee on Printing, 67th Cong., 2nd sess., p. 18.

[23]*Congressional Record*, 67th Cong., 1st sess., pp. 5775–76.

[24]Ibid., p. 5778.

[25]*New York Times*, 25 September 1921, p. 1.

the worst of the administration's sins. President Wilson, Borah continued, had only accepted the hideous Versailles Treaty because of its connection with the League,

> but now, so far as we are concerned, the league has been stricken from the document. The sole badge of respectability, the sole hope of amelioration, so far as American advocates were concerned, now vanish. With the league stricken out, who is there left in America, reared under the principles of a free government, to defend the terms and conditions of this treaty?[26]

Again Borah was making an essentially moral argument against the treaties, but this time he managed to set himself up as Wilson's moral successor, while arguing from a distinctly isolationist viewpoint.

Williams rose next, first to denounce Borah's vision as "isolated and provincial" and then to announce that he had changed his mind about the treaties. "I had a talk with my friend Carter Glass, of Virginia, this morning," he said, "and Carter and I both concluded that you could swallow this dish if you wanted to . . . that really it created a nausea that would make us throw up the food before we got it plumb down."[27] Nauseous metaphors aside, supporters of the treaties may have felt heartsick themselves because Democratic opposition was suddenly becoming organized.

In the last week of September, Wilson's known opposition to the separate peace began to crystallize party sentiments against the treaties.[28] Democratic senators went into a party caucus of 27 September divided, with Minority Leader Underwood and former Minority Leader Hitchcock both supporting the peace settlement while most others opposed it. After ninety minutes the conferees failed to reach agreement and adjourned for two days while treaty opponents framed reservations.[29] Glass, working closely with Wilson, centered the Democratic opposition to the treaties around a clever plank lifted from the 1920 Republican presidential campaign platform. "We cannot make peace," the statement read, "except in company with our allies. It would brand us with everlasting dishonor and bring ruin to us also if we undertook to make a separate peace." The declaration came, albeit out of context, from a magazine article written by Lodge in June of 1918.[30] Wilson must have enjoyed perpetrating this bit of irony on his most bitter foe, but unless the Senate Democratic leadership could be won over, the former president's revenge would not be complete.

Glass attempted to lure Hitchcock and Rhode Island Senator Peter G.

---

[26]*Congressional Record*, 67th Cong., 1st sess., pp. 5794–5800.
[27]Ibid., pp. 5803–5. See also George Coleman Osborn, *John Sharp Williams, Planter Statesman of the Deep South* (Baton Rouge: Louisiana State University Press, 1943), pp. 385–86.
[28]*New York Times*, 27 September 1921, p. 1.
[29]Ibid., 28 September 1921, pp. 1 and 3.
[30]Ibid.; Wimer and Wimer, "The Separate Peace," pp. 19–20.

Gerry to Wilson's home on S Street for a conference on the treaties. This effort fell through, Glass wrote to Wilson on 29 September, because "each of them treated my preliminary suggestion in a rather treacherous fashion." The Virginia senator suspected that one or both of them had told Senator Pomerene about the invitation and that Pomerene, a strong supporter of the separate peace, fed the story to the press. Nevertheless, Glass told Wilson, opposition to the treaties was growing:

> There have been two conferences and those of us who are opposed to the treaty are hammering hard. At the conference today things were distinctly better and it may be that we shall succeed in averting the disgrace of ratification of the treaty by Democratic votes.[31]

Either Glass held an overly optimistic view of the situation himself or he was just telling Wilson what the old man wanted to hear because things did not go "distinctly better" for the antitreaty forces at the Democratic caucus. The senators agreed to demand time for "reasonable consideration" of the treaties so that they might study the Foreign Relations Committee's reservations. The conference also reaffirmed the earlier view that the treaties should not be made a party matter. In other words, there would be no unified Democratic action. Glass believed that he had only twenty-one of the thirty-seven Democrats on his side, not nearly enough to block the Republican peace.[32]

LODGE'S TACTICS

While Democrats maneuvered behind the scenes, debate on the treaties continued in open session. In order to push the separate peace through more quickly, Lodge arranged for night sessions. On the evening of 28 September, Kellogg denied Borah's contention that the treaties would lead to political entanglements with Europe. The senator from Minnesota emphasized the need for expanded American exports to Central and Eastern Europe in order to assure prosperity at home. For good measure, at a time when the Red Scare was still fresh in many minds, Kellogg linked the treaties to the fight against the communist conspiracy. The United States should support the moderate governments in Germany, Austria, and Hungary as buffer states. Should these governments fail, he said, "the flame of revolution and anarchy which lights the skies of Russia today . . . may sweep westward to the Atlantic and may touch the Western Hemisphere."[33]

Watson of Georgia, the newest irreconcilable, answered Kellogg the

---

[31]Carter Glass to Wilson, 29 September 1921, reel 115, Wilson Papers.
[32]Evans C. Johnson, *Oscar W. Underwood: A Political Biography* (Baton Rouge: Louisiana State University Press, 1980), pp. 313–14; *New York Times*, 30 September 1921, p. 1.
[33]*Congressional Record*, 67th Cong., 1st sess., pp. 5860–62.

next day in terms which revealed the residual bitterness still present three years after the end of the war. Watson accused the administration of rank hypocrisy in rushing to make peace with the nation's enemies while refusing to deal justly with America's own political prisoners, including David T. Blodgett of Iowa, the recipient of a ten-year prison sentence for reading in public one of Watson's speeches on the unconstitutionality of the draft. "Should he be in the Senate and I in the penitentiary?" he asked sarcastically. "He did not say any more in Iowa than I have said here in the Senate, and I think that I am in somewhat better company than he. That is only an opinion of mine. [Laughter]" The Georgian ridiculed Kellogg's economic argument, pointing out the absurdity of engaging in commerce with the torpedoers of the *Lusitania* while the nation boycotted its wartime ally, Russia.[34] Watson was spoiling for a fight with the administration over the treaties, but among the irreconcilables, only Borah, Reed, Norris, and La Follette stood ready to cast votes in the negative. Most of the bitter-enders, including Johnson and every surviving member of the realist faction, favored the separate peace. Meanwhile, powerful supporters of the treaties maneuvered to assure eventual ratification.

On 30 September Lodge offered an agreement for unanimous consent to limit debate on the treaties after 14 October.[35] Underwood explained that he had negotiated the cloture resolution in accordance with the Democratic desire to give the peace careful consideration. He warned the Republicans "that unless we receive proper consideration from the majority of the Senate in the consideration of this matter they will endanger the ratification of the treaties. We have shown our good faith in the matter."[36] The minority leader had acted at the insistence of the Glass forces that there must be adequate time for debate on reservations. Still, the agreement, passed unanimously later in the day, stood as a victory for the protreaty forces as it eliminated the possibility that die-hard opponents might use the filibuster in a last-ditch effort to put off or even to kill ratification.

Senate Democrats wanted to debate the separate peace fully, but the whole subject had begun to bore the public. "There is not the interest in the German Treaty that some people here believed there would be," Johnson noted. "Indeed, I don't think our people pay much attention to it, and I think they care little about it."[37] If the *New York Times* was any reflection of popular opinion, one aspect of the treaty fight did interest the public; while the *Times* relegated reports on the debates to the middle of the paper, the involvement of Wilson made the front pages.

---

[34]Ibid., pp. 5879–81. See also C. Vann Woodward, *Tom Watson, Agrarian Rebel* (New York: Oxford University Press, 1963), p. 476.

[35]*Congressional Record*, 67th Cong., 1st sess., pp. 5888–89.

[36]Ibid.; *New York Times*, 1 October 1921, p. 1.

[37]Johnson to A. Johnson and H. Johnson, Jr., 1 October 1921, part 6, box 3, Johnson Papers.

Colby wrote to his old chief that "there is tremendous speculation everywhere about your course with reference to the German Treaty." Although he doubted that the ex-president would break his policy of silence with regard to current events, the former secretary of state found it "amusing to see the hosts of normalcy balk, shy and rear when they fancy they discern the shadow of your tall figure athwart their muddle-headed program. The persistent reports of your gain in health and vigor is giving the enemy a case of nerves."[38] Wilson had no intention of denouncing the peace treaties publicly, but he continued to fight "the enemy" in a limited way. On 4 October he congratulated Williams for changing his mind about the separate peace "which completes the international degradation which the Republicans have brought upon us."[39] If the fallen president could persuade just a few more of his old supporters in the Senate to vote against the treaties, the peace would fall short of the two-thirds majority necessary for ratification.

Senate debate resumed on 5 October when Texas Democrat Morris Sheppard denounced the separate peace, in a speech lasting for over six hours.[40] Then Senator Moses, a realist irreconcilable and former chief liaison between Lodge and the bitter-enders during the Versailles Treaty debate, spoke in favor of the treaties. Like Borah, Moses dreaded the possibility that Hughes and "that group of international bankers" might plunge the nation into the work of the Reparation Commission, but he argued that rejection of the peace could only make it easier for the administration to justify involvement in European affairs.[41] Johnson agreed, contending that his reservation prohibiting American participation on any Versailles-related body without congressional approval safeguarded the country. "Borah says in response," Johnson wrote, "that with our servile Senators and subject Congressmen, the Administration will have no difficulty in passing an Act or Joint Resolution for participation in the Reparations Commission." Johnson did not understand Borah's attitude; neither did most of the other irreconcilables.[42]

"THAT SUPREME EGOTIST"

Wilson believed that only the unified action of Senate Democrats could defeat the treaties.[43] On 10 October the former president wrote to Senator Swanson:

[38]Bainbridge Colby to Wilson, 4 October 1921, reel 115, Wilson Papers.
[39]Wilson to John Sharp Williams, 4 October 1921, ibid.
[40]*Congressional Record*, 67th Cong., 1st sess., pp. 6006–58; *New York Times*, 6 October 1921, p.19.
[41]*Congressional Record*, 67th Cong, 1st sess., pp. 6059–60; *New York Times*, 6 October 1921, p. 19.
[42]Johnson to Charles K. McClatchy, 5 October 1921, part 3, box 4, Johnson Papers.
[43]Wimer and Wimer, "The Separate Peace," p. 21.

> If the Democratic Senators will organize a caucus which can bind its members, and then care to seek my counsel, I will be glad to put at their disposal the utmost resources of my thought and judgment.
>
> Otherwise, I should not feel justified in adding such a responsibility to the present tasks of my brain.[44]

Swanson canvassed his fellow Democrats and found that few had changed their minds since the last caucus two weeks earlier. "This is frankly the situation," he wrote to Wilson, "and I do not think anything can be accomplished by calling a conference and endeavoring to get a party declaration on the matter."[45] That news must have been very disappointing to the ex-president; it appeared that the separate peace would go through, although the vote might be exceedingly close.

On 12 October Senator Knox died, thereby eliminating one sure vote for the treaty and delaying the ratification proceedings. That same day the *New York Times* reported that certain prominent Democrats—including William G. McAdoo, former secretary of the treasury and Wilson's son-in-law, and Bernard Baruch, former chairman of the War Industries Board—had pressured Democratic senators "to stand by the Versailles Treaty."[46] Additionally Hamilton Holt, the influential publisher, announced that his Woodrow Wilson Democracy political club was launching its own pressure campaign against the German treaty.[47] These last-minute efforts did have an effect. On 16 October the *Times* noted that the most optimistic conclusion from Republican leaders indicated only a three vote legal margin for the treaties. The problem lay not so much with the Republicans because only three of their senators—Borah, La Follette, and Norris—opposed the peace. But increasing Democratic opposition so worried Lodge that he called upon President Harding to use his influence on the governor of Pennsylvania in appointing a successor to Knox quickly, before the treaties came to a vote.[48] In the interim Senate treaty opponents began to offer amendments.

Senator Thomas Walsh of Montana, a Wilsonian, spoke against the treaties on 12 October. He praised Borah, observing that "the Senator who taunted his Republican colleagues with abandoning their contention of the wisdom of noninterference in European affairs is correct in the view he takes." He charged that the Republicans were pushing the United States into the affairs of Europe, but only halfway. "We ought either to enter far enough to be of service," he continued, "or we ought to stay out altogether."[49] Walsh and the other Wilsonians opposed Borah's brand of isolationism absolutely;

---

[44]Wilson to Claude A. Swanson, 10 October 1921, reel 115, Wilson Papers.
[45]Swanson to Wilson, 12 October 1921, ibid.
[46]*New York Times*, 13 October 1921, p. 3.
[47]Ibid., p. 13.
[48]Ibid., 16 October 1921, p. 1.
[49]*Congressional Record*, 67th Cong., 1st sess., p. 6250.

yet the supernationalist irreconcilables (except for Johnson) and the Wilsonians both opposed the separate peace on moral grounds. They regarded as moral anathema the essentially internationalist Republican policy of economic privileges without political and military responsibilities. When debate on the treaties resumed on 12 October, the supernationalist irreconcilables and the Wilsonians offered two very different sets of amendments, all of them designed to keep the United States either completely in or out of European affairs.

Walsh asked the Senate how the Treaty of Berlin could assume responsibility for Part 5 of the Versailles pact, dealing with German disarmament, when the nation had no vote in the League of Nations councils which judged Germany's compliance with disarmament provisions. Morally, how could the nation pledge itself to strip Germany of arms without committing itself to the League guarantees of protection? To remedy this situation, the Montana Democrat offered an amendment which pledged the United States to protect Germany so long as that vanquished nation complied with the Versailles Treaty's disarmament provisions.[50] When only six Wilsonians voted for the amendment, Walsh offered a watered-down version, but it too went down to defeat overwhelmingly.[51]

Reed of Missouri charged that "not 25 per cent of the Senators in this body have ever read this treaty. By that I mean that not 25 per cent of them have read the treaty along with the documents which it incorporates." With help from Borah, Reed fashioned an amendment which eliminated all references to the Versailles agreement in the German-American treaty. The Missourian argued that the rights gained in the treaty did not seem to be worth the risks of becoming involved in "the hell pot of European politics and embroilment, that witches' cauldron, into which every poisonous and noxious thing is being dropped daily and hourly." The Senate defeated Reed's amendment by a vote of sixty-six to seven, with only the irreconcilables (Johnson included) and two disillusioned Democrats casting ayes.[52]

A few days before the final vote, Colby "did a little shopping around on the treaty situation" for Wilson, submitting a detailed memorandum as though Wilson were still president and Colby his secretary of state. Colby reported that while most Democrats would vote against the treaties, a small group under the combined leadership of Underwood and Hitchcock planned to join the Republicans in supporting the separate peace, a move which would give the pacts the necessary two-thirds majority. In his analysis Colby tried to account for the disloyalty of Hitchcock and Underwood. Hitchcock faced a tough reelection campaign shortly "and his present wobbly course is supposed to be dictated by a desire to curry favor with the pro-German elements in his

---

[50]Ibid., p. 6361.
[51]Ibid., pp. 6364 and 6367.
[52]Ibid., pp. 6375–82; *New York Times*, 18 October 1921, p. 19.

State" as well as by advice from William Jennings Bryan. As for Senator Underwood,

> his theory of opposition-leadership is that he should not frustrate the effort of the majority to discharge the responsibilities which the voters placed upon it. . . . and that the Democrats should not take the responsibility of defeating the treaty's ratification, inasmuch as the country sighs for peace and business is anxious to see the impediments to its resumption with Germany removed.[53]

The former president could do nothing more before the Senate came to a vote; Wilson's attempt at a limited political comeback would fail, but just barely.

The Foreign Relations Committee's action in reporting the treaties to the floor with two reservations infuriated Secretary of State Hughes. He was especially angry over the amendment on American claims, which he regarded as "entirely superfluous" and "in rather crude form."[54] As time went on, however, and serious opposition developed to the peace, annoyance turned to apprehension at the Department of State. As the vote approached, Castle wrote to Commissioner Dresel that "some little doubt" existed whether the treaties would pass. "I understand," he wrote, "that, if four of the Democrats who agreed to vote for it should be over-persuaded by that supreme egotist, W[oodrow] W[ilson], who has injected himself into the fight, it will not be possible."[55] Virtually all of the prevote analysis concentrated on the crucial roles of the errant Wilsonians, Underwood and Hitchcock. The friends of the treaties also had to reckon with those other mercurial moralists, the pro-administration irreconcilables.

IRRECONCILABLE LOGIC

Johnson felt uneasy about voting with the Lodge forces and against his fellow supernationalist irreconcilables, especially his old friend Borah. "It really hurts me to disagree with him," he had written in September, "although he is a most difficult person to keep in agreement with."[56] On 18 October, the last day of debate, Johnson spoke to the Senate about his stance in rather defensive terms, noting that he had done as much as any man to prevent the

---

[53]Colby to Wilson, 14 October 1921, and memorandum, Colby to Wilson, 14 October 1921, reel 115, Wilson Papers.

[54]Hughes to Harding, 23 September 1921, reel 144, Harding Papers.

[55]Castle to Dresel, 19 October 1921, box 68, file 16, Dresel Papers. Although this letter was dated October 19, it was probably written earlier. See Wimer and Wimer, "The Separate Peace," p. 21n.

[56]Johnson to A. Johnson and H. Johnson, Jr., 23 September 1921, part 4, box 2, Johnson Papers.

nation from becoming involved in European entanglements. "No less earnestly in the future than in the past," he continued, "will I pursue this course." Johnson went on to say that although Secretary Hughes "has been one of those who, mistakenly, would have taken us into the maelstrom of Europe," President Harding's intentions, which were more isolationist (and hence, more honorable), could be trusted.[57] Later Johnson explained to his sons that "when Harding had gone right, it was the part of decency to say so," although he stood ready to oppose the administration if it erred in the future. The speech, he wrote, "angered Borah, but he is simply impossible."[58] Johnson's dilemma was that while he thought himself "as tender as most people of a moral obligation," he had chosen the pragmatic course in this particular instance rather than what the other supernationalists saw as the moral one.[59]

Across the senatorial aisle, Hitchcock was caught in a similar quandary. After Johnson spoke, Wilson's former confidant rose to defend the separate peace. He made an eloquent plea for Democrats to put aside partisan considerations and to think of the country's best interests.[60] Democratic irreconcilable Reed of Missouri would have none of the pragmatic argument, emphasizing, as had Borah, that references in the Berlin Treaty to rights under the Versailles pact gave the country the moral obligation to accept the burdens of victory. Since one of those burdens implied acceptance of the principle of reduced claims against Germany, Reed proposed an amendment to lock up all seized German property until Germany paid full claim damages to American citizens.[61] After the defeat of this amendment, Reed offered another which would reserve to the United States all rights under Versailles-related commissions regardless of whether the nation joined these bodies. This amendment also went down to defeat by a lopsided margin.[62]

The Wilsonians also offered amendments during the last days of debate. Senator King moved "to strike out the pending treaty entirely and substitute in lieu thereof the Versailles Treaty with the Lodge reservations," a move the senators tabled fifty-nine to twenty-three.[63] Finally, Senator Kenneth McKellar of Tennessee proposed an amendment which would have given the Berlin Treaty a clause corresponding to Article 231 of the Versailles pact, spelling out full German acknowledgment and acceptance for starting the Great War. The McKellar amendment, which lost badly twelve to sixty-six, produced a split among the Wilsonians.[64]

[57]*Congressional Record*, 67th Cong., 1st sess., pp. 6408–10.
[58]Johnson to A. Johnson and H. Johnson, Jr., 21 October 1921, part 6, box 3, Johnson Papers.
[59]Johnson to A. Johnson and H. Johnson, Jr., 23 September 1921, part 4, box 2, ibid.
[60]*Congressional Record*, 67th Cong., 1st sess., pp. 6410–12.
[61]Ibid., pp. 6414–18.
[62]Ibid., pp. 6419–20.
[63]Ibid., pp. 6420 and 6435.
[64]Ibid., pp. 6433–34.

La Follette, leader of the peace progressive faction of the irreconcilables, had not joined in the fight against the separate peace. Just before the treaties came to a vote, however, he gave a speech which not only summarized the position of the supernationalists and the peace progressives on the Republican peace, but foreshadowed the basic progressive approach to foreign policy in the 1920s as well. The whole idea of a separate peace, La Follette noted, smacked of fraudulence as the rights of the victors were "inseparably bound" in a moral sense to corresponding obligations. Ratification of even these separate treaties "will involve this country in the quarrels and dissensions of Europe for a period of at least 40 years to come." Tragically, La Follette concluded, renewed American involvement in Europe "will prevent this Government from devoting its efforts and the best intelligence of its statesmanship to the solution of its domestic problems without reference to the bewildering cross-currents of European imperialism and diplomacy."[65] In other words the internationalist course would push the nation into European-style imperialism, and at the same time pose a threat to democracy at home.[66] From this perspective Hughes's brand of internationalism was just as bad as Wilson's, for the results would be the same. Some, including Borah and La Follette, seemed even to prefer Wilsonian foreign policy over normalcy because no matter how misguided Wilson may have been, his policies were at least moral.[67]

PEACE AS "A DISAGREEABLE NECESSITY"

On 18 October at 7:30 P.M., the Senate voted to ratify the separate peace with Germany by a vote of sixty-six to twenty, a legal majority of eight. An identical vote was recorded for the Austrian treaty, while the Hungarian pact passed sixty-six to seventeen. Since Norris was ill, only Borah and La Follette broke from Republican ranks to vote against the Berlin Treaty. In the end Underwood, Hitchcock, and fourteen other Democrats made the difference between administration victory and continued domestic deadlock.[68] Lodge found the results "very satisfactory," writing to Commissioner Dresel that Wilson had tried to induce Democrats to vote as a unit ("a perfectly crazy plan") but "fortunately, Senator Underwood, the leader of the Democratic

---

[65]Ibid., pp. 6435–38.

[66]LeRoy Ashby, *The Spearless Leader: Senator Borah and the Progressive Movement in the 1920's* (Urbana: University of Illinois Press, 1972), p. 95. See also Albert J. Beveridge to Borah, 6 October 1921, box 94, Borah Papers.

[67]Claudius O. Johnson, *Borah of Idaho* (Seattle: University of Washington Press, 1967), p. 256.

[68]*Congressional Record*, 67th Cong., 1st sess., pp. 6438–39; *New York Times*, 19 October 1921, pp. 1 and 4.

side, took what seemed to me the sound and patriotic view" and the separate peace passed. "I regard it," he concluded, "as a great achievement and of real value to the country."[69] Meanwhile, at his home across town, Wilson dictated a note to Senator Swanson, asking for a copy of the *Congressional Record* for 18 October. The former president, confident that history would condemn those who voted for the separate peace, wanted to know their names so that he might avoid all contact with them in the future.[70]

The separate peace proved to be neither as loathsome as Wilson thought nor as great as Lodge had supposed. The *New York Times* struck a better balance when it editorialized that "the country, like the Senate, coldly acquiesces in the treaty as a disagreeable necessity."[71] If the treaties represented a victory for the administration, it was certainly a hollow one. Originally Hughes had wanted to resubmit the Versailles Treaty with new reservations, but settled for pacts based on the Knox-Porter resolution with index references to American rights and privileges. The Senate forced Hughes to compromise his peace plans further when it approved the Johnson-Lodge reservation specifying that the government could not participate in any Versailles-related commission without congressional approval. Johnson made it plain that he had framed the amendment to hamstring the internationalist secretary of state. When the reparations question subsequently created a crisis in Europe, Hughes could do little about it officially in spite of America's powerful economic position. For the Harding administration, the separate peace had been, at best, a disagreeable necessity.

Senate Republicans really had very little to boast about. They guided the treaties through the ratification process, but their performance had been uninspired. Shortly after the treaty debates, Nicholas Murray Butler, president of Columbia University, expressed dismay at the Old Guard's lack of leadership which "practically invited political guerillas like La Follette and Borah to take the leadership out of Lodge's hands and they do so at intervals in ways that are most distressing."[72] The Republican leadership was old and on its way out. Knox, who began the whole separate peace movement, did not live long enough to vote for ratification. Boies Penrose, who, in his prime, could have whipped even a Borah into line, died a few months later. Lodge had already begun on a long slide downhill both physically and mentally.[73] Even with a top-heavy Republican majority behind him, the majority leader

[69]Lodge to Dresel, 22 October 1921, box 263, file 7, Dresel Papers.
[70]Wilson to Swanson, 20 October 1921, and Swanson to Wilson, 21 October 1921, reel 115, Wilson Papers. See also Breckinridge Long Diary, 20 October 1921, Breckinridge Long Papers, box 2, folder 11, Library of Congress, Manuscript Division, Washington.
[71]"The Anticlimax Treaty," *New York Times*, 20 October 1921, p. 6.
[72]Quoted in Ashby, *The Spearless Leader*, p. 34.
[73]Ibid., pp. 34–35; Herbert F. Margulies, *Senator Lenroot of Wisconsin: A Political Biography, 1900–1929* (Columbia: University of Missouri Press, 1977), pp. 343–44; Russell, *Shadow of Blooming Grove*, pp. 457–59.

almost let Wilson block ratification—and the former president never left his house on S Street.

Ironically the Old Guard's leadership began to collapse just when it had gained ascendancy over the executive in foreign policy. Even then the moment of triumph came only when key Democrats defected from the camp of Woodrow Wilson. Former Minority Leader Hitchcock supported the peace in a bid to regain voter support back home in Nebraska; Minority Leader Underwood voted for the treaties to end the domestic deadlock. Before the World War, Underwood had opposed Wilsonian idealism in foreign policy, and he accepted the defeat of the Versailles Treaty gracefully, then helped the Republicans to return to a policy of traditional nationalism.[74] To Frank Cobb, a leading Wilsonian journalist, Underwood was "about as much of a Democrat as Penrose."[75] The Alabama senator supported the pragmatic peace, although reluctantly, since many in his party opposed it. For leading Democrats like Hitchcock and Underwood who made ratification possible, as with the administration, the treaties were only a disagreeable necessity.

The realist irreconcilables and other assorted bitter-enders, including Johnson, genuinely viewed the treaties as a great achievement. They had been fighting more or less continuously against the new internationalism since 1919, and the separate peace represented a triumph of their efforts. Johnson supported the Berlin Treaty because it terminated the state of war with Germany, ended all chances that Hughes and Hoover would return the Versailles pact to the Senate, and "contained the first official repudiation of the League of Nations."[76] The separate peace completed the irreconcilables' victory over Wilson. The Senate had designed the treaty reservations to keep Wilson's successor as chief foreign policymaker, Hughes, from assuming new internationalist obligations.

WILSON'S MORAL SUCCESSOR

Senator Borah denounced the treaties bitterly from start to finish. Even though he voted against the separate peace, the Idahoan also emerged from the ratification fight as a victor. "He is playing a long hand," Johnson had written during the debates, "and playing it well."[77] Borah objected to the treaties on grounds that Hughes's index references to the rights and privileges

---

[74]Arthur S. Link, *Wilson, The New Freedom* (Princeton, NJ: Princeton University Press, 1967), pp. 309–10 and 312.

[75]Frank Cobb to Wilson, 17 October 1921, reel 115, Wilson Papers.

[76]Johnson to McClatchy, 29 October 1921, part 3, box 4, Johnson Papers.

[77]Johnson to A. Johnson and H. Johnson, Jr., 21 October 1921, part 6, box 3, Johnson Papers.

of the Versailles pact were tantamount to acceptance of the basically unfair and immoral postwar peace system of Europe. He also judged the separate treaties to be immoral because they referred only to American rights and not to corresponding responsibilities. Borah understood that the administration's motive for claiming advantages without obligations was primarily economic and not political, yet he still objected. "This Government," he wrote, "could better afford to give up any material advantage then [sic] to give even any moral sanction to the militaristic and imperialistic principles of the Versailles Treaty."[78] Borah feared that the separate peace sacrificed the nation's moral purpose and might lead to war in the future through American involvement in Europe.

There was a striking parallel between Borah's idealistic thesis and one that President Wilson put forth on 5 March 1917 during his second inaugural address. In this important but often forgotten speech, the president looked ahead to the crucial period after the war when the victors and the vanquished would gather to make peace. The United States, in order to preserve its way of life at home, would have to stand for "the principles of a liberated mankind" on behalf of all the world.[79] During the separate peace debates, Borah praised Wilson for taking this great principle with him to Paris. Regrettably for the world, as Borah saw it, the imperialists of Europe triumphed over the president in the Versailles Treaty.[80] Wilson and Borah parted company over the Versailles pact, while continuing to respect and admire one another because of their shared idealism.[81] It was altogether fitting that they should find themselves on the same side in the fight against what both of them saw as a dishonorable and immoral peace settlement. During the struggle against the treaties, Borah's biographer Claudius O. Johnson wrote, "some observers were beginning to say that Borah was now the successor to Wilson as moral leader; nor did Borah resent the suggestion."[82]

Fortunately, at least for the supernationalists, the separate peace constituted only a beginning point for the comprehensive settlement of war-related problems. Hughes had already begun to negotiate with Japan over former German Pacific colonial possessions. When an agreement on that subject reached the Senate, Borah, Wilson's moral successor, would be ready and waiting to confront Hughes, a dedicated Republican internationalist pursuing a policy of American economic expansion largely inherited from his predecessor, Wilson.

---

[78]Borah to Edwards, 28 September 1921, box 94, Borah Papers.
[79]Woodrow Wilson, *President Wilson's State Papers and Addresses* (New York: George H. Doran, 1918, p. 370.
[80]*Congressional Record*, 67th Cong., 1st sess., pp. 5794–95.
[81]Johnson, *Borah of Idaho*, p. 256.
[82]Ibid., p. 260.

3

"THIS APPARENTLY SMALL MATTER"
The Yap Controversy and the Problem of Mandates

On 19 August 1919 President Wilson met with the Senate Foreign Relations Committee at the White House to discuss the Versailles Treaty. At one point Lodge brought up the subject of former German overseas posses-sions, asking Wilson if the Navy Department considered any of them to have strategic importance. "There is a little island," the president recalled, "which I must admit I had not heard of before."[1] The "little island" which Wilson could not remember was Yap, a cluster of ten islands totaling 38.6 square miles in area in the Western Carolines 1,100 miles east of the Philippines. Although these tiny specks in the Pacific contained neither important raw materials nor good harbors, Yap had served as the cable center for the German-Netherlands Telegraph Company, a vital link in the communications system between the United States and the Far East.[2] After the defeat of Wilson's treaty, at a time when foreign affairs did not interest Americans particularly, the United States became very concerned about Yap when the Allies turned the islands over to Japan as a mandate.

Secretary of State Hughes and the Japanese ambassador to the United States, Baron Shidehara Kijūrō, finally settled the dispute that arose over Yap with a treaty in 1922, but not before the mandates had become a major irritant in both Japanese-American and Anglo-American relations while further alienating the United States from the League of Nations. In arranging this settlement, Hughes elaborated on Wilson's basic Asia policy, designed to arrest Japanese expansion and to win further international recognition of the Open Door.

Hughes established a precedent in the Yap dispute that led to the safeguarding of American rights and privileges in other, more important man-dated areas. However, the secretary of state found implementation of the Open

---

[1]U.S., Congress, Senate, *Treaty of Peace with Germany: Hearings Before the Committee on Foreign Relations*, S. Doc. 106, 66th Cong., 1st sess., p. 506. See also Ray Stannard Baker, *American Chronicle* (New York: Charles Scribner's Sons, 1935), p. 489.

[2]Sherwood G. Lingenfelter, *Yap: Political Leadership and Culture in an Island Society* (Honolulu: University of Hawaii Press, 1975), pp. 5–7.

Door in Asia to be every bit as elusive as Wilson had before him. In the Senate irreconcilable supernationalists such as Borah and Johnson contended that Hughes's diplomacy smacked of dangerous internationalism, even as many Democrats opposed the Yap pact because it did not go far enough in asserting American rights. The Yap Treaty passed the Senate with the help of key Democrats who believed in the administration's brand of limited internationalism based on policies inherited from Wilson but refashioned by Hughes to fit Republican ideology.

ORIGINS OF THE DISPUTE

Japan and the United States had been quarreling openly over Yap for months when Hughes became secretary of state. Although Wilson seemed to lose interest in most facets of foreign policy after the bitter defeat of the Versailles Treaty, his concern for Yap never flagged. At the Paris Peace Conference, Wilson pushed hard for a mandate system to avoid the traditional imperialist practice of dividing the colonial possessions of the losers. In theory the mandate system would help to make the world safe for democracy through elimination of colonialism. Wilsonians also assumed that the Open Door policy would prevail in the mandates, thus assuring peaceful economic competition among the advanced capitalist powers in the world's underdeveloped regions. Unfortunately for Wilson and his scheme, the Allies had already divided nearly all the German and Turkish colonies through secret wartime treaties. In the end most mandates were not entrusted to neutrals, as Wilson had envisioned, but to the Allies along the lines of the secret treaties.[3] Article 22 of the League covenant awarded mandates to "advanced nations" in three categories: A—Near Eastern mandates almost ready for independence; B—mandates, especially in Central Africa, which required significant supervision before independence; and C—mandates, especially South-West Africa and the Pacific islands, which would probably never be independent.[4]

On 7 May 1919 the Council of Four, including President Wilson, mandated Germany's Pacific islands north of the equator to Japan, subject to official League confirmation. Presumably the Japanese mandate included Yap,

---

[3]Edward M. Bennett, "Mandates and Trusteeships," in *Encyclopedia of American Foreign Policy*, pp. 521–23; N. Gordon Levin, *Woodrow Wilson and World Politics: America's Response to War and Revolution* (New York: Oxford University Press, 1968), pp. 245–46; Seymour, *Colonel House*, 4:157–58. For a bitter critique of Wilson's performance, see Robert Lansing, *The Peace Negotiations: A Personal Narrative* (Boston: Houghton Mifflin, 1921), pp. 149–51.

[4]*The Treaties of Peace*, pp. 19–20. See also Bennett, "Mandates and Trusteeships," p. 521.

although the official minutes did not specify the island group.[5] Because of its importance as a cable center, Wilson and Secretary of State Robert Lansing had called for the internationalization of Yap on three separate occasions before the council's decision.[6] "I made the point," Wilson said, three months later before the Foreign Relations Committee, "that the disposition, or rather the control, of that island should be reserved for the general conference which is to be held in regard to the ownership and operation of the cables." Further questioning of the president revealed that his reservations about the Yap mandate had only been oral, but he insisted that "nobody has any doubt as to what was agreed upon."[7]

Few people gave thought to the question of Yap during the dramatic nationwide debate over the Versailles Treaty. The Wilson administration became concerned about the Japanese mandate again during preliminary organizational meetings of the International Council on Communications in late 1920, a conference the Allies had set up to discuss problems concerning cables, including the former German cable center of Yap. On 9 November 1920, more than a year and a half after the Council of Four's action, Secretary of State Colby sent official protests over the disposition of Yap to Japan, France, Great Britain, and Italy.[8]

In reply the British Foreign Office pointed out that the Council of Four's Yap decision did not include any recorded reservations.[9] Anglo-American relations had already become strained in 1920 in the wake of the Wilson administration's sharp protests over French and British sphere-grabbing at the San Remo Conference.[10] Britain's apparent support of its Japanese ally on the Yap question further undermined the bonds of friendship between the two Anglo-Saxon powers. Colby denied the British contention "that the terms of

[5]U.S., Department of State, *Papers Relating to the Foreign Relations of the United States, Paris Peace Conference*, 10 vols. (Washington: Government Printing Office, 1946), 5:506–8. For the notes of the official interpreter, see Paul Mantoux, *Les Délibérations Du Conseil Des Quatres* (24 Mars–28 Juin), 2 vols. (Paris: Editions du Centre National de la Recherche Scientifique, 1955), pp. 513–14.

[6]A. Whitney Griswold, *The Far Eastern Policy of the United States* (New Haven, CT: Yale University Press, 1966), p. 265.

[7]*Treaty of Peace with Germany*, 66th Cong., 1st sess., p. 506. See also the acting secretary of state (Norman Davis) to the ambassador in Great Britain (John W. Davis), 4 December 1920, RG 59, 862i.01/59, DSNA. See also memorandum, Leland Harrison to W. W. Cumberland, 24 May 1921, Leland Harrison Papers, box 7, Library of Congress, Manuscript Division, Washington.

[8]The secretary of state to the chargé in Japan (Bell), 9 November 1920, 862i.01/49a, DSNA. Despatches to other powers sent as 862i.01/49b, 58a, and 58b.

[9]The ambassador in Great Britain (J. Davis) to the secretary of state, 17 November 1920, 862i.01/59, DSNA.

[10]U.S., Department of State, *Papers Relating to the Foreign Relations of the United States, 1920*, 3 vols. (Washington: Government Printing Office, 1935), 2:649–68 (hereafter cited as *FRUS*, followed by appropriate year).

the mandates can properly be discussed only in the Council of the League of
Nations and by signatories of the Covenant." The powers which the Allied
and Associated Nations enjoyed over the mandates, he asserted, "accrued to
them as a direct result of the war against the Central Powers." The United
States, therefore, still had an equal voice in the mandates question even though
it did not choose to join the League.[11]

Japan responded to American objections to the Yap mandate in February
of 1921. Count Uchida, the Japanese foreign minister, informed the State
Department that his government failed to see any merit in the Wilson administration's "extraordinary and unusual interpretation" of the circumstances
surrounding the transfer of Yap to Japan.[12] The next day Undersecretary of
State Norman Davis met with Ambassador Shidehara, but the two parties
made no progress because both sides had become convinced that they were
absolutely right. "The United States," Davis noted, "could not and should
not give way in this apparently small matter."[13]

Neither side could give way in the "apparently small matter" of Yap;
much larger issues were at stake elsewhere. The Great War destroyed the
balance of power which existed until 1914 in the Far East, bringing on a
Japanese-American confrontation in its place.[14] Late in the war, Wilson
launched a diplomatic offensive to stop Japanese expansion. The American
president fought long and hard at Versailles to restore the Japanese-occupied
Shantung Peninsula to China, and lost. Wilson sent American troops into
Russia during the Civil War for many reasons, not the least of which involved
checkmating possible Japanese designs on Siberia. Other irritants between
the two countries, including immigration and a rapidly escalating naval race,
made the Yap question look comparatively insignificant.[15] However, the many
problems in Japanese-American relations in 1921 created a climate of mutual
hostility and fear that made solution of the Yap dispute much more difficult
than it might have been under more friendly circumstances.

President Wilson reviewed the Japanese-American correspondence over
Yap during his last full day in office. In a letter addressed to Secretary Colby,
but obviously intended for the incoming administration—and posterity—Wilson insisted in no uncertain terms that he had never consented to the assignment

---

[11]The secretary of state to the British secretary of state for foreign affairs (Curzon), 20
November 1920, ibid., 2:671. See also the acting secretary of state to the ambassador in Great
Britain (J. Davis), 4 December 1920, 862i.01/59, DSNA.
[12]The chargé in Japan (Bell) to the secretary of state, 27 February 1921, 862i.01/46, DSNA.
[13]Memorandum of a conversation between the Japanese ambassador and N. Davis, 28
February 1921, 862i.01/166, ibid.
[14]Griswold, *Far Eastern Policy*, p. 176.
[15]Ibid., pp. 223–68; Michael G. Fry, *Illusions of Security: North Atlantic Diplomacy,
1918–1922* (Toronto: University of Toronto Press, 1972), p. 57; Levin, *Wilson and World
Politics*, pp. 200–202, and 236–44; Charles E. Neu, *The Troubled Encounter: The United States
and Japan* (New York: John Wiley, 1975), pp. 98–101.

of the Yap mandate to Japan.[16] Wilson had already lost a world; he did not want to lose Yap too. Although the voters cast aside Wilsonianism in the 1920 election, Republican internationalists such as Hughes were not about to terminate American participation in world politics, especially where economic interests might suffer. After the White House changed hands, A. Whitney Griswold noted, "the very individuals who had led the attack on the Versailles Treaty, and repudiated Wilson's labors at Paris, now proceeded to steal his thunder and use it in Eastern Asia."[17] Harding and Hughes would begin in Asia as Wilson had ended—with Yap.

REPUBLICAN DIPLOMACY

On 16 March the State Department received a letter from the president of the League council in reply to Colby's protest over the Yap mandate. The allocation of the mandates, President Gastao Da Cunha informed the Americans, did not concern the League. Consequently the present misunderstanding "would seem to be between the United States and the Principal Allied Powers rather than between the United States and the League."[18] This position spared the State Department the embarrassment of dealing with the mandates problem through the League at a time when Secretary of State Hughes was sending out careful feelers to the White House and the Senate about possible League membership. In accordance with department procedure, Hughes did not even send a formal acknowledgement of the League despatch.[19]

Hughes was as determined as Wilson had been to protest the Yap mandate, but he believed that the former president and Colby had erred in concentrating their attention solely on the tiny island group. The secretary and his advisers contended that Japan's whole North Pacific mandate—including the Marshall, Mariana, and Caroline islands—posed a potential threat to American security in the Philippines and even Hawaii. The administration could not reverse the council's decision to mandate the island chains to Japan; still, Hughes reasoned, he could build a strong case for demanding free access to the mandated areas.[20] That would allow American authorities to inspect the islands for possible fortifications while, at the same time, setting a precedent for an American Open Door in other more economically significant mandates in the Near East and Africa.

[16]Wilson to Colby, 3 March 1921, 862i.01/172, DSNA.
[17]Griswold, *Far Eastern Policy*, p. 269.
[18]The president of the council of the League of Nations (Da Cunha) to the secretary of state, 1 March 1921, 862i.01/68, DSNA.
[19]Glad, *Illusions of Innocence*, pp. 174–75.
[20]Pusey, *Charles Evans Hughes*, pp. 446–47.

Secretary of State Hughes bypassed the whole bitter and irresolvable argument over what had or had not occurred in the Council of Four. In identical notes to Tokyo, London, Paris, and Rome the secretary began with a repetition of Wilson's assertion that the Allies should not have disposed of former German colonies without American permission. The League's confirmation of the mandates had no relevance because the United States, as a nonmember, never gave the world body binding authority in the matter. "The right accruing to the United States through the victory in which it participated," Hughes continued, "could not be regarded as in any way ceded or surrendered to Japan, or to other nations, except by treaty." Obviously the United States had made no such treaty. The American failure to ratify the Versailles pact did not detract from rights acquired earlier as one of the victors. Therefore, he concluded, the United States "cannot recognize the allocation of the Island [of Yap] or the validity of the mandate to Japan."[21] According to the logic of this argument, it really made no difference what the council had decided and whether or not Wilson had reiterated his reservations when the Supreme Council allocated the German islands, including Yap, to Japan.[22]

The Hughes note undercut the arguments of the other Allies completely. From a legal standpoint, the secretary transformed Wilson and Colby's weak and defensive case into a strong and irrefutable one. On 12 April as he waited for Allied reaction to the notes, Hughes held a stormy meeting with Britain's ambassador, Sir Auckland Geddes. The British ambassador complained about remarks made at one of Senator Lodge's dinner parties "to the effect that Sir Maurice Hankey had been guilty of a 'trick' in writing up the minutes of the meeting of May 7, 1919, relating to the mandate to Japan, or at least of a 'subtlety.'" Geddes also connected this gossip with an incident earlier in the year when Hughes had accused the Allies of giving Yap to Japan "behind the back" of America. The secretary tried to minimize the importance of such unofficial remarks as he switched the subject to the Allies' indifferent attitude toward American rights. Ambassador Geddes said that the 1916 secret treaty with Japan committed his government to favor the Japanese mandate in the North Pacific, a statement which Hughes found "most extraordinary." If the matter had already been decided, what was the Council of Four discussing in May 1919? Why were the Allies relying on the minutes of May when the secret treaty formed the real basis for the Japanese mandate? In closing the interview, Hughes expressed outrage over the British refusal to support the idea of equal opportunity in the mandates for America.[23] The Geddes interview

---

[21]The secretary of state to the chargé in Japan (Bell), 2 April 1921, 862i.01/46, DSNA. See also Beerits's memorandum, "The Mandates Controversy," box 171, folder 16, pp. 3–4, Hughes Papers; Hughes to Harding, 4 April 1921, reel 143, Harding Papers.
[22]Hughes, *Autobiographical Notes*, p. 233. See also *Christian Science Monitor*, 20 April 1921.
[23]Memorandum of a conversation between the secretary of state and the British ambassador (Geddes), 12 April 1921, 862i.01/117 1/2, DSNA; Hughes, *Autobiographical Notes*, p. 233. See also memorandum of a conversation between the secretary of state and the British ambassador (Geddes), 7 April 1921, box 175, folder 76a, Hughes Papers.

made it clear to Hughes that Japan had a full commitment from Britain on the Yap mandate.

The conversation between the secretary and the British ambassador further strained Anglo-American relations. In his report to the Foreign Office, Geddes emphasized Hughes's ignorance of foreign affairs, while characterizing him as "abnormal mentally and subject to attacks of mild mania." This new American policymaker, the ambassador concluded, symbolized America's compulsive megalomania. The ambassador's report confused the British secretary of state for foreign affairs, Lord Curzon, who could only conclude that Geddes, a physician and university lecturer, had "opened up a style of diplomatic terminology that was new and frightening."[24] Unfortunately Geddes's opposite number at the Court of St. James's, George Harvey, proved to be every bit as eccentric and opinionated as the British ambassador.[25] At a time when Anglo-American relations were not good, these erratic agents added to the mutual misperceptions and mistrust.[26] Ambassador Geddes put a quick end to any notions Hughes may have held of using the British as middlemen in easing the crisis with Japan.

The first positive diplomatic results of the 2 April notes came in mid-May, when Italy and France gave informal assurances of their support for the Americans on the question of the Japanese mandate.[27] Initially Japan replied to the Hughes note rather indecisively, but in terms which definitely left the door open for further discussion after Undersecretary of State Henry P. Fletcher explained to the Japanese ambassador "that the position of this Administration was much more fundamental than that maintained by the former Secretary of State."[28] Then, on 3 June, Ambassador Shidehara called on the secretary at the State Department to announce that Japan was now ready to negotiate the Yap dispute.

BREAKTHROUGH AND COMPROMISE

Early in their discussions, Ambassador Shidehara inquired whether the United States contested the entire North Pacific mandate or just the mandate

---

[24]Fry, *Illusions of Security*, pp. 65–66.
[25]Buckley, *Washington Conference*, p. 37; [Gilbert], *The Mirrors of Washington*, pp. 49–51.
[26]Robert Jervis, *Perception and Misperception in International Politics* (Princeton, NJ: Princeton University Press, 1976), pp. 331–38.
[27]The ambassador in Italy (Johnson) to the secretary of state, 13 May 1921, 862i.01/130, and the ambassador in France (Wallace) to the secretary of state, 17 May 1921, 862i.01/133, DSNA; memorandum of a conversation between the undersecretary of state and the French ambassador (Jusserand), 20 April 1921, box 174, folder 74a, Hughes Papers.
[28]Memorandum of a conversation between the undersecretary of state and the Japanese ambassador (Shidehara), 13 April 1921, box 176, folder 85a, Hughes Papers; *New York Times*, 24 May 1921, p. 5.

over Yap. Secretary Hughes replied that equality of opportunity in all of the former colonial possessions of the Central Powers interested his government, but as a practical matter the problem between Japan and America boiled down to Yap because of its strategic location. Noting that there had been talk of internationalizing the island for cable purposes, Shidehara volunteered "that this might be arranged but that if the United States pressed for anything more, it would be extremely difficult." This did not satisfy Hughes, who insisted on "equality in the enjoyment of all privileges afforded by the island."[29]

The two sides met again on 18 June; Shidehara offered a tentative draft calling for free American access on the basis of equality with regard to the Yap-Guam cable, an overture Hughes found unacceptable since it excluded other forms of communication.[30] On 19 August Hughes handed Shidehara a memorandum commenting in detail on the Japanese proposals. The United States insisted on equal rights of residence and acquisition of property on Yap, free entry and exit, no cable censorship, no taxes, and no discriminatory police regulation. Hughes did agree to drop the demand for a wireless station if Japan would operate its radiotelegraphic service on a cooperative basis.[31] Three weeks later Shidehara reported that his government found the American request for rights, privileges, and exemptions on Yap to be substantially acceptable.[32] The secretary of state and the Japanese ambassador would continue to negotiate for several more months before arriving at an understanding, but they had now agreed on the basic framework of a settlement.

Even as Hughes and Shidehara began to make real progress on the Yap problem during the summer of 1921, the American secretary of state worked to undermine the cornerstone of Japan's foreign policy, the Anglo-Japanese alliance. In the years after the Great War, most American leaders agreed that the alliance encouraged Japanese aggression while forcing America into the role of Japan's major opponent in the Far East.[33] Secretary Hughes stepped up Wilson's campaign for modification of the Anglo-Japanese alliance in June, after the Associated Press reported that the British government was

---

[29]Memorandum of a conversation between the secretary of state and the Japanese ambassador (Shidehara), 3 June 1921, 862i.01/141 1/2, DSNA; "The Mandates Controversy," box 171, folder 16, pp. 6–7, Hughes Papers.

[30]Memorandum of a conversation between the secretary of state and the Japanese ambassador (Shidehara), 18 June 1921, 862i.01/145 1/2, and memorandum, Japanese embassy to Department of State, 18 June 1921, 862i.01/144 1/2, DSNA; memorandum, Japanese embassy to State Department, 18 June 1921, *FRUS, 1921*, 2: 291–92; "The Mandates Controversy," box 171, folder 16, pp. 7–8, Hughes Papers.

[31]Memorandum of a conversation between the secretary of state and the Japanese ambassador (Shidehara), 19 August 1921, 862i.01/154 1/2, DSNA; "The Mandates Controversy," box 171, folder 16, pp. 7–8, Hughes Papers.

[32]Memorandum, Japanese embassy to Department of State, 8 September 1921, 862i.01/173, DSNA.

[33]Buckley, *Washington Conference*, pp. 27–28; Fry, *Illusions of Security*, p. 69; Griswold, *Far Eastern Policy*, pp. 275–80; Neu, *Troubled Encounter*, pp. 102–3; Pusey, *Charles Evans Hughes*, p. 491. For an excellent summary of the State Department's attitudes toward Japan, see memorandum, John V. A. MacMurray to the secretary of state, 20 October 1921, and Harding to Hughes, 21 October 1921, reel 180, Harding Papers.

keeping the State Department fully informed on the renewal of the alliance and had promised "to guard against the inclusion of anything inimical to American rights."[34] At his next press briefing, Hughes denied categorically that the British Foreign Office had given him any such assurances, a statement which brought an embarrassed Geddes to the State Department for a consultation the next day.[35]

Speaking "in a personal way and informally," the secretary told Geddes in no uncertain terms that renewal of the Anglo-Japanese alliance "would be fraught with mischief." When the ambassador inquired if the United States might be interested in a tripartite alliance, Hughes replied that while a formal alliance was quite out of the question, he favored the British and Americans "having and maintaining common policies." To drive home the importance of cooperating with the United States in the Far East at a time when the suppression of a nationalist revolt in Ireland preoccupied Britain, Hughes said that termination of the Anglo-Japanese alliance "would give great aid and comfort" to congressional opponents of a resolution to recognize the Irish Republic.[36] Sir Auckland understood the veiled threat that Britain had better fall into line with American foreign policy in the Far East or else face American opposition on the Irish question. Prudently omitting any reference to Ireland, the ambassador reported to his superiors the next day that renewal of the Anglo-Japanese alliance, even in modified form, would have a very unfortunate effect on British-American relations.[37]

Hughes's missive to Geddes occurred during the opening week of a British imperial conference, where leaders of the empire planned to discuss the future of the Anglo-Japanese alliance. The British also knew that American leaders, including President Harding and Senator Borah, favored an international disarmament conference, a forum the United States might use to put further pressure on the alliance between Japan and Britain.[38] Furthermore, Canada proved to be a strong advocate within the Imperial Conference of the American position. Fearing that their nation might become another Belgium in the event of an Anglo-American war, Canadian Prime Minister Arthur Meighen and his principal aide in foreign affairs, Loring C. Christie, demanded that Britain give top priority to improving relations with Washington.[39]

---

[34]The secretary of state to the ambassador in Great Britain (Harvey), 22 June 1921, *FRUS, 1921*, 2:313.

[35]Pusey, *Charles Evans Hughes*, p. 492.

[36]Memorandum of a conversation between the secretary of state and the British ambassador (Geddes), 23 June 1921, *FRUS, 1921*, 2:314–16. Hughes reiterated the point formally two weeks later. See memorandum of a conversation between the secretary of state and the British ambassador (Geddes), 6 July 1921, box 175, folder 76a, Hughes Papers. On the Irish factor in Anglo–American relations, see Thomas John Noer, "Irish Independence and American Diplomacy," M.A. thesis, Washington State University, 1968, pp. 116–40.

[37]Geddes (Washington) to Curzon, 24 June 1921, *DBFP*, 14:311–12.

[38]Griswold, *Far Eastern Policy*, pp. 285–86.

[39]Fry, *Illusions of Security*, pp. 130–35.

In spite of his outspoken criticism of Japan as the Prussia of the Far East, British Prime Minister David Lloyd George favored continuation of the alliance. He also wanted to steer a middle course that would avoid having to choose between Japan and the United States.[40] An invitation from the Harding administration to participate in a conference on the limitation of armaments provided the prime minister with a way out of his dilemma: Britain could use the gathering to open negotiations with Japan and the United States on the cancellation or revision of the Anglo-Japanese alliance in a manner that would pacify all concerned.[41]

The General Staff of the Japanese armed forces favored renewal of the alliance, as did the cabinet, because it had served the nation well for twenty years. Japanese officials sent the Crown Prince to Britain during the summer of 1921, breaking a 2,500-year-old tradition, as a demonstration of their eagerness to retain the partnership.[42] However, as the junior partner in the alliance, the Japanese found themselves dependent on Britain's decision. Japan had a mixed reaction to the proposed American disarmament conference. Spending 50 percent of government revenues on military items, Japan welcomed the chance to cut back on the arms race, but some officials feared that other powers, including the United States, might use the conference to deprive the Imperial Government of wartime gains in China and the North Pacific.[43] Consequently, on 26 July, Japan accepted the American invitation with the hope "that introduction . . . of problems such as are of sole concern to certain particular powers or such matters that may be regarded [as] accomplished facts should be scrupulously avoided."[44]

When Hughes appeared to regard the Japanese qualification as a mere suggestion and not a precondition of participation, the Imperial Government leaked a memorandum outlining Japanese newspaper opinions on the conference to reiterate its position that certain problems were out of bounds. "Japan's Chinese and Siberian policy," the memorandum read, "has already been decided upon and the Shantung and Yap question has surely been settled under the terms of the peace treaty with Germany." Some members of the press in Japan thought that Hughes's insistence on including these "settled" issues in the agenda was a plot "on the part of America who seems to be aiming at the lion's share of continental Asia regardless of the fact that she persists in the Monroe Doctrine with regard to Central and South America."[45] On 10 September the State Department finally announced the conference

---

[40]Ibid., p. 140; Peter Rowland, *Lloyd George* (London: Barrie and Jenkins, 1975), p. 541.
[41]Buckley, *Washington Conference*, p. 34.
[42]Fry, *Illusions of Security*, p. 110; I. H. Nish, "Japan and the Ending of the Anglo-Japanese Alliance," in *Studies in International History*, eds. K. Bourne and D. C. Watt (Hamden, CT: Archon, 1967), pp. 371–75.
[43]Buckley, *Washington Conference*, pp. 37–38; Nish, "Anglo-Japanese Alliance," p. 379.
[44]The chargé in Japan (Bell) to the secretary of state, 26 July 1921, *FRUS, 1921*, 1:45.
[45]The chargé in Great Britain (Wheeler) to the secretary of state, 6 August 1921, ibid., 1:52.

agenda under two headings: limitation of armaments and Pacific and Far Eastern questions, the latter category including questions concerning China, Siberia, and the mandated islands. The department's memorandum noted that Pacific mandates would be discussed unless the concerned parties resolved the problem earlier, a hint from Hughes to Japan that time remained to settle the Yap dispute privately before the glare of public diplomacy intruded on the bilateral talks, presumably to the detriment of Japanese interests.[46]

On 15 September Hughes presented another memorandum to Ambassador Shidehara on Yap and the other North Pacific mandates. The assumption contained in the ambassador's note of 8 September that the United States did not object to Japan's mandate per se, the secretary observed, "is true in a qualified sense" because the Americans would not protest as long as the two nations came to an agreement which protected American interests. To begin with, the United States wanted all the rights and privileges set forth in the League mandate agreement.[47] The previous year, during negotiations with the British over exploitation of petroleum in Palestine and Mesopotamia, the State Department proposed that the British guarantee the Open Door in all of their A and B mandates as they had in the East Africa trust territory.[48] While the United States wanted to see the Open Door extended to all mandates, Hughes told Shidehara that he would not insist on applying the policy to the Pacific islands "in view of the paucity of existing or potential economic resources." Instead the United States merely requested free access to all waters of the mandates and application of all Japanese-American treaties still in force to the North Pacific islands.[49]

On the surface the American position seemed quite reasonable, especially considering that the Japanese-American commercial treaty of 1911 accorded only most-favored-nation treatment to the United States with respect to commerce, navigation, and customs duties.[50] After careful study of the Hughes memorandum, the Imperial Government concluded that acceptance of the free access principle and the application of all existing bilateral treaties together "will practically lead to the recognition, in essential particulars, of the principle of equal opportunity for all nations." Japan might apply the Open Door to the North Pacific mandate "provided that the other Mandatories of C class shall likewise agree to extend equal treatment to all nations in the territories under their respective Mandates." Unless the Allies opened all class C mandates

---

[46]The secretary of state to the ambassador in Great Britain (Harvey), 10 September 1921, ibid., 1:67.

[47]Memorandum, the secretary of state to the Japanese ambassador (Shidehara), 15 September 1921, 862i.01/173, DSNA.

[48]See FRUS, 1920, 2:649–75; Quincy Wright, Mandates Under the League of Nations (Chicago: University of Chicago Press, 1930), pp. 476–79.

[49]Memorandum, the secretary of state to the Japanese ambassador (Shidehara), 15 September 1921, 862i.01/173, DSNA.

[50]Wright, Mandates, p. 452.

for equal economic opportunity, the 17 October memorandum concluded, Japan could not make such a concession.[51] Hughes replied to the Japanese memorandum immediately, treating the Imperial Government to another of his high-powered and airtight legalistic briefs. "The question of equality of opportunity," the secretary insisted, "is not in fact at issue." Japanese rights of administration over the North Pacific mandate emanated from the Principal Allied and Associated Powers, including the United States. If Japan had obtained the islands without American aid, they would be open to United States trade under current bilateral treaties. Surely the Imperial Government did not contemplate granting less favorable conditions to the United States in an area which the Americans had helped Japan to acquire![52] Once again the secretary of state had presented Japan with an unanswerable argument.

YAP AND THE WASHINGTON CONFERENCE

The Japanese government had not replied to Hughes's latest memorandum when the Washington Conference opened in mid-November. In spite of his earlier implied threat, Hughes did not include the Far Eastern mandates in the final agenda out of a belief that the two sides were on the verge of an agreement. On 2 December Japan proposed that the American and Japanese delegations invite the British to a conference on C mandates. The Japanese wanted to discuss the application of existing treaties to mandates as well as free access of foreign nationals to such areas, the two very issues that remained unsettled in the Yap controversy.[53]

Sensing an obvious Japanese trap, Hughes declined to participate in the trilateral meeting, although he did take the opportunity to clarify the American position. If Japan assured American nationals and their vessels of free access to the harbors and surrounding waters of the mandated islands, the United States would not ask for special arrangements, a position suggesting that the principle of access interested the United States more than actual entry. In order to assure Japan that the United States was not singling it out, Hughes offered to draw up a side-letter to the Yap Treaty stating that if his government should make commercial treaties applicable to Australia and New Zealand (holders of the Pacific mandates south of the equator), the Americans would

[51]Memorandum, the Japanese embassy to the Department of State, 17 October 1921, *FRUS, 1921*, 2:301–2; memorandum of a conversation between the secretary of state and the Japanese ambassador (Shidehara), 17 October 1921, box 176, folder 85a, Hughes Papers. See also "The Mandates Controversy," box 174, folder 60, ibid.

[52]Memorandum, the Department of State to the Japanese embassy, 18 October 1921, *FRUS, 1921*, 2:302–4.

[53]Memorandum, the Japanese embassy to the Department of State, 2 December 1921, 862i.01/158 1/2, DSNA.

seek the same rights in these mandates as they had in the islands assigned to Japan.[54] Hughes's offer of a side-letter and his assurances about American intentions did not amount to real concessions, but they might make the settlement more acceptable to Japan.

Meanwhile Hughes, former British Secretary of State Arthur Balfour, Shidehara, former French Premier René Viviani, and others worked at the Washington Conference to replace the Anglo-Japanese alliance with a consultative pact. Secretary Hughes used the resulting Four-Power Pact to hasten the mandate settlement with Japan. On 8 December the secretary invited Balfour to his home to discuss the mandate situation. The United States stood ready, Hughes noted, to make a treaty with League members to secure equal rights in the mandated territories. If the British did not wish to begin negotiations at once, would they agree to an exchange of notes recognizing an American reservation of rights in the Pacific mandates? Balfour replied that he "understood perfectly" the American concern that the Quadruple Treaty should not affect claims in any way.[55] The two men then met with Viviani and the Japanese to hammer out the final draft of the Four-Power Pact. When Ambassador Shidehara inquired if the proposed treaty covered mandated territories, Hughes took the opportunity to put additional pressure on Japan to make concessions over Yap, noting that the United States would not sign the multilateral pact without a prior settlement of the North Pacific mandate question.[56]

Two days later on 10 December, at the conclusion of a meeting on the Shantung problem, Ambassador Shidehara approached the chief of the State Department's Far Eastern Division, John V. A. MacMurray. The Imperial Government had just sent the ambassador new instructions: Japan now had no objections to applying existing bilateral treaties to the North Pacific mandated islands. American citizens and their vessels would be assured of free access to the waters surrounding the trust territories. Japanese authorities would also be happy to accept the secretary's suggestion of a side-letter on potential American trade terms with mandates of British Dominions south of the equator.[57] Shidehara confirmed formally that his government had accepted the American terms in a memorandum of 12 December.[58] Immediately Hughes

---

[54]The secretary of state to the Japanese ambassador (Shidehara), 5 December 1921, ibid.

[55]Memorandum by the technical adviser of the American delegates (Blakeslee) of a conversation at the home of the secretary of state, 8 December 1921, *FRUS, 1922*, 1:8–12. See also Balfour (Washington delegation) to Curzon, 9 December 1921, *DBFP*, 14:547–48; and memorandum of an interview at 1529 18th Street, 8 December 1921, box 169, folder 5, Hughes Papers.

[56]Memorandum by the secretary to the British empire delegation of a conversation at the home of the secretary of state, 8 December 1921, *FRUS, 1922*, 1:14.

[57]Memorandum, MacMurray to the secretary of state, 10 December 1921, 862i.01/179, DSNA.

[58]The Japanese ambassador (Shidehara) to the secretary of state, 12 December 1921, 862i.01/158, ibid.

announced to the press that the United States and Japan had reached agreement on the North Pacific mandates.[59] On 11 February 1922 the two powers signed a formal convention verifying their earlier agreement.[60] Unlike the bilateral peace treaties which Hughes negotiated with Germany, Austria, and Hungary, the Yap pact was an agreement between victors. Although negotiating from a position of strength, Hughes could not dictate a settlement to Japan as he had to the former Central Powers. Both sides compromised while still gaining their major objectives. Japan won American recognition of the North Pacific mandate; the United States acquired operational rights in the islands and a precedent for demanding similar privileges in other more important mandates in the Near East and Africa. Hughes did not press for the Open Door in the Japanese mandate because prospects for trade and investments seemed insignificant. He used a combination of principles inherited from Wilson, his own legalistic arguments, and creative diplomacy to effect a settlement of the Yap dispute at a time when Japanese-American relations had become badly strained. The State Department hoped to use the Yap Treaty as a precedent for gaining Allied recognition of American rights in former German and Turkish colonial regions containing oil, minerals, and rich trade possibilities. First, the bilateral pact had to undergo the scrutiny of the Senate where several irreconcilables and Wilsonians waited to challenge Hughes's brand of internationalism.

RATIFICATION: A "DISMAL PROLOGUE"

Senator Borah began the postwar American disarmament movement in December 1920 when he introduced a resolution calling on the president to invite Japan and Great Britain to a conference on naval reductions.[61] Nevertheless, much of what went on at the Washington Conference horrified the Idaho senator and his fellow supernationalist irreconcilables. Fearing that the "whiskered Wilson" had presided over his own little Versailles conference complete with secret diplomacy and new entangling alliances, the bitter-enders prepared, although not enthusiastically, to do battle against the Yap Treaty and other pacts that came out of the Washington Conference.[62] "It is a hopeless and a heart-breaking situation," Johnson of California wrote, looking toward the

[59]Statement issued to the press by the secretary of state, 12 December 1921, *FRUS, 1922*, 1:31–33.
    [60]Convention between the United States and Japan, signed at Washington, 11 February 1922, *FRUS, 1922*, 2:600–604.
    [61]Ashby, *Spearless Leader*, pp. 105–7.
    [62]Ibid., pp. 108–9; Howard A. DeWitt, "Hiram Johnson and American Foreign Policy, 1917–1941" (Ph.D. diss., University of Arizona, 1972), pp. 171–80.

ratification debates. Four months earlier he had supported the separate peace because President Harding seemed to be headed in the right direction. But now Harding had become a captive of the strong-willed internationalists in the cabinet, leaving Johnson with a sense of helplessness. "It's a horrible thing for me to contemplate, and yet I feel powerless to prevent it," he observed; "I can only weakly voice my opposition."[63] The irreconcilables had practically dictated policy to the White House during the separate peace debate, administering several behind-the-scenes defeats to Hughes. This time, Johnson realized, they could do nothing except to protest the secretary of state's fait accompli.

In mid-February 1922, shortly after the end of the Washington Conference, Majority Leader and delegate Lodge presented the resulting treaties, including the bilateral Yap agreement, to the Senate. The Republican leadership decided to put the Yap Treaty up for consideration first as a test for the multilateral pacts.[64] On 20 February the Foreign Relations Committee sent the treaty to the full Senate with only Democrat Key Pittman of Nevada voting against a favorable report, although as the *New York Times* noted, "several 'irreconcilables' let it be known that they would have a good deal to say when the treaty is made the unfinished business of the Senate."[65]

With some exceptions, the same factions of irreconcilables and Wilsonian Democrats who opposed the separate peace treaties lined up against the Yap agreement. On 24 February during the first day of debate, Pittman charged that the Yap Treaty surrendered American economic opportunities to Japan.[66] Joseph France, the bitter-ender from Maryland who voted for the separate peace, argued that Japanese sovereignty over Yap "takes away from the United States a point of great military advantage to us."[67] Two days later Minority Leader Underwood defended the Japanese-American pact against attacks from the irreconcilables. Then Johnson denounced the Yap Treaty as "the dismal prologue" to the multilateral pacts of the Washington Conference. Tracing Japan's claim on the North Pacific islands back to the Anglo-Japanese agreement of 1916, the California senator noted that ratification of the Yap pact meant "that we stamp with our approval the bargains that were made before we entered into the World War and that were stealthily withheld from our Government, bargains in relation to peoples who were helpless, and their territory."[68] He, for one, would never give legal sanction to the immoral secret treaties.

While Wilsonian opponents of the treaties contended that the Yap agreement did not do enough to protect American rights, the irreconcilables believed

---

[63]Johnson to A. Johnson, 18 February 1922, part 6, box 3, Johnson Papers.
[64]Buckley, *Washington Conference*, p. 178; *Washington Post*, 2 March 1922.
[65]*New York Times*, 21 February 1922, p. 19.
[66]*Congressional Record*, 67th Cong., 2nd sess., pp. 2997–3003.
[67]Ibid., p. 3011.
[68]Ibid., pp. 3093–98.

that the pact went too far in that direction. "When we took the Philippines," Borah told the Senate, "we repealed the Declaration of Independence, and now we are about to disregard the teachings of Washington in order to protect those islands." The Harding administration negotiated the treaty in order to defend America's overseas empire. "Thus, step by step, after we have entered upon this course of imperialism," he concluded, "we are compelled to adopt all the methods and customs and practices of imperialists."[69] Borah and the other supernationalists saw Hughes's foreign policy as a continuation of the expansionism and imperialism of Theodore Roosevelt, William Howard Taft, and Woodrow Wilson, policies which these progressive senators had opposed in the past and would continue to resist in the future at all cost.[70]

On 1 March, the final day of debate, Pittman offered several reservations, all of which failed to pass, and then, irreconcilable Watson spoke at length against the treaty, linking it to "great confederated banks."[71] Once the Georgia Democrat finished his speech, the debate was over. Lodge, in a switch from his tactics during the separate peace debate, followed a strategy of not challenging the irreconcilables and Wilsonians directly. Instead he let them have their say while protreaty forces stayed off the floor. "We have not been able to get any of them in the ring," Watson sputtered in frustration to a nearly empty chamber; "they will not fight."[72] Indeed Lodge had no need to; he had the votes, including a majority of those who had once been irreconcilables, and the antitreaty forces lacked leadership. On 28 February Senator Glass, Wilson's unofficial spokesman, issued a statement which the press interpreted to mean that the former president would not take any part in the controversy.[73]

The Yap Treaty passed sixty-seven to twenty-two, a legal majority of seven.[74] Sixteen of the twenty-two senators casting no votes had also voted against the Berlin Treaty; only five of the irreconcilables (Borah, France, Johnson, Reed, and Watson) joined the Wilsonians in voting against the Yap agreement. Again, as with the separate treaties, the realist faction of the irreconcilables and a significant number of Democrats, led by Minority Leader Underwood, voted with the majority to put the Japanese-American treaty over the top. The vote, the *New York Times* observed, "has greatly encouraged the friends of the treaties directly resulting from the [Washington] Conference . . . who believe that the ratification of these treaties is now assured."[75] Ratification discouraged Johnson, as he watched the irreconcilable alliance

[69]Ibid., p. 3142.
[70]Ashby, *Spearless Leader*, pp. 101–2, and 109.
[71]*Congressional Record*, 67th Cong., 2nd sess., pp. 3182–93.
[72]Ibid., p. 3188.
[73]*New York Times*, 28 February 1922, p. 1.
[74]*Congressional Record*, 67th Cong., 2nd sess., pp. 3193–94. See also Richard Lowitt, *George W. Norris: The Persistence of a Progressive, 1918–1933* (Urbana: University of Illinois Press, 1971), pp. 146–47.
[75]Johnson, *Underwood*, pp. 321–22; *New York Times*, 2 March 1922, p. 1.

crumble before his eyes. "I wish that we had time to present this this [*sic*] thing to the people," he wrote two weeks later during the debate on the Washington Conference treaties, "but there is not time, and it can't be done, and then the fact is, there would be nobody to present it but myself, anyway."[76] For Johnson, Borah, and a handful of other die-hard irreconcilables, Hughes and Harding had indeed stolen Wilson's thunder in the Far East.

HUGHES, WILSON, AND THE FAR EAST

The Yap settlement pleased Norman Davis, who had handled much of the correspondence on the mandates for Wilson and Colby in late 1920 and early 1921. After the Washington Conference, Davis told a gathering of the Council on Foreign Relations that he had been confident that once leaders of the Harding administration confronted the facts and problems of United States foreign policy "they would reach substantially the same conclusions and see the wisdom of adopting the same true American course" as the Wilsonians. "My belief," Davis noted, "has been substantially confirmed, except as to our ratification of the Treaty of Versailles and entrance into the League of Nations."[77] Hughes clearly adopted "the same true American course" which Wilson had followed in the Yap dispute. Both men insisted on the recognition of American rights in the North Pacific as a check upon Japanese expansionism and to establish the principle of equal economic opportunity in all mandated regions. The Republican secretary of state used his legal skills to advantage as he picked up Wilson's arguments and improved upon them to force Japan into a compromise.

Davis was not the only observer of Republican foreign policy to remark on similarities between Hughes and Wilson. Two leading members of the British delegation at the Washington Conference, Maurice Hankey and Arthur Balfour, also saw the resemblance. Hankey wrote to Prime Minister Lloyd George:

> Meeting as we have done in Mr. Hughes' private room, and listening to Mr. Hughes' delivering speeches with that strange mixture of high moral purpose and practical bargaining, which I had always thought peculiar to President Wilson, I have to rub my eyes to know if I am not back in the old rooms in Paris. . . . In spite of the total physical dissimilarity, Mr. Hughes' mind is in some respects so like President Wilson's that Balfour nearly always unconsciously refers to Hughes as "Wilson." In fact, he does it so often that I have ceased to correct him.[78]

---

[76]Johnson to H. Johnson, Jr., 16 March 1922, part 6, box 3, Johnson Papers.

[77]Norman H. Davis, "Comments Upon the Conference on the Limitation of Armaments and Far Eastern Questions" (New York: Council on Foreign Relations, 1922), pp. 7–8.

[78]Hankey (Washington delegation) to Lloyd George, undated, *DBFP*, 14:572.

Hankey had observed that Wilson, the idealistic schoolmaster, and Hughes, the high-powered corporation lawyer, both cloaked their pursuit of the national interest in moral terms because the balance of power concept was European in origin and, hence, anathema to them. Each man championed the principle of equality of economic opportunity as the moral underpinning for American expansionism. Yet the Open Door had a built-in paradox in that it was never real and only an elusive and theoretical concept.[79]

Wilson and Hughes both paid lip service to the Open Door principle even as they bargained it away for practical reasons. In the Lansing-Ishii Agreement of 1917, the United States recognized Japan's special interest in China to alleviate growing Japanese-American tensions during a time of emergency, the Great War. The ambiguous wording of the agreement allowed the administration to abandon the Open Door temporarily while continuing to pursue the principle through other means.[80] Four years later Hughes asked for Japanese recognition of the Open Door in mandated areas, but settled for equal treatment with respect to electrical communications and the application of existing treaties with Japan to the mandated islands. That meant accepting only most-favored-nation treatment with respect to commerce, navigation, and certain duties, terms which together did not mean an Open Door, that is, full equality of treatment regarding trade and investment.[81] Nevertheless Hughes told the American Historical Association in late 1922 that "the Open Door policy is not limited to China. Recently we have had occasion to apply it to mandated territories."[82] Thus Hughes, like Wilson, continued to espouse the Open Door as a slogan while settling for less as a means of practical diplomacy.

Although Hughes could not cite the Yap settlement as a precedent to demand the Open Door in all mandates, he did indicate to the Allies that they should also make bilateral treaties safeguarding the rights of the United States in mandated territories. Using the Yap Treaty as a beginning point, the secretary negotiated treaties with the French to protect American rights in the Cameroons and Togoland in 1923 and in Syria and Lebanon in 1924. Unlike the Japanese trust territories in the North Pacific, the French mandates held significant economic potential; so Hughes asked for and received recognition from France of the Open Door principle. In 1923 Belgium agreed to similar

---

[79]Richard W. Van Alstyne, "The Open Door Policy," in *Encyclopedia of American Foreign Policy*, p. 720.

[80]Burton F. Beers, *Vain Endeavor: Robert Lansing's Attempts to End the American–Japanese Rivalry* (Durham, NC: Duke University Press, 1962), pp. 114–19; Lloyd Gardner, "A Progressive Foreign Policy, 1900–1921," in *From Colony to Empire: Essays in the History of American Foreign Relations*, ed. William A. Williams (New York: John Wiley and Sons, 1972), pp. 228–29; Griswold, *Far Eastern Policy*, pp. 217–20, and 223.

[81]Wright, *Mandates*, p. 452.

[82]Charles Evans Hughes, "Some Aspects of Our Foreign Policy," in *The Pathway of Peace: Representative Addresses Delivered During His Term as Secretary of State (1921–1925)* (New York: Harper and Brothers, 1925), p. 53.

terms covering East Africa. Jealous of the predominant American position in the world petroleum market, the British put up much stiffer resistance when Hughes attempted to open the door to their trusts.[83]

Hughes had to negotiate a series of bilateral treaties covering American rights in the mandates because the United States did not ratify the Treaty of Versailles. Allied recognition of American rights and privileges remained unsecured even after the treaties of Berlin, Vienna, and Budapest came into force. The secretary and his successors spent many years confirming American rights in the trust territories, but Hughes laid most of the crucial groundwork during the Yap negotiations. Yap had been "an apparently small matter" as Davis observed, but Davis, Colby, Wilson, and Hughes refused to yield because there were much larger stakes involved elsewhere. Once Japan made a settlement, France, Belgium, and eventually Great Britain followed suit. The mandates controversy continued in another form when the United States sent diplomatic observers to the Lausanne Conference of 1922–23, convened to settle war-related problems in the Near East. Hughes would use the conference not only to establish diplomatic and economic relations with a new Turkey, but also to confront the Allies over their closed door imperial strategy in an area containing much of the world's petroleum.

---

[83]Hughes to Harding, undated, and Harding to Hughes, 3 February 1923, reel 144, Harding Papers; memorandum of a conversation between the secretary of state and the chargé of the British embassy (Chilton), 8 July 1922, box 175, folder 75b, and "The Mandates Controversy," box 171, folder 16, p. 17, Hughes Papers; Hyde, "Charles Evans Hughes," 10:240–41; Stephen H. Longrigg, *Syria and Lebanon Under French Mandates* (New York: Oxford University Press, 1958), pp. 109–11; Pusey, *Charles Evans Hughes*, p. 449.

4

HUMAN RIGHTS, PETROLEUM, AND THE NATIONAL INTEREST
The Long Road to Renewal of Diplomatic and Commercial Relations Between the United States and Turkey

When Harding became president, he had every intention of keeping the United States out of Near Eastern politics. Wilson's crusade for an independent Armenia had ended a few months earlier in 1920 when Soviet Russia and Turkey overran the area of Eastern Anatolia set aside by the Allies on paper for the Armenians.[1] Harding, like Wilson and many other Americans, held great sympathy for the plight of Armenia, but the new president refused to do more than send off a personal check for sixty dollars to Near East relief to support an Armenian child for one year.[2] "I quite agree that there is a deplorable condition in Armenia," Harding wrote to Hughes in regard to a plea for action from a philanthropic group, ". . . but I very much fear the petitioners have a conception of the influence and power of this Republic which is born of an earlier attempt to direct the affairs of the world."[3] Clearly the president meant that his administration would not be following Wilson's lead in regard to the Near East. Whereas Wilson wanted to save the world, Harding would be content with one Armenian child.

Philanthropic and missionary groups pressured the administration continually to intervene in the Near East for humanitarian reasons throughout 1921 and 1922. Meanwhile the State and Commerce departments urged American oil companies to form a consortium, promising them support in a bid to open the door to Near Eastern petroleum resources. In late 1922 after the

---

[1] M. S. Anderson, *The Eastern Question, 1774–1923* (London: St. Martin's Press, 1966), p. 369; Roderic H. Davison, "Turkish Diplomacy From Mudros to Lausanne," in *The Diplomats, 1919–1939*, ed. Gordon A. Craig and Felix Gilbert, 2 vols. (New York: Atheneum, 1972), pp. 186–87; Trask, *Response to Turkish Nationalism*, pp. 27–28.
[2] George B. Christian to John B. Larner, 13 April 1921, and Harding to Hughes, 30 June 1921, reel 189, Harding Papers.
[3] Harding to Hughes, 2 May 1921, reel 178, ibid.

Turkish defeat of Britain's client state Greece had completely altered the balance of power in the Near East, the Allies realized that they would have to modify the severe terms of the Treaty of Sèvres. Secretary of State Hughes suddenly faced a seemingly impossible task: He had to defend the nation's economic and humanitarian interests in the Near East without accepting correlative political responsibilities. Hughes decided to send a team of unofficial observers to the Lausanne Conference to promote the Open Door and to work on behalf of Christian minorities in the Near East. Once the Allies had settled up with Turkey, the Americans took the opportunity to negotiate a Turkish-American treaty of amity and commerce. Despite the skilled efforts of Joseph C. Grew in negotiating the treaty with the underdeveloped Moslem nation of Turkey, on terms of relative equality, the Senate rejected the pact. Ironically the Senate reversed itself after Grew renegotiated the pact on less favorable terms, thus ending several years of feverish Near Eastern diplomacy which eclipsed all previous American economic and philanthropic activities in the Levant including those of Wilson.

AMERICA WATCHES AND WAITS

Even as Wilson retreated from American involvement in the Near East during his last months in office and his successor worked to keep the nation out of the region altogether, the American high commissioner at Constantinople, Admiral Mark Lambert Bristol, continued to urge the State Department to pursue an aggressive policy for the sake of American economic and humanitarian interests. Formally the United States conducted diplomacy with Turkey through the Swedish embassy, which had taken charge of American interests when the Turks broke ties in 1917; in practice Admiral Bristol acted as senior United States representative at Constantinople.[4] While the administration had unofficial diplomatic relations with the sultan's Ottoman Empire government, it did not recognize, even tacitly, Mustafa Kemal's rival nationalist government at Ankara.

In 1919 British Prime Minister Lloyd George and the Supreme Council at Paris approved a Greek plan to dismember Western Anatolia from the Ottoman Empire by force. Shortly after the Greek offensive began, Mustafa Kemal, an inspector in the Turkish army, arrived in Anatolia to unite local resistance groups into a national movement. Less than two years later, his Grand National Assembly had become the real government for most of Turkey through a series of military victories against Greece and several diplomatic

---

[4]Evans, *United States Policy*, p. 323; Trask, *Response to Turkish Nationalism*, pp. 28–29.

maneuvers designed to play Soviet Russia against the Allies and the Allies against each other.[5] Just before Wilson left office, Kemal's government made overtures to the United States through Bristol for the renewal of diplomatic relations. Bristol recommended to Washington that if the two Turkish regimes did not soon reconcile their differences, the State Department should dispatch a representative of the high commissioner to Ankara to monitor Kemalist activities.[6] On 20 June 1921 the commissioner again suggested sending an unofficial representative to the interior, pointing out that the Allies all had informal missions there. "Unless we are prepared to sit and allow [the] Allies to secure all the commercial advantages in Anatolia," he concluded, "we should take action."[7] Secretary Hughes seemed to agree that such a representative could prove useful, but left the matter to dangle a while longer.[8] In frustration, Allen W. Dulles, one of Bristol's aides, wrote his friend Ellis Loring Dresel:

> We have no indications from Washington that any real interest is being taken in Near Eastern Questions. I really don't blame the Department for this. The Allies by their selfish policy of trying to promote their own commercial interests have so messed up the whole situation that dynamite or poison for all the inhabitants of the Near East is about the only solution.[9]

Dulles's comments typified the ambivalent American attitude of disgust with European politics on the one hand and a fear on the other that America might be hurt economically if it did not join in the scramble for commercial concessions.

In October the admiral notified Hughes that Hoover's Commerce Department had authorized Julian Gillespie, assistant to the trade commissioner, to proceed to Ankara. Gillespie would be a safe man to use as an observer,

---

[5]Briton Cooper Busch, *Mudros to Lausanne: Britain's Frontier in West Asia, 1918–1923* (Albany: State University of New York Press, 1976), pp. 62–309 passim; Davison, "Turkish Diplomacy," pp. 172–82; Paul C. Helmreich, *From Paris to Sèvres: The Partition of the Ottoman Empire at the Peace Conference of 1919–1920* (Columbus: Ohio State University Press, 1974), pp. 290–332; Harry N. Howard, *Turkey, the Straits, and U.S. Policy* (Baltimore: Johns Hopkins University Press, 1974), pp. 99–101; Lord Kinross, *Ataturk: A Biography of Mustapha Kemal* (New York: William Morrow, 1965), pp. 343–75; George Lenczowski, *The Middle East in World Affairs* (Ithaca, NY: Cornell University Press, 1952), pp. 84–110; Bernard Lewis, *The Emergence of Modern Turkey* (London: Oxford University Press, 1961), pp. 246–49; Howard M. Sachar, *The Emergence of the Middle East, 1914–1924* (New York, Alfred A. Knopf, 1969), pp. 433–42.
[6]The commissioner at Constantinople (Bristol) to the secretary of state, 9 February 1921, RG 59, 711.67/15, DSNA.
[7]The commissioner at Constantinople (Bristol) to the secretary of state, 20 June 1921, 711.67/17, ibid.
[8]The secretary of state to the American commissioner at Constantinople (Bristol), 22 June 1921, 711.67/17, ibid.
[9]Allen Dulles to Dresel, 27 June 1921, box 113, file 2, Dresel Papers.

Bristol wrote, because he did not represent the State Department, so the Turks could not misinterpret the mission to mean diplomatic recognition. "We cannot keep open the door of economic opportunity in Anatolia," he wrote, again emphasizing economic considerations, "merely by a policy of aloofness due to the fear of constructive recognition of a government which is in real control of the country."[10] Hughes finally gave his assent to Gillespie's dual mission as trade representative and unofficial diplomat.[11]

In spite of Bristol's care in choosing a Commerce Department official for his representative, the Kemalist government made elaborate plans to send a Turkish diplomatic mission to the United States. With American religious, philanthropic, and missionary groups still in an uproar over actions of the "Terrible Turk" against Christian Armenia, Hughes could ill afford to have Kemal's representatives in Washington. He ordered Bristol to discourage the Ankara mission.[12] Bristol did so, but in relating the episode to the department, he took the opportunity to make a detailed critique of America's "hide bound and conservative" Near Eastern policy, observing that as the China of the Near East, Turkey deserved attention. When the Treaty of Sèvres came up for revision, the United States should take an active part in initiating "American ideas of fair play, free opportunity, and the Open Door." In addition the American commissioner recommended that the nation recognize Kemal's regime, make a new commercial treaty with it, and abandon all hope of establishing an independent Armenia.[13] All of Bristol's suggestions would become administration policy, but not until after a year of hesitation and indecision.

Gillespie returned to Constantinople in early 1922 after a month in Ankara full of enthusiasm for the possibility of closer Turkish-American relations. In his report to the Commerce Department, he noted that the Turks wanted the United States to develop their natural resources, including the oil-rich region of Mosul claimed jointly by Turkey and Britain.[14] The Gillespie mission impressed the State Department sufficiently to appoint a foreign service officer, Robert W. Imbrie, as a permanent unofficial representative at Ankara.[15]

While Admiral Bristol emphasized economic considerations in his

---

[10]The American commissioner at Constantinople (Bristol) to the secretary of state, 28 October 1921, 711.67/20, DSNA.
[11]The secretary of state to the American commissioner at Constantinople (Bristol), 1 November 1921, 711.67/20, ibid.
[12]The secretary of state to the American commissioner at Constantinople (Bristol), 15 November 1921, 711.67/24, ibid.
[13]The American commissioner at Constantinople (Bristol) to the secretary of state, 17 December 1921, 711.67/24, ibid.
[14]The American commissioner at Constantinople (Bristol) to the secretary of state, 23 February 1922, RG 59, 867.01/81, DSNA.
[15]Evans, *United States Policy*, p. 338.

despatches to Washington, he spent much of his time trying to protect American lives and property and prevent massacres of civilians during Turkey's bitter struggle against Greece.[16] On 18 July 1921 Bristol reported that the Kemalist Turks, in anticipation of a major Greek attack, had ordered the deportation of some fifteen thousand Greeks from the port of Samsoun into the interior. The admiral sent a vigorous written protest directly to Kemal "in the name of humanity" out of a fear that these innocent Greeks would be slaughtered.[17] Bristol's action alarmed Warren D. Robbins, chief of the Near Eastern Division in the Department of State, because "an official protest from Bristol might be understood by the oriental Mustafa Kemal as coming directly from the State Department."[18] Although the Turks denied they were deporting the Greeks from Samsoun, Bristol claimed that his appeal to Kemal stopped a possible massacre.[19]

More than a year later, in September 1922, as Kemal began the final Turkish offensive, Bristol made plans to evacuate Americans caught in the path of the fighting. On 4 September, with the Turks bearing down on the ancient city of Smyrna, the American consul requested that the secretary of state intervene with Ankara to allow for a Greek evacuation.[20] After consulting with the president, Acting Secretary of State William Phillips decided only to request authorization from the Navy Department for Bristol to send one or two destroyers solely for the protection of American lives and property.[21] The American commissioner then ordered three destroyers to Smyrna just as Kemal's forces entered the city. Captain A. J. Hepburn of the U.S.S. *Simpson* sent sixty marines ashore to protect the American consulate, the Y.M.C.A., and the American college.

On 14 September 1922 enraged Turkish soldiers slaughtered thousands after Greek partisans set fire to the city. The navy evacuated all American citizens successfully as well as "women of native born Americans" to Athens on the *Simpson*.[22] With the taking of Smyrna, the Turks controlled all of

---

[16]The American commissioner at Constantinople (Bristol) to the secretary of state, 2 June 1921, RG 59, 767.68/98, DSNA.
[17]The American commissioner at Constantinople (Bristol) to the secretary of state, 18 and 25 July 1921, 767.68/123 and 138, DSNA.
[18]Robbins to Hughes, 19 July 1921, 767.68/129, ibid.
[19]The American commissioner at Constantinople (Bristol) to the secretary of state, 25 July, 2 and 4 August 1921, 767.68/128, 138, and 141, ibid.
[20]The American consul at Smyrna (Horton) to the secretary of state, 4 September 1922, 767.68/276, ibid.
[21]The acting secretary of state (Phillips) to the acting secretary of the Navy (Roosevelt), 5 September 1922, 767.68/274, ibid.
[22]The American commissioner at Constantinople (Bristol) to the secretary of state, 9 September 1922, 767.68/297; the American consul at Smyrna (Horton) to the secretary of state, 9 September 1922, 767.68/304; Captain A. J. Hepburn, U.S.S. *Simpson*, to Bristol, 11 September 1922, 767.68/312; the American commissioner at Constantinople (Bristol) to the secretary of state, 14 September 1922, 767.68/319, ibid.

Asiatic Turkey except the Straits' zone, which they could not take without a direct confrontation with Great Britain. The great powers would have to revise the Treaty of Sèvres now, for as an American naval intelligence officer in Constantinople had put it a month earlier with the handwriting already on the wall, "The one point on which the Allied officials here seem to agree is that their respective home governments have made an awful mess of things."[23]

"A CANDID FRIEND" AT LAUSANNE

Admiral Bristol continued to urge Hughes to pursue an independent and aggressive policy in the Near East as a counter to the muddled imperialism of the Allies.[24] The Anglo-American clash over a possible Open Door for the Near East had simmered down since early 1921, although the two sides had not settled their differences. In the wake of the Greek defeat, Hughes wanted to know what the British planned next. Fortunately Sir Edward Grigg, Lloyd George's personal secretary, provided the American embassy in London with exact details of secret cabinet meetings. Through this source the secretary of state learned that France had offered to cooperate militarily with Britain if Kemal chose to occupy Constantinople. The cabinet also discussed calling a Near Eastern peace conference and the possibility of issuing an invitation to the United States.[25]

On 18 September Undersecretary Phillips reported that Britain was concentrating its entire Mediterranean and Atlantic fleets in the region around the Straits. The United States, he noted, had an interest in possible Allied military intervention because war would endanger American treaty rights.[26] President Harding resisted the State Department's advice to become more actively involved in the Near East. "I should be very slow to commit this nation to any sort of participation," he noted, "except as we express concern for American Nationals whose lives and property are endangered by the activities of the Turkish-Nationalist Armies."[27] Limited American participation in the peace process might be another matter if it could be accomplished discreetly.

---

[23]Naval Intelligence Report, 10 August 1922. Enclosure in the American commissioner at Constantinople (Bristol) to the secretary of state, 17 August 1922, 767.68/268, ibid.

[24]The American commissioner at Constantinople (Bristol) to the secretary of state, 2 August 1922, 767.68/260, ibid.

[25]The American ambassador in Great Britain (Harvey) to the secretary of state, 16 and 19 September 1922, 767.68/326 and 332, ibid.; Evans, *United States Policy*, pp. 377–78.

[26]The undersecretary of state to the secretary of state (on U.S.S. *Maryland*), 18 September 1922, 767.68/333A, ibid.

[27]Harding to Phillips, 19 September 1922, 767.68/635, ibid.

Allen Dulles, successor to Robbins as chief of the Near Eastern Division, wrote to Phillips on 19 September that the British embassy's first secretary had inquired unofficially if the Americans would care to give "an informal hint" of their attitude toward participating in a peace conference on the Near East. Dulles promised only to relay the message, one which Secretary Hughes chose to ignore.[28] Two days later Ambassador Harvey telegraphed that the British had also sent out feelers to him about American participation.[29] Again Hughes made no response to British hints, feeling that involvement in a Near Eastern conference could be dangerous for the administration politically. The secretary decided to observe events a while longer before committing the administration one way or the other.

British Secretary of State Lord Curzon decided to proceed without the Americans. On 23 September Britain, France, and Italy invited the Ankara government to negotiate a final treaty of peace with the Allies. Tentatively the conference would include France, Britain, Italy, Japan, Yugoslavia, Rumania, Greece, and Turkey, but not the United States or Turkey's only real ally, Soviet Russia.[30] Curzon wanted the Russians to stay away from Lausanne to keep the Turks isolated and to stop the Soviets from opposing the British plan of only limited Turkish control over the Straits and freedom for all warships to enter the Black Sea.[31]

On 26 September at a State Department press conference, Hughes endorsed the Allied proposal for freedom of the Straits, praised the Big Three for their concern over Christian minorities, and declined comment on the issue of American participation.[32] The news conference encouraged Curzon, who asked the British ambassador in Washington to press the administration for an authoritative statement. But Hughes's comments affirming freedom of the Straits and freedom of worship had been strictly for domestic consumption, not for the benefit of the Allies.

Several pressure groups urged the administration to participate in the peace conference. Missionary and philanthropic groups, shocked by the burning of Smyrna and rumors of Turkish atrocities against Christianity, pressured the administration to stop the Terrible Turk's reign of terror.[33] For very different

---

[28]Dulles to Phillips, 19 September 1922, 767.68119/26, ibid.
[29]The ambassador in Great Britain (Harvey) to the secretary of state, 21 September 1922, 767.68/342, ibid.
[30]British secretary's note of a conference between the French president of the council, the British secretary of state for foreign affairs, and the Italian ambassador in Paris, 23 September 1922, *DBFP*, 18:88–96.
[31]Edward H. Carr, *A History of Soviet Russia*, vol. 3, *The Bolshevik Revolution* (New York: Macmillan, 1953), pp. 485–86; Harry N. Howard, *The Partition of Turkey: A Diplomatic History* (Norman: University of Oklahoma Press, 1931), p. 270; George F. Kennan, *Russia and the West Under Lenin and Stalin* (Boston: Mentor Books, 1962), pp. 217–18.
[32]*New York Times*, 27 September 1922, p. 1.
[33]See, for example, James Barton to Hughes, 4 October 1922, and Edward Caldwell Moore to Hughes, 5 October 1922, 767.68119/12 and 4, DSNA.

reasons, Rear Admiral Colby M. Chester also urged American participation. "The Turks need almost everything which America can wish to sell them," he wrote in *Current History*, "and they are the best of people to deal with."[34] As head of the Ottoman-American Development Company, Chester wanted peace in the Near East to make Turkey safe for American investments. The arguments of Chester and of other American businessmen carried great weight with the Harding administration, committed as it was to opening economic doors to foreign resources and markets wherever they might be closed. The combined pressures of Protestant groups and business lobbyists forced Harding and Hughes to rethink their policy of noninvolvement in the Near East.

On 10 October 1922 Turkey and Britain came to armistice terms just seventy-five minutes before the British could carry out their threat to attack the Turks at Chanak.[35] The next day Allen Dulles wrote a memorandum for Secretary Hughes emphasizing that American participation in the upcoming peace conference deserved prompt consideration. The United States had many unique interests in Turkey which needed to be safeguarded. Dulles proposed that the United States send observers to the conference to perform the twin tasks of watching over American interests and negotiating a new bilateral treaty with the Turks. If the department waited until after the conclusion of the peace conference, the Turks might try to drive a harder bargain. More important, the division chief reasoned, "we have a greater hold upon the Allies both financially and otherwise than we have upon Turkey and we can use our influence upon the Allies if we negotiate simultaneously or concurrently with them to secure proper protection of our interests."[36]

Secretary Hughes wrote a fourteen-page letter to President Harding regarding possible participation in the Near Eastern peace, basing it in large part on Dulles's recommendations.[37] Negotiations with Turkey, which the United States would have to undertake sooner or later, the secretary noted, "will necessarily be greatly influenced, if not practically controlled, in considerable measure, by the result of negotiations between the Allied Powers and the Turkish authorities." A key American objective was preservation, so far as possible, of the Capitulations, extraterritorial rights which gave foreigners in Turkey many privileges and immunities that the Kemalists found obnoxious and degrading. The department advocated continued use of Capitulations to protect U.S. educational and philanthropic institutions.[38] Hughes and Dulles

---

[34]Colby M. Chester, "Turkey Reinterpreted," *Current History* (September 1922): 939–47.

[35]Busch, *Mudros to Lausanne*, pp. 354–58; Davison, "Turkish Diplomacy," p. 198; Walder, *The Chanak Affair*, pp. 310–18.

[36]Dulles to Hughes, 11 October 1922, 767.68119/196, DSNA.

[37]See Dulles to Hughes, 16 October 1922, 767.68119/197, ibid.

[38]Hughes to Harding, 24 October 1922, 767.68119/62a, and Hornbeck to A. C. Millspaugh, 20 May 1922, 767.68/218, ibid. For the Turkish attitude toward the Capitulations, see Article 6 of the Turkish National Pact in J. C. Hurewitz, ed., *Diplomacy in the Near and*

had few illusions about the protection of the missionaries' clients, the Asian Christians, feeling that wholesale evacuation offered the most feasible solution. The secretary found it only "barely possible" that an Armenian homeland could be resurrected.[39] In regard to the Straits, Hughes and his Near Eastern expert found that during times of peace, America, like the Allies, stood to gain from unrestricted passage of merchant vessels. Hughes also favored unrestricted movement for warships to protect American interests, but he wanted no part of maintaining freedom of the Straits forcibly because that might push the country into another European war. The two men more than matched their disinclination for political commitments with great enthusiasm for protection of economic interests against the Allies, with Hughes writing:

> We should aim to secure an abandonment of the policy of spheres of influence and to establish definitively the policy of the open door and recognition of American interests on an equal footing with the interests of other powers throughout the entire Ottoman Empire.

The secretary of state had nothing less in mind than launching a frontal diplomatic assault on postwar Allied economic strategy in the Near East. In conclusion Hughes explained to Harding that while he did not find full participation at the peace conference to be either "natural or appropriate," America could play the part of "a candid friend" ready to interpose words for protection of legitimate interests through expert observation, a ruse which Wilson and Colby had used during their retreat from European affairs in late 1919.[40]

On 27 October Britain, France, and Italy issued formal and simultaneous invitations to the United States for full participation and to Soviet Russia and Bulgaria for discussion of the Straits question.[41] Immediately Hughes cabled two aide mémoires based on his letter to the president to the embassies in Paris, London, and Rome. The secretary asked the ambassadors to hand the first of the two documents, which indicated the general nature of American interests, to the respective foreign ministers, while making guarded use of portions of the second aide mémoire to learn the reactions of the Allies to specific areas of concern. Puzzled over the meaning of observer status, Lord Curzon hoped Hughes would work toward a "sharing of responsibility for maintaining [the] great open waterway as a wide-open door," an ironic turn

---

Middle East: A Documentary Record, 1535–1956, 2 vols. (Princeton, NJ: D. Van Nostrand, 1956), 2:75. See also Lucius Ellsworth Thayer, "The Capitulations of the Ottoman Empire and the Question of their Abrogation As It Affects the United States," *Journal of International Law* 17 (April 1923): 207–33.

[39]Hughes to Harding, 24 October 1922, 767.68119/62A, DSNA.

[40]Ibid. For the role of the observer during the Wilson administration, see Glad, *Illusions of Innocence*, p. 178; and Smith, *Aftermath of War*, pp. 54–55.

[41]British embassy to the Department of State, 27 October 1922, 767.68119/36, DSNA.

of phrase in light of the British closed-door petroleum policy.[42] Owing to the political chaos in Rome, Ambassador Child could not contact any responsible Italian officials.[43] From France, Ambassador Myron T. Herrick reported Premier Raymond Poincaré's "gratification" with the American response.[44] In this opening round of formal exchanges, both the Americans and the Allies acted cautiously, generally feeling one another out; yet all parties realized that the spheres quarrel should wait until after they had presented the Turks with a solid Western front to drive the best possible bargain.

Kemal gave Curzon reason to believe that the Americans might be driven into the Allied camp completely. On 7 November Admiral Bristol reported that Ankara had put Armenians and Greeks on one month's notice to leave Turkey or face deportation to the interior. While promising that the American navy would not interfere in the refugee problem, the admiral told Hughes that he would pressure the Kemalists "to assure humane attitude toward Christian population."[45] Well aware of the American public's preoccupation with Near Eastern Christians, Lord Curzon had Ambassador Geddes ask Secretary Hughes to support a British ultimatum to the Turks threatening war if the deportations did not stop, a request the secretary turned down flatly. Geddes referred to Wilson's hopes for an Armenian mandate, implying that responsibility for the current crisis could be traced to Washington. Hughes's temper flared as he told the ambassador "that what troubled the dreams of the British statesmen was their maintenance of their imperial power, the question of India, the question of Egypt, of the Suez Canal, and their relations to the Near East in connection with their vast imperial domain."[46] British imperial ambitions and problems, Hughes fumed, had nothing to do with American actions.

The Hughes-Geddes interview illustrated that four years of Anglo-American economic tensions could not be glossed over with an appeal to American idealism. The secretary considered the minorities question one of secondary importance when compared with international recognition of a Near Eastern Open Door and negotiation of a new bilateral treaty with Turkey. For internal political reasons, these goals had to be accomplished without involving the United States too deeply in European diplomacy. This complication made an already difficult task even more formidable; American observers had to

---

[42]The American ambassador in Great Britain (Harvey) to the secretary of state, 31 October 1922, 767.68119/54, ibid.
[43]The American ambassador in Italy (Child) to the secretary of state, 30 October 1922, 767.68119/49, ibid.
[44]The American ambassador in France (Herrick) to the secretary of state, 2 November 1922, 767.68119/67, ibid.
[45]The American commissioner at Constantinople (Bristol) to the secretary of state, 7 November 1922, *FRUS, 1922*, 2:950–51.
[46]Memorandum by the secretary of state of a conversation with the British ambassador, 10 November 1922, ibid., 2:952–55.

side with the Allies on issues where their interests coincided (the Straits, Capitulations, and minorities) without imperiling the primary objective of negotiating the best possible Turkish-American treaty. In order for the plan to work, the United States needed a tightly knit team of crafty diplomatic observers and strong leadership from Washington. Neither would be forthcoming during the first phase of the peace conference.

THE LAUSANNE CONFERENCE, PHASE I

Harding and Hughes decided to send three observers as well as a full staff of experts and stenographers to the Near East peace conference at Lausanne. They chose Child—one of Harding's closest friends and the ambassador to Italy—as chief observer along with Admiral Bristol and Grew, who, as minister to Switzerland, could arrange the mission's accommodations while performing regular duty.[47] Hughes did not give his observers either specific orders or full briefings before the conference. Three days before the talks convened, he sent the mission extracts from his 27 October aide mémoires, the Allied invitations, the American reply, and several envelopes of past diplomatic correspondence and old treaties relating to the Near East, promising to send further instructions as specific situations arose.[48]

In the absence of direct orders, the observers could not engage in important preconference bargaining. While the other powers busied themselves with intrigue, Child spent most of his time prior to the opening session "thrashing out with Grew what our duties will be and how to fulfill them."[49] Grew took tea with his old friend Sir Horace Rumbold, the second ranking member of the British delegation, who revealed that the conference would deal first with territorial and military questions and then tackle the Straits, Capitulations, and minorities.[50] Ninety minutes before the conference opened, Child and Grew met with Italian Prime Minister Benito Mussolini over coffee. Mussolini told the Americans that the Big Three had agreed to divide the conference into committees dealing with territories, minorities, and economic and financial affairs. The prime minister also confided that growing Anglo-French

---

[47]Russell, *The Shadow of Blooming Grove*, p. 439; the secretary of state to the ambassador in France (Herrick), 15 November 1923, 767.68119/36, DSNA; Grew to Margaret Perry, 13 November 1922, Joseph C. Grew Papers, bMS Am. 1687.5, Letter Books, 1922, vol. 2, Houghton Library, Harvard University, Cambridge, MA (hereafter cited as Grew Papers).

[48]The secretary of state to American mission, Lausanne, 17 November 1922, 767.68119/195A, DSNA. See also Richard W. Child to his parents, 15 November 1922, Richard W. Child Papers, box 2, folder 1922, Library of Congress, Manuscript Division, Washington.

[49]Richard W. Child, *A Diplomat Looks at Europe* (New York: Duffield, 1925), p. 83.

[50]Grew Diary, 19 November 1922, 20:152–53, Grew Papers.

tensions over the German reparations question threatened to break up the hoped-for Allied united front.[51]

On 21 November, the day after the purely ceremonial opening session, Lord Curzon took control of the conference proceedings for himself with the announcement that the conference would break up into committees and that his committee alone would begin its work immediately.[52] Curzon's unofficial presidency, which ended any possibility of an open democratic conference, meant that important decisions would not be made in the conference room, but in the privacy of the delegates' hotel suites. The Americans decided to adjust their strategy to the new situation. During a meeting with Child, Djelal-ed-Din Arif Bey of the Turkish delegation promised recognition of the Open Door, an American share in the Mosul oil fields, and protection of missionary and philanthropic institutions, property, and archeological projects. Encouraged, the American observers decided to become Turkey's "friends and advisers" in order to capitalize on the special Turkish trust in the United States.[53]

Meanwhile the Allies, hoping to create a split between Turkey and the United States, agreed not to support any American measures on behalf of the Armenians.[54] Curzon had clamped a lid of secrecy over the conference while unofficially exempting French, British, and Italian correspondents from the news blackout. When the verbatim remarks of a Greek delegate appeared in the press, Lord Curzon accused an American reporter of causing the leak. Venting his anger, Child then told Curzon that he would personally break secrecy and pull his nation out of the conference unless the Allies treated the American press more fairly.[55] Curzon acted quickly to repair the damage, telling Child on 23 November that the British Foreign Office had already begun to abandon efforts to obtain zones, concessions, and special privileges and now was prepared to support the Open Door policy in the Near East, a move which made the Americans anxious to put the question of the Open Door before the entire conference.[56]

At the end of the 25 November session, when the discussion of territorial

---

[51]Child, *A Diplomat Looks at Europe*, p. 85; Grew Diary, 20 November 1922, 20:154, Grew Papers; De Novo, *American Interests*, pp. 135 and 142.

[52]Harold Nicolson, *Curzon: The Last Phase, 1919–1925* (New York: Harcourt, Brace, 1939), p. 292; Child, *A Diplomat Looks at Europe*, p. 86; Grew Diary, 21 November 1922, 20:159, Grew Papers.

[53]American mission, Lausanne, to secretary of state, 22 November 1922, 767.68119/174, DSNA; Grew Diary, 21 November 1922, 20:161, Grew Papers.

[54]American mission, Lausanne, to the secretary of state, 23 November 1922, 767.68119/184, DSNA.

[55]Child, *A Diplomat Looks at Europe*, pp. 89–90; Grew Diary, 22 November 1922, 20:164, Grew Papers; American mission, Lausanne, to the secretary of state, 23 November 1922, 767.68119/187, DSNA.

[56]American mission, Lausanne, to the secretary of state, 24 November 1922, 767.68119/189, DSNA; Hughes to Harding, 25 November 1922, box 24, Hughes Papers. See also Grew Diary, 23 November 1922, 20:165, Grew Papers.

questions began to wind down, Child read a brief statement. After referring to the postwar Allied sphere-carving in highly critical terms, he offered the conference the Open Door as an alternative to special privilege, "a foundation for a greater equity in the relation of nation with nation, and the basis for a more progressive economic development of territories."[57] Child's statement created quite a stir. "His remarks," Harold Nicolson of the British delegation wrote, "were so foolish and irrelevant that the diplomatists who witnessed this unhappy scene gazed at each other in bewildered embarrassment."[58] The irrelevance of Child's speech to the debate over Western Thrace and the Aegean islands, coupled with the subject of the Open Door, led many to believe that the observers were making their opening bid for Turkey's petroleum resources.[59] In justification of the speech, Child cabled Hughes that the British had been trying to trade their claims on Mosul to Turkey in exchange for monopoly oil concessions. "It is necessary," the delegation concluded, "to have immediate guidance of the Department not received in any form, as to the definite arrangements desired if we are to protect adequately American interests."[60] Hughes's meager instructions and rumors about the oil situation stampeded the observers into the ill-timed Open Door speech, making the United States appear greedy while tipping the American hand to Lord Curzon.

The British secretary of state issued a statement which not only supported the American position, but declared the San Remo Agreement of 1920 for the division of Mosul oil to be null and void as well, thus adding to the illusion of an American victory.[61] In reality nothing had changed since Curzon's statement did not affect the American consortium's negotiations with the Turkish Petroleum Company in London where the Allies still held most of the high cards.[62] While lulling the Americans into a false sense of security, Curzon juggled the agenda so that Mosul would be the last subject discussed when the British no longer would need American support on other important issues such as the Straits.[63]

The Straits debate opened on 4 December, pitting the fanatically anti-Russian Lord Curzon against Ismet Pasha, the chief Turkish delegate, and Georgii Chicherin, the Anglophobic Russian commissar for foreign affairs.

[57]American mission, Lausanne, to the secretary of state, 25 November 1922, 767.68119 T&M/6, DSNA.

[58]Nicolson, *Curzon: The Last Phase*, p. 297.

[59]Grew Diary, 25 November 1922, 20:171, Grew Papers; Waldo H. Heinrichs, Jr., *American Ambassador: Joseph C. Grew and the Development of the United States Diplomatic Tradition* (Boston: Little, Brown, 1966), p. 69.

[60]American mission, Lausanne, to the secretary of state, 26 November 1922, 767.68119/201, DSNA.

[61]Child, *A Diplomat Looks at Europe*, p. 93; Grew Diary, 25 November 1922, 20:172, Grew Papers.

[62]Gibb and Knowlton, *The Resurgent Years*, p. 294.

[63]Curzon to E. Crowe, 27 November 1922, DBFP, 18:338–39; American mission, Lausanne, to the secretary of state, 1 December 1922, 767.68119/228, DSNA.

The British had already concluded private agreements with Rumania, Bulgaria, and Greece (Curzon's "cat's paws," as Child put it), so the debate really boiled down to a contest for Ismet's allegiance.[64] Ismet did not wish to alienate Russia, Turkey's only ally, yet he shared Kemal's fundamental distrust of Bolshevism.[65] The Americans, still basking in the afterglow of their Open Door "victory" and 100 percent behind freedom of the Straits, urged the Turks privately to come into the Allied camp.[66] After Child read a statement calling for virtually unlimited freedom of the Straits and the Black Sea in war and peace, Curzon and, more importantly, Ismet both rushed to congratulate the Americans for their position.[67] The debate on the Straits continued, but Turkey had veered away from its alliance with Soviet Russia.[68]

The Americans helped to turn the tide in favor of freedom of the Straits and the Black Sea without clear guidance from Washington. Child recorded in his diary what went through his mind as he read the speech:

> I found myself thinking that few outsiders would ever believe how little "instruction" has come to me from Washington. When Dwight . . . arrived on November 28, as representative of the Department of State, we "tore open" the pouches. Instead of any instructions of interest we found a mere heap of academic material and references.[69]

The observers found this lack of direction from Hughes especially harmful to American interests in the area of minorities.

International recognition of the Open Door and negotiation of a new bilateral Turkish-American treaty, the two primary goals at Lausanne, did not interest the American public nearly as much as protection of Christian minorities in Turkey. Several philanthropic and church lobbyists shadowed the observers at Lausanne in hopes of averting a diplomatic betrayal.[70] While the observers would do what they could for Near Eastern Christians, they also had long-range American economic interests to consider.[71] The American

[64]Child, *A Diplomat Looks at Europe*, p. 100; Grew Diary, 4 December 1922, 20:183–86, Grew Papers.

[65]Davison, "Turkish Diplomacy," p. 203.

[66]Child, *A Diplomat Looks at Europe*, p. 101; Grew Diary, 5 and 6 December 1922, 20:187–88 and 190–91, Grew Papers.

[67]The American mission, Lausanne, to the secretary of state, 6 December 1922, 767.68119 T&M/13, DSNA; Grew Diary, 6 December 1922, 20:189–90, and Grew to Annie Grew, 7 December 1922, Letter Books, 1922, vol. 2, Grew Papers. See also War Diary, 3 December 1922, Mark L. Bristol Papers, box 4, Library of Congress, Manuscript Division, Washington (hereafter cited as Bristol Papers).

[68]Curzon to Crowe, 6 December 1922, *DBFP*, 18:374–75; Grew to Hugh Gibson, 13 December 1922, and Grew to Boylston Beal, 14 December 1922, Letter Books, 1922, vol. 1, Grew Papers; Howard, *The Straits*, pp. 117–19; Nicolson, *Curzon: The Last Phase*, p. 313.

[69]Child, *A Diplomat Looks at Europe*, p. 101.

[70]War Diary, 27 November 1922, box 4, Bristol Papers; Grabill, *Protestant Diplomacy*, pp. 270–71.

[71]Grew Diary, 10–21 December 1922, 20:209, Grew Papers.

delegation split over the minorities question, with Bristol favoring an autonomous Armenia in Cilicia while Child regarded any sort of homeland program as futile.[72] Because Washington offered little guidance, the observers compromised among themselves. On 12 December Child made a speech calling for "prevention rather than mere relief and guarantees of safety of minorities rather than mere succor to their misery," although he made no specific proposals and no mention of Armenia.[73]

Publicly Curzon threatened to close the conference down if Turkey did not agree to an Armenian homeland. Privately the British secretary promised that if the Turks agreed to join the League of Nations, where he hoped they might be split further away from Moscow and permanently separated from Mosul province, the Allies would drop the Armenian homeland issue.[74] On 14 December Ismet announced that his country would apply for League membership, and Curzon immediately created a subcommittee on minorities for the express purpose of burying the Armenian issue.[75] Outraged church and relief lobbyists telegraphed Hughes, demanding action, but the secretary only asked his observers for their recommendations; his order against initiating proposals still held.[76] When Hughes told the American diplomats in early January to sound out the French on Allen Dulles's idea to carve an Armenian state out of Syria, the observers cabled back that the homeland issue was all but dead.[77] The Americans could only rise in impotent protest when the Allies traded Armenia away for Turkish membership in the League because of the self-imposed limits of diplomatic observation.

The observers handicapped American diplomacy at Lausanne further through their inability to work as a team on key problems. Admiral Bristol, who understood the Turks better than either the State Department or the other observers, realized that the Kemalists demanded an end to the Capitulations as a matter of national pride and recommended that the Americans stand with Ankara to further good diplomatic and economic relations.[78] Fearing that American special privileges in China, Egypt, and other countries could be affected by Turkish abrogation of the Capitulations without adequate judicial

---

[72]Child, *A Diplomat Looks at Europe*, p. 103; Caleb Frank Gates, *Not To Me Only* (Princeton, NJ: Princeton University Press, 1940), pp. 287–89; Grabill, *Protestant Diplomacy*, pp. 270–72.

[73]War Diary, 12 December 1922, box 4, Bristol Papers; the American mission, Lausanne, to the secretary of state, 13 December 1922, 767.68119 T&M/16, DSNA.

[74]Heinrichs, *Grew*, p. 70; Nicolson, *Curzon: The Last Phase*, pp. 314–17.

[75]War Diary, 14 December 1922, box 4, Bristol Papers; Curzon to Crowe, 14 December 1922, *DBFP*, 18:391.

[76]The secretary of state to the American mission, Lausanne, 26 December 1922, *FRUS, 1923*, 2:934.

[77]Dulles to Hughes, 4 January 1923, 767.68119 T&M 3/15; the secretary of state to the American mission, Lausanne, 6 January 1923; the American mission, Lausanne, to the secretary of state, 9 January 1923, 767.68119 T&M 3/16, DSNA.

[78]War Diary, 30 November and 11 December 1922, box 4, Bristol Papers.

safeguards, Hughes had the observers stand with the Allies, a policy Bristol found distasteful in the extreme.[79] Child and Bristol quarreled over a proposed American statement, forcing Grew to mediate a compromise. When the Turks did not respond to the American note, Child drew up another with much stronger wording. In retaliation the admiral refused to sign it, secretly urging the Turks through an intermediary not to accept the final Allied plan for the Straits.[80] America's harder line offended the Turks without budging them; they continued to insist on being treated as equals.[81]

On 15 January, with the conference deadlocked hopelessly over the Capitulations, Lord Curzon asked Child for help. The American ambassador brought the British foreign secretary and Ismet together for an awkward and unproductive meeting.[82] Then, after what Grew described as "a somewhat heated situation" between the admiral and Child, Bristol agreed to try his hand as peacemaker. Several hours of futile arguing with the Turk led Bristol to confide to his diary "that Ismet was not employing Oriental tactics," meaning that Turkey would decline to sign the treaty if it did not get all it wanted.[83]

Lord Curzon's temper grew shorter in January as Ismet refused to give in to British threats. The Allied united front all but collapsed when France invaded the Ruhr to punish Germany for nonpayment of reparations.[84] On 21 January with the united front in shambles, Curzon decided that he no longer had anything to lose by reopening the Mosul question.[85] During his speech the British secretary of state referred to the validity of the Turkish Petroleum Company's monopoly in Mosul and to the magnanimous British negotiations in London designed to give all interested parties a share in the disputed region's petroleum.[86] Secretary Hughes had already turned down Britain's latest offer to the American consortium on the ground that it violated the Open Door. On 8 January Hughes instructed the observers to oppose any British attempts to obtain official recognition of the T.P.C. claims in the

---

[79]The secretary of state to the American mission, Lausanne, 22 December 1922, 767.68119 F&M 1/7, DSNA; Harding to Hughes, 21 December 1922, reel 144, Harding Papers. See also MacMurray to Hughes, 12 December 1922, 767.68119 F&M/-, and Dulles to Hughes, 4 December 1922, 767.68119/375, DSNA. For Bristol's attitude, see War Diary, 2 January 1923, box 4, Bristol Papers.

[80]Grew Diary, 14 January 1923, 22:13–15, Grew Papers; Heinrichs, *Grew*, pp. 73–74. See also War Diary, 14 January 1923, box 4, Bristol Papers.

[81]The American chargé in Constantinople (Dolbeare) to the secretary of state, 11 January 1923, 767.68119/364, DSNA.

[82]Child, *A Diplomat Looks at Europe*, p. 118; Grew Diary, 15 January 1923, 22:16–17, Grew Papers. See also Curzon to Crowe, 15 January 1923, *DBFP*, 18:448–49.

[83]Grew Diary, 17 January 1923, 22:20, Grew Papers; War Diary, 17 January 1923, box 4, Bristol Papers.

[84]Grew Diary, 20 January 1923, 22:23–25, Grew Papers.

[85]Curzon to Lindsay, 21 January 1923, *DBFP*, 18:258–60; American mission, Lausanne, 22 January 1923, 767.68119/379, DSNA; Nicolson, *Curzon: The Last Phase*, p. 328.

[86]War Diary, 23 January 1923, box 4, Bristol Papers; Grew Diary, 23 January 1923, 22:29–30, Grew Papers; Shwadran, *Middle East, Oil*, p. 225.

conference.[87] The Americans sent two notes of protest to the British delegation and while Curzon made no reply, he did drop the plan to validate the Allied monopoly concession through the treaty, thus setting the stage for a bitter Anglo-American controversy in the coming months.[88]

On 31 January Lord Curzon handed the Turks a draft treaty with the announcement that he would be leaving for London in four days.[89] The Allies and Turkey both made some small concessions, but juridical Capitulations, Turkish economic arrangements, and Mosul all remained unsettled. Up until the last moment the Europeans and the Americans, save for Admiral Bristol, remained confident that Ismet would sign. At the hour of Curzon's deadline, as everyone crowded into the conference room for the signing, the Turkish delegation walked out of the hotel past the astonished Allies. Even then the Americans refused to give up. They talked Ismet into allowing foreign juridical advisers to be stationed in three cities in exchange for Allied concessions on the economic clauses. The observers then sped to the railway station, only to see Curzon's train fading into the distance.[90]

The Americans did not have much to show for their two and one half months of observation. Turkish-American treaty negotiations had not yet begun; Lord Curzon had opened the door a crack and then rudely slammed it shut through the insistence, both at Lausanne and in London, that the T.P.C. claims be recognized as valid; and the human rights of Near Eastern Christians had not been secured. However, the observers did gain a limited understanding of the new Turkey. Bristol's views made a great impression on Grew, who noted that "patience was the necessary element which Curzon lacked and now I know that without that quality it is useless to try to deal with the Turk."[91]

The American diplomats served only as observers, not as delegates, which weakened their influence both as policymakers and peacemakers. Hughes debilitated their diplomatic effectiveness further through his lack of concise instructions because without specific orders, the mission was forced

---

[87]The secretary of state to the president of the Standard Oil Company of New Jersey (W. C. Teagle), 15 December 1922, *FRUS, 1922*, 2:348–49; Hornbeck to Hughes, 6 January 1923, 767.68119 F&E 4/12, and the secretary of state to the American mission, Lausanne, 8 January 1923, 767.68119 F&E 4/12, DSNA. See also DeNovo, *American Interests*, pp. 192–94; and Feis, *Diplomacy of the Dollar*, p. 55.

[88]War Diary, 23 January 1923, box 4, Bristol Papers; the secretary of state to the American mission, Lausanne, 30 January 1923, 2:240–41, and American mission, Lausanne, to the secretary of state, 3 February 1923, *FRUS, 1923*, 2:241–42; Grew Diary, 23 January and 3 February 1923, 22:31 and 55, Grew Papers.

[89]Grew Diary, 22 January 1923, 22:27–28, Grew Papers; American mission, Lausanne, to the secretary of state, 31 January 1923, 767.68119/391, and Grew to Phillips, 22 January 1923, 767.68119/332½, DSNA.

[90]War Diary, 4 February 1923, box 4, Bristol Papers; Child, *A Diplomat Looks at Europe*, pp. 122–23; Grew Diary, 4 February 1923, 22:56–59, Grew Papers.

[91]Grew Diary, 4 February 1923, 22:60, Grew Papers. See also Grew to Phillips, 5 February 1923, Letter Books, 1923, vol. 2, ibid.

to ad lib policy. Finally, the observers' many quarrels among themselves made matters even worse. According to Grew he "had to act as a sort of oil reservoir and poured it on the wheels constantly and liberally," instead of devoting his time to safeguarding American interests.[92] When the Lausanne Conference reconvened in April, Hughes would choose Grew as the sole observer with instructions to participate more actively on behalf of American interests, a move which augured well for American Near Eastern diplomatic policy.

INTERREGNUM

Ismet Pasha and Admiral Bristol conversed at length as the two men returned to the Near East on the *Orient Express* in February 1923. The Turkish diplomat inquired if the United States would care to open bilateral treaty negotiations immediately. Bristol replied that talks could begin once Turkey had made peace with the Allies and not before, a response Ismet found disappointing, for Turkey would need a big power ally when the Near Eastern peace talks resumed.[93]

On 8 March 1923, after the Turkish Grand National Assembly refused to accept the Lausanne Treaty as it stood, Ismet, with the full backing of Kemal, telegraphed moderate Turkish counterproposals to the Allies.[94] Child learned through Mussolini that Curzon had requested an immediate conference in London to discuss the Turkish counterpoints without inviting the United States.[95] By the time the State Department finally ascertained the substance of those deliberations in early April, Hughes realized that the Allies did not want the United States observing again at the resumed conference.[96] In the interim the secretary had replied to British inquiries regarding specific objections to the economic clauses of the Lausanne Treaty, referring to Articles 65, 94, 96, and 97 which, according to Stanley K. Hornbeck of the Office of the Economic Adviser, might confirm, indirectly, the prewar claims of the Turkish Petroleum Company and other Allied firms.[97] After reading the Amer-

[92]Grew to Castle, 24 February 1923, Letter Books, 1923, vol. 1, ibid.

[93]War Diary, 8 February 1923, box 4, Bristol Papers; the commissioner at Constantinople (Bristol) to the secretary of state, 15 February 1923, 711.672/14, DSNA.

[94]The commissioner at Constantinople (Bristol) to the secretary of state, 12 March 1923, 767.68119/466, DSNA; Rumbold to Curzon, 7 March 1923, *DBFP*, 18:579–80. See also Davison, "Turkish Diplomacy," pp. 205–6; Martin Gilbert, *Sir Horace Rumbold: Portrait of a Diplomat, 1869–1941* (London: Heinemann, 1973), p. 287; and Howard, *Partition of Turkey*, p. 280.

[95]The American ambassador in Italy (Child) to the secretary of state, 17 March 1923, 767.68119/472, DSNA.

[96]Dulles to Hughes, 4 April 1923, 767.68119/537, ibid.

[97]Hornbeck to Hughes, 21 February 1923, 767.68119/530, and Department of State to British embassy, 31 March 1923, 767.68119/500a, ibid.

ican objections, Lord Curzon recommended to Premier Poincaré of France that the United States be excluded, since it opposed certain economic clauses in the treaty.[98] A vote in the Grand National Assembly, however, made Poincaré think twice about snubbing the United States.

On 9 April 1923 the Assembly voted overwhelmingly to accept the Chester concession of the Ottoman-American Development Company of Delaware. The project, which dwarfed all other Turkish grants, authorized the American company to build a nationwide network of railroads; to exploit all oil and mineral rights adjacent to the proposed routes; to sell farm equipment; and to construct oil pipelines, refineries, power plants, and port facilities all over Turkey.[99] The Chester concession encompassed an area so vast that it came into conflict with several prewar concessions granted to the Allies. While the Turks certainly wanted the American project to be carried out, they hoped to use the concession to gain American support at Lausanne and, hence, to sow discord among the Western powers.[100]

"The granting of the Chester concession," Hughes wrote, "may be understood to mark the triumph in Turkey of the Open–Door policy, as against such policies as inspired the tripartite agreement and the Bagdad railroad concession." The New York Times noted more realistically that "the door, technically, is still open, but there is little room for anybody but Chester in the vestibule."[101] The grant threatened to put the American observer at Lausanne in a most embarrassing position; no longer could the United States protest righteously against the Allied monopoly in Mesopotamia without hearing justifiable accusations of rank hypocrisy. To make matters worse, the Chester concession called for investments in excess of three hundred million dollars and the company had no capital.[102]

Meanwhile the Turkish Petroleum Company had made a new offer to the American consortium in London designed to meet Hughes's Open Door guidelines. Both the State and Commerce departments objected to the compromise because the T.P.C. reserved the right to reject new applicants to the

---

[98]Curzon to Phipps, 9 April 1923, DBFP, 18:677–78.

[99]The American commissioner at Constantinople (Bristol) to the secretary of state, 16 April 1923, and the Ottoman-American Development Company to the secretary of state, 25 July 1923, FRUS, 1923, 2:102–4 and 1215–40.

[100]War Diary, 12 January 1923, box 4, Bristol Papers; Davison, "Turkish Diplomacy," p. 206; DeNovo, American Interests, p. 225; Howard, Partition of Turkey, p. 280; Longrigg, Oil in the Middle East, p. 46. For evidence on Turkish sincerity regarding the Chester concession, see memorandum from the Eastern European Division to Christian Herter, 20 July 1923, box 134, Hoover Papers, HHL.

[101]The secretary of state to the commissioner at Constantinople (Bristol), 20 April 1923, FRUS, 1923, 2:1207; "The Golden Fleece," New York Times, 22 April 1923, part 2, p. 6.

[102]The American commissioner at Constantinople (Bristol) to the secretary of state, 16 April 1923, FRUS, 1923, 2:1203–4. See also DeNovo, American Interests, p. 225; Feis, Diplomacy of the Dollar, p. 56; Heinrichs, Grew, p. 81; Shwadran, Middle East, Oil, pp. 22; and "That Chester Concession," Current Opinion (June 1923): 661.

multinational consortium.[103] Secretary Hughes decided to continue his public policy of impartiality regarding the indirectly competing Chester concession and the Jersey Standard consortium. In the coming months, though, he would pursue a policy which favored subtly the established companies negotiating with the Allied monopoly.[104]

Hughes had already decided that the United States would observe again at Lausanne with or without an invitation.[105] Following a suggestion from Allen Dulles, the secretary named Grew as the only observer.[106] In his instructions to Grew, Secretary Hughes stressed the importance of blocking the Allies from confirming the T.P.C.'s prewar claims.[107] To best serve America's Near Eastern interests, Grew would have to oppose the prewar concessions while simultaneously working with the Allies in order to obtain a substitute for the Capitulations. He also had to pick just the right time to initiate bilateral negotiations with Turkey to get the best possible terms. The American minister could not merely sit on the sidelines observing events as during the first phase of the conference. He had to become very involved in all aspects of the conference as he bargained separately with Turkey. If he played both sides against the middle, Grew could emerge with a Near Eastern Open Door and a Turkish-American treaty acceptable to the Senate. Despite an excellent personal effort, Grew came home with neither.

AGAIN LAUSANNE

"The first difficult problem we had on our hands," Grew later explained, "was, strange as it may seem, the necessity of establishing friendly relations with our British colleagues."[108] The American observer pledged to the new chief British delegate, Sir Horace Rumbold, complete cooperation with the Allies on the Capitulations. Unsoftened by the American promise, Sir Horace continued to oppose American requests for admission to the subcommittees,

---

[103]Hughes to Hoover, 31 March 1923, box 286, Hoover Papers, HHL; Wilson, *American Business*, p. 193

[104]The secretary of state to the American commissioner at Constantinople (Bristol), 20 April 1923, *FRUS, 1923*, 2:1207.

[105]The secretary of state to the ambassador in France (Herrick), 12 April 1923, 767.68119/536, DSNA.

[106]Hornbeck to Hughes, 4 April 1923, 767.68119/537, and the secretary of state to the American minister in Switzerland (Grew), 9 April 1923, 767.68119/508, ibid.

[107]The secretary of state to the American minister in Switzerland (Grew), 19 April 1923, 767.68119/548, ibid.

[108]"Informal Talk at the Consular Dinner at the Hotel Victoria, Interlaken," Grew Diary, 2 September 1923, 22:21, Grew Papers.

where the powers negotiated details of the treaty.[109] To win the confidence of the Europeans, Grew promised not to take any action on the Turkish-American treaty without giving the Allies full information.[110] On 26 April an angry Ismet demanded to know when the bilateral negotiations would begin. When Grew implied that Turkey had to make a fair settlement on the Capitulations first, Ismet replied that such a policy "would act like a cold 'douche' on the Chester concession."[111] The next day the American diplomat announced that the United States would stand by its hard line policy opposing abrogation, a statement which pleased the British Foreign Office immensely.[112]

On 29 April Grew recommended to Secretary Hughes that the United States offer to proceed with the negotiation of a treaty of amity and commerce with Turkey.[113] Grew planned to stall the Turks with informal discussions that would form a basis for formal talks in order to keep Ismet happy temporarily while the observer attempted to gain access to the subcommittees. As soon as Hughes approved his strategy, Grew held a friendly meeting with the chief Italian delegate, Giulio Montagna, who proposed that the United States and Italy might work together harmoniously in the Near East. Complaining that Britain and France treated Italy with "scant consideration," Montagna spoke emotionally of the Italian need for territorial expansion into Asia Minor.[114] Grew saw that a covert Italian-American alliance might allow him to gain access not only to the subcommittees, but to Allied secrets as well.

While Grew continued to support the Allies during the debate on the Capitulations, Rumbold blocked Montagna's efforts on behalf of American entrance into the subcommittees. In desperation the American observer tried slowing the conference down by reserving the right to make detailed comments at committee sessions.[115] Within a few days, France and Italy forced the British to give in.[116] Grew thanked Montagna, promising the aging career diplomat, worried about his future under the Fascists, that Ambassador Child would put in a good word to his friend Mussolini.[117] From the time of Grew's promise until the Allies left Lausanne in July, the Americans had complete access to

---

[109]*DBFP*, 18:690, note 7.

[110]"Informal Talk," Grew Diary, 22:22, Grew Papers.

[111]Grew Diary, undated, 22:84, Grew Papers.

[112]American mission, Lausanne, to the secretary of state, 27 April 1923, 767.68119 P/6, DSNA.

[113]The American mission, Lausanne, to the secretary of state, 29 April 1923, 711.672/31, and the secretary of state to the American mission, Lausanne, 30 April 1923, 711.672/36, ibid.

[114]The American mission, Lausanne, to the secretary of state, 1 May 1923, 767.68119/564, ibid.; Grew Diary, undated, 22:87–90, Grew Papers.

[115]The American mission, Lausanne, to the secretary of state, 3 and 4 May 1923, 767.68119 E/10 and 11, DSNA.

[116]The American mission, Lausanne, to the secretary of state, 4 May 1923, 767.68119 E/12, ibid.

[117]Dulles to Phillips, 10 May 1923, 711.672/35, ibid.; Heinrichs, *Grew*, p. 83. A handwritten note at the bottom of the Dulles memorandum reads: "June 18. This has been done."

Allied secrets. By 4 May with Americans admitted to the subcommittees and Montagna providing a steady flow of intelligence, Grew finally had the freedom to observe the Allies fully and to negotiate the basis for a bilateral treaty with Turkey. Within a few days, however, the conference faced a grave crisis which threatened renewed warfare in the Near East.

Greece's military dictatorship wanted to consolidate its position at home with a spectacular gain in foreign policy. Greek Foreign Minister Apostol Alexandris came to Lausanne to urge immediate consideration of Greek affairs and to refuse payment of any indemnity to Turkey.[118] The foreign minister spoke openly of war, hinting to Montagna that he had the full support of a great power behind him. Rumbold's stony silence throughout the meetings on the crisis led Grew to the conclusion that Athens had the tacit backing of Britain, which hoped to use the Greeks to weaken Turkey's position at the peace table.[119] On 24 May the Greek delegation threatened to leave if the conference did not settle the reparations question quickly in Greece's favor. The British battleship *Iron Duke* and an escort of twenty destroyers entered the Straits as elements of the British press threatened Turkey with war. Grew played a crucial part in the settlement, shuttling between the Greek and Turkish delegations and bringing the two sides face-to-face in the bridal suite of the Hotel Château d'Ouchy, where the Turks agreed to accept Karagatch in Western Adrianople in lieu of Greek reparations.[120] The American role in the Greek crisis further dissipated earlier ill feelings against the United States over the Chester concession. In addition the crisis gave secondary Turkish and American personnel the opportunity to begin informal conversations on the bilateral treaty.[121]

The solution of the Greco-Turkish reparations question made the delegates eager to press on with remaining business. On 28 May the Allies relinquished all claims for reparations against Turkey.[122] Two days later the Allies agreed that foreigners would be subject to Turkish laws and courts while Ismet acquiesced in the appointment of at least four foreign legal advisers to his nation's judiciary.[123] The conference still faced other problems, but

---

[118]The American consul in Greece (Atherton) to the secretary of state, 9 May 1923, 767.68119/574, DSNA; "Informal Talk," Grew Diary, 22:26, Grew Papers.

[119]The American mission, Lausanne, to the secretary of state, 16 May 1923, 767.68119/586, DSNA; "Informal Talk," Grew Diary, 22:26–27, Grew Papers.

[120]"Informal Talk," Grew Diary, 22:27–31, Grew to A. Grew, 28 May 1923, and Grew to Dulles, 28 May 1923, Letter Books, 1923, vol. 2, Grew Papers. The American mission, Lausanne, to the secretary of state, 21 and 27 May 1923, 767.68119/587 and F/18, DSNA; Heinrichs, *Grew*, p. 85; Sacher, *Emergence of the Middle East*, p. 451.

[121]The American mission, Lausanne, to the secretary of state, 16 and 23 May 1923, 711.672/49 and 58, DSNA.

[122]The American mission, Lausanne, to the secretary of state, 28 May 1923, 767.68119/608 and 609, ibid.; Howard, *Partition of Turkey*, p. 311.

[123]The American mission, Lausanne, to the secretary of state, 31 May and 4 June 1923, 767.68119 P/44 and P/48, DSNA. See also DeNovo, *American Interests*, p. 147; and Heinrichs, *Grew*, 85–86.

basically Turkey had what it wanted. Settlement of the Capitulations issue also meant that the Americans and the Allies had no more significant interests in common.

On the evening of 5 June, Ismet brought Grew the alarming news that the Allies had been pressing Turkey at informal meetings to accept a generalized treaty clause confirming all prewar concessions. The American observer gave Ismet a pep talk on Turkish sovereignty and a warning that such underhanded concessions to the Europeans "might have an unfortunate reaction in the United States."[124] Grew planned to use Ismet and Montagna to fight for American interests, but on 15 June, after the Italian diplomat admitted that he had failed to persuade the Allies to withdraw the objectionable clause, the American observer convinced France's chief delegate, General Maurice Pellé, to give him a copy of the proposed concessions clause which Rumbold was refusing even to show the Americans.[125] Allen Dulles then telephoned an American protest to the British embassy in Washington while Secretary Hughes instructed his ambassadors in Rome, Paris, and London to inform the respective foreign offices orally that the United States strongly opposed the Allied scheme.[126] On 6 July Montagna told Grew that Rumbold was now willing to change the offensive clause, or if necessary, to drop it altogether. The observer had been waiting for that moment since mid-June, when he had drawn up a list of fifteen arguments against confirmation of the prewar concessions in the treaty. He then dangled the list before the Allies, threatening to elaborate on it in open session after passing out copies of the protest to the press. Faced with this "proverbial sword of Damocles," as Grew called it, the Europeans decided to drop the clause completely.[127]

Rumbold decided to try another tack, secretly replacing the generalized clause with three others specifically confirming the prewar concessions of the Régie Générale des Chemins de Fer, the Vickers-Armstrong Company, and the Turkish Petroleum Company.[128] Immediately Montagna smuggled out a draft of the new article to his American friend, who did all he could to further strengthen Ismet against renewed Anglo-French pressure.[129] The Allies held another private meeting where they reworked the T.P.C. clause to read: "The rights granted in 1914 to the Turkish Petroleum Company, limited, are valid and maintained," wording which legal experts told Grew "meant literally and exactly nothing" except as a face saving gesture because Turkish authorities

---

[124]The American mission, Lausanne, to the secretary of state, 6 June 1923, 867.602 Ot81/342, DSNA.

[125]The American mission, Lausanne, to the secretary of state, 16 June 1923, 867.602 Ot81/351, ibid.; "Informal Talk," Grew Diary, 23:35–36, Grew Papers.

[126]The chief of the Near Eastern Division to the secretary of the British embassy, 19 June 1923, the secretary of state to the ambassador in France (Herrick), 23 June 1923, *FRUS, 1923*, 2: 1022–25.

[127]"Informal Talk," Grew Diary, 23:36–37, Grew Papers.

[128]*DBFP*, 18:942, note 20; "Informal Talk," Grew Diary, 23:37, Grew Papers.

[129]"Informal Talk," Grew Diary, 23:37, Grew Papers; the American mission, Lausanne, to the secretary of state, 9 July 1923, 867.602/98, DSNA; Heinrichs, *Grew*, p. 89.

had never made the grant official.[130] Grew cabled Washington to urge acceptance of the proposed formula, but the British compromise made Hughes wary. After sleeping on the matter, the American observer and his staff also began to have doubts. A few hours later, Hughes sent the longest telegram that the Americans had seen during the entire conference, with a style and content which, Grew later recalled, "indicated clearly the august hand which wrote it and it left nothing whatever to the imagination."[131] After scolding Grew for faulty analysis, the secretary ordered the observer to continue his protests.[132] Anglo-American relations grew tense as Grew held stormy sessions with Rumbold, while encouraging Ismet to hold out.[133] On 17 July the British finally capitulated, this time dropping all mention of the Turkish Petroleum Company's claims.[134] A week later, after speedy adjustment of minor items, all powers attending the conference, with the exception of the United States, signed the Lausanne Treaty, returning the Near East to peace four days short of nine years after the outbreak of the Great War.

Grew managed to overcome many of the handicaps of mere observation through slick behind-the-scenes diplomacy. He exploited Montagna's insecurity successfully to gain valuable intelligence and a friendly voice within the Allied councils. The American observer also used Turkish nationalism to advantage when he induced Ismet to hold out against European pressures on the prewar oil claims question. Near the end of the conference, Secretary Hughes had to step in to firm Grew up against a last British effort on behalf of the Turkish Petroleum Company, but all in all, the observer guarded American interests with skill.

The American observer fought long and hard against confirmation of the prewar Allied monopolies and for the Open Door policy; yet this victory proved to be Pyrrhic. The Ottoman-American Development Company never became solvent financially because Secretary Hughes refused to give encouragement to potential backers. On 2 May 1923 Otto Kahn of Kuhn, Loeb and Company came to Hughes, not to obtain a federal guarantee, but for "a feeling expressed through the authorities of the Government that it was to the interest of the United States that this should be undertaken."[135] Hughes's silence,

---

[130]The American mission, Lausanne, to the secretary of state, 10 July 1923, 867.602/101, DSNA; "Informal Talk," Grew Diary, 23:37–38, Grew Papers.

[131]"Informal Talk," Grew Diary, 23:38–39, Grew Papers.

[132]The secretary of state to the American mission, Lausanne, 10 July 1923, 867.602/101, DSNA. See also Hughes to Harding, 23 July 1923, box 24, Hughes Papers.

[133]The American mission, Lausanne, to the secretary of state, 14 and 16 July 1923, 767.68119/687-688, DSNA; "Informal Talk," Grew Diary, 23:39, Grew Papers.

[134]"Informal Talk," Grew Diary, 23:40, Grew Papers. See also the American mission, Lausanne, to the secretary of state, 17 July 1923, 767.68119/690, DNSA.

[135]The secretary of state to the American mission, Lausanne, 4 May 1923, 867.602 Ot 81/310a, DSNA; memorandum of an interview with Otto Kahn of Kuhn, Loeb and Company, 2 May 1923, box 176, folder 91, Hughes Papers.

which stood in marked contrast to Secretary Hoover's "go out and get it" speech to the Standard consortium, caused the banking community to back off from the Chester concession. The secretary would not aid the Chester project at a time when he was holding out against Allied confirmation of the T.P.C. claim in the name of the Open Door and while sanctioning and encouraging the private London negotiations between that same monopoly and the Standard consortium. Therefore Grew's Open Door triumph over the Allies at Lausanne turned out to be only theoretical.

The State Department sent observers to the conference to watch over American interests and to negotiate a bilateral treaty with Turkey. The battle against the Allied closed door diverted Grew and Ismet from their bilateral negotiations. All along the Turks had been eager to negotiate a treaty with the United States both to gain American support at the conference and to normalize relations with the investment-hungry Americans. But once the conference ended, the Turks no longer had any pressing need to give the U.S. special concessions, especially in the light of rumors reaching Ankara about the financially troubled Chester project.

NEGOTIATING THE TURKISH-AMERICAN TREATY

Grew and Ismet began their treaty discussions in earnest shortly after the final showdown with the Allies over the concessions. On 20 July the chief Turkish diplomat asked if the bilateral talks could be wrapped up in a few days or whether the Americans preferred to sign a treaty based on what had already been accomplished. This query took Grew aback since the two men had not yet come to terms on most-favored-nation treatment, naturalization, modifications in a judicial declaration, the Capitulations, claims, the Straits, treaty language, minorities, sanitary matters, and taxes.[136] The observer had already written to Castle in regard to the bilateral treaty that "we have several difficulties still ahead of us, and I am by no means sure that they can all be surmounted successfully," but even Grew did not expect to be deadlocked so quickly on so many issues.[137]

The United States offered Turkey conditional most-favored-nation status, that is, granting the same privileges already given to America's other best customers on a limited basis. Ismet said that Turkey associated this phrase with the Capitulations; instead he preferred to have national treatment, an

---

[136]Joseph C. Grew, *Turbulent Era: A Diplomatic Record of Forty Years, 1904–1945*, ed. Walter Johnson, 2 vols. (Boston: Houghton Mifflin, 1952), p. 590.
[137]Grew to Castle, 6 July 1923, Letter Books, 1923, vol. 2, Grew Papers.

unconditional form of most-favored-nation status. Grew, who had learned to respect the Turkish obsession with sovereignty, promised to work on a substitute phrase. The Americans wanted their own judicial adviser to the Turkish courts, while the Turks believed that there were already too many foreign counselors. The two sides also clashed over naturalization. Ismet wanted to uphold a Turkish law in the treaty which prohibited former Turkish citizens from returning home; Grew, representing a nation of immigrants, explained in vain that the Senate would never accept such a provision. The Allies had relinquished their wartime claims against Turkey, a precedent Ismet urged the Americans to follow, but Hughes, fearing possible repercussions in pending claims cases against Germany, Austria, and Hungary, refused to hear of it. The secretary wanted Grew to obtain a declaration from Ismet on the protection of minorities similar to the one in the Lausanne Treaty, only omitting references to the League of Nations' supervision in order not to offend the Senate, a suggestion Ismet vetoed because he did not want to offend the Grand National Assembly.[138] The deadlock between Ismet and Grew had much to do with politics in Ankara and Washington: Both men were trying to please chauvinistic legislatures concerned with the setting of possibly unpleasant precedents and the loss of face.

Grew had demanded all along that Ismet accept the idea of submitting claims to a mixed arbitral tribunal. On 25 July Hughes telegraphed that if Ismet would not agree to the tribunal concept, the department could live with an exchange of notes calling for early agreement on the claims question.[139] Ironically Hughes's despatch crossed the wires with one Grew had composed. The diplomat asked for permission to drop the naturalization question from the treaty, recommending that the department settle for the same judicial declaration and formula specifically abolishing the Capitulations that the Allies had agreed to at the peace conference, contingent upon Ismet's promise to write a letter guaranteeing religious freedom to minorities, a proposal the secretary found acceptable.[140] On 29 July the Turks conceded for the first time that they could hardly refuse to pay justifiable claims, although Ismet's definition of justifiable claims was so narrow that Grew rejected it.[141] The

[138]The American mission, Lausanne, to the secretary of state, 21 July 1923, 711.672/124, the American mission, Lausanne, to the secretary of state, 23 June 1923, 767.68119P/64, and the secretary of state to the American mission, Lausanne, 26 June 1923, 767.68119P/64, DSNA; the American mission, Lausanne, to the secretary of state, 20 June 1923, *FRUS, 1923*, 2:1091–92; the secretary of state to the American mission, Lausanne, 11 June 1923, 767.68119 P/55A, and the American mission, Lausanne, to the secretary of state, 21 June 1923, 767.68119 P/57, DSNA; Grew, *Turbulent Era*, 1:590–96.
[139]The secretary of state to the American mission, Lausanne, 25 July 1923, 711.672/132, DSNA.
[140]The American mission, Lausanne, to the secretary of state, 25 July 1923, 711.672/137, and the secretary of state to the American mission, Lausanne, 26 July 1923, 711.672/138, ibid.
[141]The American mission, Lausanne, to the secretary of state, 29 July 1923, 711.672/146, ibid.

next day the chief Turkish negotiator presented Grew with a modified version of his formula calling for negotiation of acceptable claims categories and the consideration of the claims under the agreed-upon categories on a case-by-case basis.[142] Grew wavered, but Hughes told him to accept. "You are too near together," he concluded, "to justify breaking or even suspending negotiations."[143]

On 1 August Grew told Ismet that his government had accepted the Turkish claims formula. The Turks, however, no longer found their own proposal satisfactory; Ismet wanted to limit claimants to those who had been American citizens at the time of the particular claim. The American diplomat finally convinced Ismet to drop this point in return for the elimination of the word *entitled* from the claims formula.[144] After receiving instructions from Ankara, the Turks insisted once again that claimants had to have been American citizens at the time of the claim. Grew rejected this proposal and offered, as Hughes had authorized ten days before, to drop all mention of claims from the treaty except to state that the problem would be settled in the future.[145]

Grew, Ismet, and two other Turkish diplomats signed the Turco-American Treaty of Amity and Commerce along with an extradition agreement on 6 August 1923.[146] Two days earlier Ismet had transmitted three Turkish declarations to the Americans regarding judicial administration, sanitary matters, and the protection of foreign educational, philanthropic, and religious institutions identical to those agreed upon at the Lausanne Conference.[147] Article 1 of the bilateral treaty provided for the resumption of official diplomatic relations. Article 2 abrogated Capitulations, while the next six articles (3–8) set down conditions for the establishment and residence of individuals and corporations upon the basis of reciprocity. Article 9 guaranteed American merchant vessels, warships, and aircraft unlimited freedom of the Straits on a most-favored-nation basis. Other articles dealt with taxes, duties, diplomatic immunities, property rights, and the abrogation of all previous treaties.[148]

The American diplomat negotiated a bilateral pact that was equal to or more favorable to American interests in every area covered in the Allies'

---

[142]The American mission, Lausanne, to the secretary of state, 30 July 1923, 711.672/149, ibid.

[143]The secretary of state to the American mission, Lausanne, 31 July 1923, 711.672/149, ibid.

[144]Grew, *Turbulent Era*, pp. 596–99. See also the American mission, Lausanne, to the secretary of state, 2 August 1923, 711.672/152, DSNA.

[145]The American mission, Lausanne, to the secretary of state, 5 August 1923, 711.672/156, DSNA; Grew, *Turbulent Era*, pp. 599–600.

[146]The American mission, Lausanne, to the secretary of state, 6 August 1923, 711.672/158, DSNA.

[147]The Turkish mission, Lausanne, to the American mission, Lausanne, 4 August 1923, 711.672/170, ibid.

[148]The American mission, Lausanne, to the secretary of state, 29 January 1924, 711.672/254½, ibid.; Grew, *Turbulent Era*, pp. 603–5.

Treaty of Lausanne. The endless wrangling over the prewar Allied concessions during the peace conference caused the Americans to wait too long before bargaining seriously with Turkey on the bilateral level. "After the Allied treaty was concluded," Grew explained to his mother, "we could not hope to get much better terms than they did, and with the Allies the Turks had matters all their own way."[149] During the first phase of the peace conference, Grew regarded Ismet as little more than a wily carpet dealer who would haggle until the last moment and then give in. After the bilateral treaty, the American judged the very same Turkish diplomat as "Napoleonic—the greatest diplomatist in history. He has played every one of us to a standstill. And he has done it fairly and squarely."[150] Grew's change in attitude allowed him to protect American interests more effectively because without his understanding of Turkish national aspirations and character, he might have stalked away from Lausanne as Lord Curzon had—lacking a treaty of any kind. Grew also contributed significantly to the more flexible position taken by Hughes toward Turkey during the final stages of the bilateral talks. Once the diplomats finished negotiating the treaty, Hughes had to sell that change in attitude to the American people and the Senate.

THE STRUGGLE FOR RATIFICATION

Many years after the ratification controversy, Grew explained to the American Philosophical Society what happened to the bilateral treaty: "I brought it home to Washington, well pleased and expecting the accolade 'Well done thou good and faithful servant.' But, alas, alas, domestic politics intervened."[151] Grew might have forgotten that during the negotiation of the treaty he had written to his mother that "I doubt if it ever goes through the Senate," a statement which turned out to be prophetic.[152] From the outset Secretary Hughes realized that ratification would not be easy; two years earlier the Senate had passed the separate peace treaties with Germany, Austria, and Hungary, but only by slim margins. Majority Leader Lodge had urged ratification of those treaties chiefly because "we secure all that is desirable for the United States and are not called upon to make any embarrassing concessions."[153] The Turkish-American treaty contained many "embarrassing conces-

[149]Grew to A. Grew, 19 August 1923, Letter Books, 1923, vol. 2, Grew Papers.

[150]Quoted in Heinrichs, *Grew*, p. 94.

[151]Joseph C. Grew, "The Peace Conference of Lausanne, 1922–1923," U.S., *Department of State Bulletin* (26 September 1955): 498.

[152]Grew to A. Grew, 30 July 1923, Letter Books, 1923, vol. 2, Grew Papers.

[153]*Congressional Record*, 67th Cong., 1st sess., p. 5791.

sions" to an underdeveloped Moslem nation which had a very bad reputation in regard to treatment of its Christian minorities.

Hughes withheld any decision on political strategy during the first two weeks of August 1923 as the nation mourned the death of Warren G. Harding. When President Calvin Coolidge indicated that he too would let Hughes run American foreign policy, the Department of State began a low-key campaign for ratification.[154] Opponents of the Turkish-American pact had already organized lobbies. Wilson's former ambassador to Germany, James W. Gerard, headed the largest of these pressure groups, the American Committee Opposed to the Lausanne Treaty, although Vahan Cardashian, an Armenian-American lawyer, dominated the committee's activities.[155] On 24 November Dr. James L. Barton, president of the American Board of Commissioners for Foreign Missions, and one of a group of church lobbyists who had journeyed to Lausanne only to leave in disgust after the sellout of Armenia, pleasantly surprised the department with his vigorous endorsement of the treaty.[156] Three days later Hughes asked Admiral Bristol in Constantinople to solicit the views of American businessmen and missionaries in Turkey.[157] Bristol wrote back that the American community there favored early ratification with near unanimity.[158]

The influential Foreign Policy Association backed the bilateral treaty, but only with reluctance. James G. McDonald, chairman of the association, explained to Allen Dulles that "we are very critical of the excessive diligence with which our representatives at Lausanne worked on behalf of American petroleum companies."[159] Once again, as during negotiation of the bilateral treaty, Grew's successful fight against confirmation of the Turkish Petroleum Company's prewar claims had come home to haunt the administration. Cries against the department's work on behalf of the oil companies did not die down even after Turkey cancelled the Chester concession and the Standard consortium's negotiations in London with the T.P.C. remained deadlocked for some time after Lausanne.[160] Many Americans continued to oppose the Turkish-American treaty because they thought that somehow Grew and Hughes

---

[154]*New York Times*, 15 August 1923, p. 1.

[155]Trask, *Response to Turkish Nationalism*, pp. 37–38. See also Daniel, "The Armenian Question," p. 270.

[156]Barton to Hughes, 24 November 1923, U.S., Presidents, Public Papers of the Presidents of the United States, microfilm, Calvin Coolidge, reel 193, National Archives, Washington (hereafter cited as Coolidge Papers).

[157]The secretary of state to the American commissioner at Constantinople (Bristol), 27 November 1923, 711.672/225B, DSNA.

[158]The American commissioner at Constantinople (Bristol) to the secretary of state, 8 December 1923, 711.672/231, ibid.

[159]Quoted in Dulles to James G. McDonald, 2 April 1924, 711.672/276a, ibid.

[160]On the death of the Chester concession, see the American commissioner at Constantinople (Bristol) to the secretary of state, 21 December 1923, *FRUS, 1923*, 2:1251–52.

had sold out Armenia for petroleum, in spite of the fact that the United States still did not have access to any Near Eastern oil fields.

During the 1924 presidential campaign, Senator King of Utah and a small faction of Democrats made a partisan issue out of the treaty. "We condemn the Lausanne Treaty," the Democratic National Party Platform stated; "it barters legitimate American rights and betrays Armenia, for the Chester oil concession."[161] The treaty gave the Democrats a foolproof, emotional campaign issue as well as a chance to embarrass the Coolidge administration. The president, who could not refute the generalized charges short of revealing the entire classified Lausanne correspondence, remained silent on the subject throughout the campaign while the Democrats used the treaty to attack administration foreign policy as a whole.[162] On 8 December 1924 after Coolidge's election victory, Secretary Hughes wrote to Senator Borah, chairman of the Foreign Relations Committee after the death of Lodge, urging prompt action on the treaty.[163] Eleven days later Borah told Hughes that he had made little progress in bringing the treaty to the floor "owing to the pronounced opposition."[164] At this point the secretary decided that the department would have to mount a major campaign aimed at the Senate to salvage Grew's work.

Hughes enlisted Commerce Secretary Hoover and former Undersecretary of State Norman Davis to convince the senators, including Borah (who had never endorsed the treaty because of his own suspicions about petroleum diplomacy), that the lack of formal relations with Turkey was crippling American economic interests.[165] The secretary of state forwarded a despatch to the Foreign Relations Committee from Admiral Bristol reporting that American business and philanthropic leaders in Turkey favored ratification.[166] Dr. James Barton began to prowl the congressional corridors, faithfully reporting the results of his efforts to Allen Dulles.[167] President Coolidge capped the campaign with a lavish White House dinner for former Ambassador Child.[168] On 10 February the Foreign Relations Committee voted nine to one in favor of the treaty with minor reservations on the control of immigration and the treatment of shipping.[169] In March the treaty received a setback when Secretary Hughes

---

[161]Porter and Johnson, *National Party Platforms*, p. 250.

[162]Daniel, "The Armenian Question," p. 271; Trask, *Response to Turkish Nationalism*, pp. 44–45.

[163]Hughes to Borah, 8 December 1924, 711.672/325A, DSNA.

[164]Borah to Hughes, 19 December 1924, 711.672/331, ibid. See also Borah to Barton, 26 November 1924, box 153, Borah Papers.

[165]Hughes to Borah, 3 January 1925. Enclosure in 711.672/335, DSNA. See also Hughes to Borah, 17 April 1923, box 129, Borah Papers for Borah's queries about the Chester concession.

[166]The American commissioner at Constantinople (Bristol) to the secretary of state, 6 January 1925, 711.672/337, DSNA.

[167]See, for example, Dulles to Hughes, 31 January 1925, 711.672/345, ibid.

[168]*New York Times*, 22 January 1925, pp. 1–2.

[169]The secretary of state to the American commissioner at Constantinople (Bristol), 21 February 1925, 711.672/350A, DSNA.

resigned, turning over the department to the much less capable Frank B. Kellogg, a man fellow Republican Johnson characterized as "weak and timid . . . and un-American."[170] After Borah advised the administration of the "very considerable opposition" in the full Senate, the State Department made no further efforts on behalf of the treaty through 1925.[171]

The fight over the treaty heated up early in 1926 as the department put together a booklet on Turkish-American relations for distribution to the Senate and to outstanding treaty opponents while Dr. Barton and other philanthropic and missionary lobbyists also escalated their efforts on behalf of ratification.[172] The Gerard-Cardashian group had published a pamphlet on the horrors of the bilateral pact prominently featuring a letter from the late Woodrow Wilson denouncing the treaty as "indeed iniquitous." Back in late 1923, Gerard tried to involve Wilson in the fight against renewing Turkish-American relations, but the former president refused even to allow publication of his private correspondence on the subject. After Wilson's death in 1924, Gerard used one of the letters anyway after editing out the old man's statement that the Democrats did not have to worry about the treaty because God would punish the Republicans for it.[173] In April 1926 Gerard and Cardashian gave wide publicity to a petition signed by 110 Episcopal bishops denouncing the treaty. The petition outraged Senator Borah, who finally declared himself in favor of the pact publicly.[174]

On 7 May Borah expressed pessimism over the final fate of the treaty in a conversation with a State Department official. "Senator Swanson," Borah noted, "who is as a rule careful in his statements, had said recently that he had enough Democratic votes to defeat the treaty."[175] Still Borah believed that the treaty had "a fighting chance" and recommended that the administration insist on an immediate vote.[176] President Coolidge and Secretary Kellogg

---

[170]Johnson to A. Johnson and H. Johnson, Jr., 21 January 1925, part 6, box 4, Johnson Papers.
    [171]Borah to Coolidge, 13 February 1925, box 178, Borah Papers. See also N. Davis to Hoover, 17 March 1925, box 613, Hoover Papers, HHL.
    [172]U.S., Department of State, *A Summary of Views Concerning the Present Status and Future Prospects Concerning the American–Turkish Treaty of Lausanne* (Washington: n.p., n.y.), 711.672/404, DSNA.
    [173]Wilson to Gerard, 2 October 1923, Wilson to Gerard, 13 December 1923, Gerard to Wilson, 21 December 1923, and Wilson to Gerard, 22 December 1923, reel 129, Wilson Papers. For the edited version of the letter of 13 December 1923 see the American Committee for the Independence of Armenia, *The Lausanne Treaty and Kemalist Turkey* (New York: n.p., n.y.), p. 3.
    [174]The secretary of state to the American commissioner at Constantinople (Bristol), 6 April 1926, 711.672/417a, DSNA; Borah to Bishop William T. Manning, 5 April 1926, box 252, Borah Papers.
    [175]G. Howland Shaw to Kellogg, 7 May 1926, 711.672/459, DSNA. See also Borah to Coolidge, 10 May 1926, reel 193, Coolidge Papers.
    [176]The secretary of state to the American commissioner at Constantinople (Bristol), 22 May 1926, 711.672/464, DSNA.

decided to gamble that the situation might improve later in the year, although Borah warned that further postponement "would be about, if not equal, to having it defeated."[177] Shortly after New Year's Day 1927, Senator Borah presented the case for the treaty to the Senate. Senator King, leading the forces opposed to the treaty, attacked the Department of State, Dr. Barton, and the Kemalist regime. At one point in his oration, King dramatically pulled a letter from his pocket and quoted an American missionary in Constantinople as saying that there were "Christian girls in slavery in Turkish harems."[178] On 18 January 1927 the treaty, which Grew had negotiated three and one half years earlier, fell six votes short of ratification.[179]

DIPLOMATIC AFTERMATH

Immediately Kellogg instructed Admiral Bristol to call on Ismet in Ankara to explain the Senate's vote in terms of domestic politics and then to negotiate an executive agreement on the resumption of diplomatic relations.[180] A month later, on 17 February 1927, Admiral Bristol and Teufik Aras of the Turkish Foreign Ministry exchanged notes calling for favorable treatment of American commerce and the resumption of relations.[181] Congress, with the predictable exceptions of Senators King and Swanson, did not object because there had been an adverse public reaction to the rejection of ratification. *Literary Digest* reported that thirteen out of fifteen leading newspapers surveyed printed editorials critical of the Senate action.[182] Secretary Kellogg appointed Grew as the first postwar ambassador to Turkey; the former observer duly renegotiated the bilateral treaty that he had made with Ismet Pasha several years earlier. "By that time," Grew later noted, "the Armenians in our country had shot their bolt, and, while this second treaty was not one-half as favorable to American interests as the first one, it passed the Senate *viva voce*."[183]

---

[177]Borah to Kellogg, 18 June 1926, box 764, Borah Papers.

[178]*New York Times*, 14 January 1927, p. 8.

[179]The secretary of state to the American commissioner at Constantinople (Bristol), 18 January 1927, 711.672/539, DSNA.

[180]The secretary of state to the American commissioner at Constantinople (Bristol), 18 January 1927, 711.672/539, DSNA; Henry Chalmers to Hoover, 19 February 1927, box 613, Hoover Papers, HHL.

[181]The American commissioner at Constantinople (Bristol) to the secretary of state, 17 February 1927, 711.672/566, DSNA.

[182]"Why the Democrats Defeated the Turkish Treaty," *Literary Digest*, 29 January 1927, pp. 10–11. See also General Committee of American Institutions and Associations in Favor of Ratification of the Treaty with Turkey, *American Public Opinion Condemns the Failure to Ratify the American–Turkish Treaty* (New York: n.p., 1927), 711.672/568, DSNA.

[183]Grew, "The Peace Conference of Lausanne," p. 498.

Although the Republicans came into power in 1921 determined to reverse Wilson's policy of growing American involvement in the Near East, they succeeded only in changing the emphasis from humanitarian to commercial concern. Diplomats such as Admiral Bristol and Allen Dulles made the administration aware that the United States had to keep a close watch on the European powers which had conspired to make the Near East a closed-door region. The Lausanne Conference afforded the nation the opportunity to safeguard American interests against the Allies while arranging for a new treaty with revitalized Turkey. Diplomatic observation, a "half a loaf" approach designed to protect American rights without becoming involved in international political understandings, did not work particularly well. Mere observation weakened American diplomatic influence at a gathering where the great powers made the important decisions in private among themselves and not at the conference sessions.

During the first phase of the conference, Hughes imposed so many limitations upon his diplomats that they became helpless to stop the British from trading Armenia and other issues of human rights for Turkey's promise to join the League as part of Lord Curzon's plan to wrest control of Mosul away from the Turks. At the reconvened conference, Hughes gave Grew more freedom of action in order to protect American interests. This allowed Grew to block confirmation of monopolistic prewar Allied concessions in the name of the Open Door. Grew's triumph over British policy paved the way for an Anglo-American rapprochement which would have far-reaching implications in the European reparations quarrel, but otherwise the American victory on behalf of the Open Door turned out to be valueless.

In March 1925 the T.P.C. renegotiated its prewar concession with a new landlord, the British-backed king of Iraq. Once Turkey had cancelled the American Chester concession, Hughes faced the prospect of either seeing America shut out of Iraq altogether or compromising his own Open Door principles by acquiescing in the Standard consortium's deal with the monopolistic Turkish Petroleum Company. The secretary, choosing "to deal with these problems from a practical rather than from a theoretical point of view if we are to be of any real assistance to American business interests," agreed to a face-saving subleasing arrangement which made a mockery of the Open Door.[184] Due to local disturbances in the claims area, the multinational cartel did not exploit the oil monopoly until the 1930s, when it reorganized itself under a new arrangement which scrapped the subleasing provisions completely.[185]

At Lausanne Hughes held out stubbornly for principles which American

---

[184]Hughes to Coolidge, 31 October 1923, reel 26, Coolidge Papers; Gibb and Knowlton, *The Resurgent Years*, p. 297.

[185]DeNovo, *American Interests*, pp. 198–202; Feis, *Diplomacy of the Dollar*, pp. 58–59; Gibb and Knowlton, *The Resurgent Years*, pp. 297–308; Glad, *Illusions of Innocence*, p. 318.

companies never used in practice. In his pursuit of the elusive Open Door, the secretary laid the administration open to charges which led to the defeat of the bilateral treaty, for he made it easy for critics to conclude that there had been a deal involving Armenia and petroleum. While the observers did not swap blood for oil, they did pursue economic considerations much more diligently than they did humanitarian concerns, a policy which soured many on a basically sound treaty, one in which the United States received terms that equalled or bettered the Allied settlement in every area. Although the Department of State and protreaty pressure groups made significant progress in reversing years of hatred against "the Terrible Turk," the treaty went down to defeat at the hands of a minority in the Senate. After using diplomatic observation with only mixed results at Lausanne, Hughes modified this formula for protecting American interests without becoming politically involved with Europe by using businessmen to represent American interests during a serious crisis over German reparations. This time, instead of standing on abstract principles while all but ignoring very real opportunities to aid in the peace process, the secretary would show more resourcefulness, both in diplomacy and domestic politics, in outmaneuvering Congress first to effect bilateral claims agreements with the former Central Powers and then to mastermind a bold plan for the economic recovery of Europe.

5

AMERICAN CLAIMS AND
EUROPEAN REPARATIONS
Wilsonian Ends Through Republican Means

Hughes and Wilson shared the belief that the traditional foreign policy of aloofness from world affairs had passed into history with American participation in the Great War. Both hoped to see the United States in the forefront of a newly liberalized international commercial order based not on European-style imperialism—or revolutionary socialism—but the Open Door, a system which would, in theory, promote peaceful competition among the industrialized powers as well as respect for the rights of underdeveloped peoples. Continued economic growth became linked with the creation of a steady world order. In keeping with this new spirit, Hughes noted shortly after becoming secretary of state that his department was "earnestly desirous of aiding in the reestablishment of stable conditions and thus of contributing to the welfare of other peoples upon which our own prosperity must ultimately depend."[1]

The lingering bitterness of the Great War constituted the greatest threat to a stable world in 1921 as Wilsonianism yielded to normalcy. The Allies, determined to salvage their international investment empires by shifting war and reconstruction costs to the former Central Powers and the United States, pushed for high reparations, cancellation of their American debts, and closed trade doors. In contrast Wilson and his Republican successors argued for reparations only on the basis of Germany's capacity to pay, a solution to the war-debt problem independent of reparations, and the Open Door. At Paris Wilson gave in to the French demand for a relatively weak Reparation Commission, one without the power either to confine reparations to a definite time period or to base them on the German capacity to pay, hoping that the matter could be settled later through the League. The European Allies then embarked on a program of economic reconstruction financed largely with German indemnities. In early 1923 France and Belgium occupied the Ruhr when Germany

---

[1]Hughes, "Some Aspects of the Department of State," in *Pathway to Peace*, p. 266. For Wilson's view, see Levin, *Wilson and World Politics*, p. 237.

suspended payments. Even as the French attempted to squeeze reparations out of Germany at bayonet point, the United States vetoed reconstruction loans to France in order to force a debt settlement. These events forced the Allies back to the bargaining table to discuss war indemnities largely on American terms.

Seizing the opportunity Secretary Hughes worked diligently to solve the reparations problem as a way of promoting European economic and political stability. In essence the Republican Dawes Plan fulfilled Wilsonian expectations in its ends and partially in its means. Acting for the good of the world (and hence of the United States) Hughes stepped forward as the arbiter of Europe, much as Wilson had at Paris. The secretary emerged with a plan strikingly similar to the outline the American president had proposed six years earlier. In the end, however, the narrow framework in which Hughes chose to operate limited the effectiveness of an otherwise sound plan.

EUROPE TESTS THE NEW ADMINISTRATION

Many European leaders seemed as anxious as the Republicans for the end of Wilson's second term. The Allies held some hope that the new administration might inaugurate a generous reconstruction program as an alternative to the makeshift policy of coercion against Germany. With equally unwarranted optimism, the former Central Powers looked to America for protection against the overbearing and insecure victors.[2] When Harding came to the White House in March 1921, Europe faced a crisis over reparations. Two months earlier at a conference in Paris, the Allies had agreed on tentative reparations figures and a payment plan, a scheme meant more to mollify outraged public opinion in France, Britain, Belgium, and Italy than to provide a permanent solution to the postwar economic tangle.[3] On 1 March German Foreign Minister Walter Simons met with British Prime Minister Lloyd George and French Premier Briand to present counterproposals, which, considering the mood of the Allies, turned out to be very unrealistic. Lloyd George gave Simons until 7 March to accept the Paris proposals or come up with an acceptable alternative plan of his own, otherwise the Allies would occupy key German towns on the right bank of the Rhine and apply economic sanctions.[4] Subsequently Simons

    [2]Fry, *Illusions of Security*, pp. 124–25; Walter A. McDougall, *France's Rhineland Diplomacy, 1914–1924: The Last Bid for a Balance of Power in Europe* (Princeton, NJ: Princeton University Press, 1978), p. 150.
    [3]Dresel to Castle, 3 March 1921, box 6, Castle Papers.
    [4]Ibid.; note of an allied conference held in London, 3 March 1921, *DBFP*, 15:257–65. See also Carl Bergmann, *The History of Reparations* (Boston: Houghton Mifflin, 1927), pp. 57–65; and David Felix, *Walter Rathenau and the Weimar Republic: The Politics of Reparations* (Baltimore: Johns Hopkins University Press, 1971), pp. 14–15.

presented a warmed-over version of his earlier plan and, as promised, the Allies occupied Düsseldorf, Duisburg, and Ruhrort, impounding customs receipts in lieu of German reparations payments.[5] In desperation Simons turned to the Americans.

On 21 March 1921, as the Allies occupied the Rhineland, communists revolted in the Ruhr, and Central Germany and Poland threatened each other with war over Upper Silesia, Simons gave American commissioner Dresel a carefully worded note stating that his nation intended to pay reparations to the best of its ability. Dresel and experts at the State Department recognized that the Germans might be using the informal statement as a means of reopening talks with the Allies.[6]

Castle advised Hughes to take a public stand on reparations because "all of Europe waits for an expression of the American attitude." The United States, Castle warned, must not offer to mediate since the Germans might capitalize on the American desire for increased trade to drive a wedge between the victors. Policymakers should keep in mind that the economic revival of Europe as a whole, and not just of Germany, would best serve American economic interests. Castle went on to recommend "an unequivocal statement that the United States stands with the Allies in demanding reparation as full as possible for the damage inflicted in the war" as the surest way for the new administration to bring peace to Europe.[7] From Paris Roland W. Boyden, Wilson's chief observer on the Reparation Commission, offered similar counsel, noting that "time must be allowed for forgetfulness, for development of results, before anyone can possibly intervene usefully."[8] After weighing this advice, Hughes sent a candid, if noncommittal, reply to Simons on 29 March making it quite clear that the United States, like the Allies, held Germany morally responsible for reparations.[9]

Three weeks later, on 20 April, Simons formally requested that President Harding act as a mediator on the reparations question, an appeal which Commissioner Dresel found to be "entirely tactless and mistaken."[10] The next day the Germans gave Dresel another memorandum outlining a new set of proposals. The German secretary of state asked the American diplomat to transmit

[5]Notes of an Allied conference, London, 7 March 1921, *DBFP*, 15:326–32. See also Bergmann, *The History of Reparations*, pp. 67–68; Gordon A. Craig, *Germany, 1866–1945* (New York: Oxford University Press, 1978), p. 439; and Eyck, *Weimar Republic*, pp. 173–77.
[6]The commissioner at Berlin (Dresel) to the secretary of state, 23 March 1921, RG 59, 462.00 R29/565, DSNA. See also Dresel to Castle, 24 March 1921, box 6, Castle Papers.
[7]Memorandum, Castle to Hughes, 25 March 1921, 462.00 R29/1501, DSNA.
[8]Boyden to Harrison, 25 March 1921, box 2, Harrison Papers.
[9]The secretary of state to the commissioner at Berlin (Dresel), 29 March 1921, 462.00 R29/565, DSNA; Dresel to Castle, 31 March 1921, box 6, Castle Papers.
[10]The commissioner at Berlin (Dresel) to the secretary of state, 20 April 1921, 462.00 R29/647 and 648, DSNA; Dresel to Castle, 21 April 1921, box 6, Castle Papers.

the document "for the purpose of confidential information regarding Germany's point of view and not to be used as a bases [*sic*] of decision in regard to mediation by the American Government."[11] Castle and Assistant Secretary of State Leland Harrison advised Hughes to turn aside the German request for mediation. They also suggested that the time might be right to propose a strengthening of the Reparation Commission with the understanding that all nations would accept its verdict. "Under these circumstances," the division chief concluded, "I feel that the United States should be formally represented on the Commission and that our representative should have full authority to act."[12]

Secretary Hughes had to take the domestic American political situation fully into account. Only a few days earlier, the irreconcilables had threatened to block Harding's domestic program if Hughes pressed for passage of the Versailles Treaty and, much to Hughes's chagrin, the president gave in. Bitter-enders such as Borah and Johnson had become obsessed with keeping America off the Reparation Commission; participation in the work of that "Senegambian in the woodpile," as Borah put it, would lead inevitably to political entanglement with Europe and, eventually, to "backdoor" entry into the League.[13] From a political viewpoint, therefore, Hughes realized that he could not afford to take Castle's advice to join the commission, although he did agree with it. The secretary turned down Simons's request for mediation, promising only to bring the new German proposals to the attention of the Allies if the foreign minister's note provided "a proper basis for discussion."[14] One hour after wiring his refusal to Dresel, Hughes sent another despatch which went much further in the direction of Castle's advice. The secretary ordered the commissioner to tell Simons confidentially that the administration "would be willing with the concurrence of the Allied Governments to participate in the negotiations if Germany will seek their resumption on a sound basis."[15] Before any new reparations conference, though, Hughes would have to consult America's wartime allies.

On 25 April Secretary Hughes presented the German proposals to British Ambassador Geddes and French Ambassador Jusserand, emphasizing, as Wilson had at Paris, that although Germany should be made to pay for its aggression, the world economy needed German productive power.[16] Three days later

---

[11]The commissioner at Berlin (Dresel) to the secretary of state, 21 April 1921, 462.00 R29/655, DSNA.
    [12]Memorandum, Castle to Hughes, 21 April 1921, 462.00 R29/1530, DSNA; Castle to Dresel, 25 April 1921, box 6, Castle Papers; Harrison to Fletcher, 20 April 1921, box 9, Harrison Papers.
    [13]Quoted in Maddox, *Borah and American Foreign Policy*, p. 121.
    [14]The secretary of state to the commissioner at Berlin (Dresel), 21 April 1921, 462.00 R29/648, DSNA.
    [15]Ibid.
    [16]Memorandum of a conversation between the secretary of state and the British and French ambassadors, 25 April 1921, *FRUS, 1921*, 2:48–49. See also Geddes (Washington) to Curzon, 25 April 1921, *DBFP*, 16:570.

the British and French representatives returned to inform the secretary that their governments found the German proposals unacceptable.[17] Hughes then wired the bad news to Simons, who, according to Dresel, "appeared much perturbed."[18] Indeed the German foreign minister had good reason to be upset, for within the span of a few days the Reparation Commission had arrived at a final German indemnity of 132 billion gold marks and the Americans had killed his last desperate initiative. On 5 May the Allied Supreme Council once again declared Germany to be in default of the Treaty of Versailles, threatening occupation of the Ruhr Valley in one week unless the Germans complied with the treaty conditions completely.[19] Reich Chancellor Konstantin Fehrenbach and his foreign minister had no choice but to surrender to Allied demands and then resign, thus ending the crisis.[20]

Ironically, in trying to drive a wedge between the Allies and the United States for the benefit of Germany, Simons brought the Europeans and the Americans closer together.[21] Impressed with the new secretary of state's willingness to act as a go-between, the Allies decided on 3 May to invite the Harding administration to send representatives to the Supreme Council, the Council of Ambassadors, and the Reparation Commission.[22] After consultations with the president, Hughes announced that George Harvey, the newly confirmed ambassador to Britain, would represent the United States on the Supreme Council. For the more politically sensitive positions, the secretary of state resorted to the use of observers: The ambassador to France immediately resumed his duties as unofficial observer in the Council of Ambassadors while Boyden began again to sit in on the Reparation Commission in an unofficial capacity.[23]

The irreconcilables protested, but could do nothing, at least for the moment. Believing that Harding and Hughes had acted at the behest of international bankers, Johnson called the decision to resume observation of the Reparation Commission "a body blow in our international relations [which] . . . will inevitably make us a part of entangling alliances abroad."[24] In a few

[17]Memorandum of a conversation between the secretary of state and the British ambassador (Geddes), 28 April 1921, and memorandum of a conversation between the secretary of state and the counselor of the French embassy (De Béarn), 28 April 1921, *FRUS, 1921*, 2:51–52.

[18]The secretary of state to the commissioner at Berlin (Dresel), 2 May 1921, 462.00 R29/684, and the commissioner at Berlin (Dresel) to the secretary of state, 3 May 1921, 462.00 R29/720, DSNA.

[19]Resolution of the Supreme Council of the Allied Powers, 5 May 1921, *FRUS, 1921*, 2:56–57.

[20]The British ambassador (Geddes) to the secretary of state, 11 May 1921, 462.00 R29/768, DSNA; Dresel to Castle, 14 May 1921, box 6, Castle Papers; Craig, *Germany, 1866–1945*, pp. 440–41; Felix, *Walter Rathenau*, p. 20.

[21]Memorandum of a conversation between the secretary of state and the counselor of the French embassy (De Béarn), 28 April 1921, *FRUS, 1921*, 2:51–52.

[22]Notes of an Allied conference held at 10 Downing Street, 3 May 1921, *DBFP*, 15:544–53.

[23]The secretary of state to the American embassy, London, 6 May 1921, 462.00 R29/729, DSNA.

[24]Johnson to A. Johnson and H. Johnson, Jr., 10 May 1921, part 6, box 3, Johnson Papers.

months time, during the Senate debate on the separate peace, the irreconcilables insisted on an amendment giving Congress a veto over formal American participation in any commission connected with the Versailles Treaty.

Hughes's handling of the German appeals for mediation pleased Western European Division Chief Castle. In following his advice, the secretary had rejected the German appeal, yet taken the opportunity to put observers back on key treaty-related bodies. "The Secretary understands," Castle wrote to Dresel, "as apparently some Senators do not, that this country is vitally interested in the whole settlement whether or not individual aspects of it appear to touch American interests."[25] Castle hoped that American participation in the work of the Reparation Commission would resign Germany to its punishment while restraining the Allies. He had also suggested that Hughes work to strengthen the commission in order to let the specialists, not Allied politicians, make key decisions, although the secretary did not go that far. Even with Americans once again sitting in and occasionally participating, the Reparation Commission could not solve the indemnity problem because it had no real power.[26] In 1922, when the Germans suspended payments again, Europe faced another crisis. Secretary Hughes would eventually propose an alternative vehicle for settlement; first, he had to square American accounts with the former Central Powers.

THE CLAIMS SETTLEMENT

In early 1922 Secretary of State Hughes prepared to set up tribunals for the adjustment of American claims against Germany, Austria, and Hungary under provisions of the separate peace treaties. The problem, he explained in a letter to President Harding, was that the separate peace provided for mixed arbitral tribunals modeled on the Versailles pact, but the Senate consented to ratification with the understanding that Congress would approve American participation in any Versailles Treaty-related body. Therefore the State Department could not settle the claims matter without a joint resolution.[27] Dutifully Harding dispatched letters to Chairman Lodge of the Senate Foreign Relations Committee and Chairman Stephen G. Porter of the House Foreign Affairs Committee formally requesting action.[28] Three days later Porter wrote back that, after careful consideration, the Republican leadership had concluded

---

[25]Castle to Dresel, 9 May 1921, box 68, file 15, Dresel Papers.
[26]Ibid.
[27]Hughes to Harding, 12 January 1922, reel 215, Harding Papers.
[28]Harding to Lodge, and Harding to Porter, 20 January 1922, ibid.

"that the Democrats in the Senate will filibuster and use the resolution to secure, if possible, some partisan advantage."[29] Regardless of whether Porter's letter reflected the situation in the Senate accurately, where Republicans held a healthy fifty-nine-to-thirty-seven advantage, or if the leadership had found significant Republican opposition to Hughes's scheme, the president understood the message from Capitol Hill: The secretary of state would have to prepare some other means for adjusting claims.[30]

Hughes saw no alternative but to negotiate separate bilateral claims agreements beginning with Germany. The secretary worked closely with the new American ambassador in Berlin, Alanson B. Houghton, a loyal Republican from New York and former chairman of the board of Corning Glass Works, in developing the idea of a German-American commission which would determine the amount of American claims.[31] Houghton soon found that Reich Chancellor Josef Wirth and Foreign Minister Walter Rathenau advocated a policy of "fulfillment" as a means of showing to the world the unfairness and impractical nature of the Versailles settlement.[32] The Germans also desired renewal of commercial relations with the United States.[33] During the spring of 1922, Ambassador Houghton used the German desideratum to hurry along a claims agreement, telling foreign office officials, as Dresel had during negotiation of the separate peace, that a commercial treaty would have to wait until after the current problem had been solved. On 5 May Houghton reported agreement on the idea that the mixed claims commission should be a small body composed of only two or three members. "I suggested," the ambassador noted, "that it might be possible to name a second American of high position and said I thought a request . . . along these lines would have good effect on Congress."[34]

Less than a month later, on 2 June, at Houghton's prompting, the German Foreign Office proposed that the president of the United States appoint "a prominent American citizen whose capabilities and character are beyond criticism" to be chairman of a claims commission composed of one other American and one German representative.[35] Hughes then wired the ambassador

[29]Porter to Harding, 23 January 1923 [sic], ibid.

[30]Pusey, Charles Evans Hughes, pp. 442–43.

[31]"The Separate Peace with Germany," box 172, folder 25, p. 23a, Hughes Papers. See also Frank Costigliola, "The United States and the Reconstruction of Germany in the 1920s," Business History Review 50 (Winter 1976): 479.

[32]Houghton to Castle, 8 July 1922, box 6, Castle Papers; Costigliola, "Reconstruction of Germany," p. 480; Felix, Walter Rathenau, pp. 80–81.

[33]The chargé in Germany (Dresel) to the secretary of state, 22 February 1922, FRUS, 1922, 2:240–41.

[34]The ambassador in Germany (Houghton) to the secretary of state, 5 May 1922, ibid., 2:243; Castle to Dresel, 16 February 1922, box 6, Castle Papers.

[35]The ambassador in Germany (Houghton) to the secretary of state, 3 June 1922, FRUS, 1922, 2:245.

a draft claims treaty and, after a brief delay caused when nationalist fanatics assassinated Rathenau, the two sides settled in to bargain over fine points.[36]

The idea of a mixed German-American claims commission did not sit well with Democratic Minority Leader Underwood. On 20 July he introduced a bill which would have, in effect, treated American claims against Germany as a purely domestic matter. Underwood wanted an exclusively American commission to use German property seized during the war and still held by the alien property custodian to settle claims without consulting Germany. "I have no bitterness against our late enemies," the senator explained, "but it would be far from my disposition to see the heirs of the people who were murdered in the sinking of the *Lusitania* go before a mixed tribunal."[37] The Underwood proposal struck Hughes as confiscatory and against accepted tenets of international law.[38] The secretary fired off an angry letter to Senate Judiciary Committee Chairman Knute Nelson charging that the bill amounted to ex parte confiscation "at variance with the principles and practice generally observed by nations in their relations with each other, and I should think it unfortunate if such a course were initiated by this Government."[39]

While the Senate debated Underwood's bill, Hughes fretted that even if it did not pass, the Alabama Democrat would have aroused enough opposition to the administration's claims plan to block ratification. He decided to proceed with the negotiations and to treat the finished project as an executive agreement which did not need the advice and consent of the Senate. On 29 July the secretary ordered Ambassador Houghton to impress upon the Germans that they would be far better off agreeing at once to the administration's proposal than facing the alternative of the one-sided Underwood bill.[40] The chief stumbling block had been the German refusal to accept private debts as legitimate claims of war. Houghton's argument that Germany would be worse off with the Underwood proposal "overcame a considerable and not unjustifiable reluctance on the part of the German Government to accept the inclusion of private debts."[41] Cleverly Hughes used Underwood's bill to cajole the Germans into a quick agreement; the Senate might be more difficult to convince.

Secretary of State Hughes had to move very cautiously in regard to claims because an open controversy with the Senate could prove disastrous for administration foreign policy as a whole. Therefore the secretary asked

---

[36]The secretary of state to the ambassador in Germany (Houghton), 22 June 1922, ibid., 2:246–49; Felix, *Walter Rathenau*, pp. 171–72.

[37]*Congressional Record*, 67th Cong., 2nd sess., pp. 10443–49; Johnson, *Underwood*, pp. 329–30.

[38]"The Separate Peace," box 172, folder 25, p. 23b, Hughes Papers.

[39]*Congressional Record*, 67th Cong., 2nd sess., pp. 13056–57.

[40]The secretary of state to the ambassador in Germany (Houghton), 29 July 1922, *FRUS, 1922*, 2:255–56.

[41]The ambassador in Germany (Houghton) to the secretary of state, 2 August 1922, ibid., 2:257.

President Harding to set up an interview with the one politician he thought capable of leading a full scale antiadministration revolt. A few days later, Hughes made his case before Senator Borah, arguing for the executive agreement setting up the German-American claims commission, a settlement far more equitable than the loathsome alternative of confiscation. Borah, who shared in the consensus of the American elite that general prosperity depended on the economic recovery of Germany and who also believed that the Allies had been far too harsh with the Germans, agreed with the Hughes plan in principle. But, the senator inquired, did the president have the authority to take this course without consulting Congress? Hughes explained that executive action had settled claims since the days of Thomas Jefferson. Borah left the meeting pledged not to oppose Hughes's agreement with Germany.[42] While Underwood grumbled, most of the Senate, following Borah's lead, accepted the administration argument.[43] When the minority leader's bill came up for a vote in late September, only eighteen senators voted for it and, by that time, the executive agreement had been functioning for more than a month.[44]

The German-American claims agreement signed 10 August 1922 provided for a mixed claims commission composed of one representative from each country and an American umpire empowered to settle American claims and debts against Germany incurred since 31 July 1914. In a side letter, the United States waived its right to claim soldiers' pensions.[45] Hughes arranged for immediate publication of the agreement along with the announcement that Harding had named Associate Justice William R. Day as umpire. "In making the announcement," President Harding suggested to Hughes, "please *emphasize* the request to us to name umpire. It is so unusual that its significance is worth bringing well to the fore."[46] Hughes did so, without, of course, mentioning that Houghton had all but insisted that Germany make the request for domestic American political reasons.[47] A few months later, during a campaign swing for Lodge, the secretary would refer to Germany's gesture as

[42]Castle to Houghton, 4 August 1922, box 6, Castle Papers; "The Separate Peace," box 172, folder 25, p. 23c, Hughes Papers; Maddox, *Borah and American Foreign Policy*, pp. 123–24; Pusey, *Charles Evans Hughes*, pp. 443–44.

[43]*New York Times*, 12 August 1922, p. 3.

[44]*Congressional Record*, 67th Cong., 2nd sess., p. 13071; Johnson, *Underwood*, pp. 330–31.

[45]Agreement between the United States of America and Germany, signed at Berlin, 10 August 1922, the German chancellor (Wirth) to the American ambassador in Germany (Houghton), 10 August 1922, and the American ambassador in Germany (Houghton) to the German chancellor (Wirth), 10 August 1922, *FRUS, 1922*, 2:262–66.

[46]Hughes to Harding, and Harding to Hughes, 10 August 1922, ibid., 2:261–62.

[47]*New York Times*, 11 August 1922, p. 1. Hughes's leading biographer and Hughes himself both repeat the myth of Germany's "unique gesture." See Pusey, *Charles Evans Hughes*, p. 444; and "The Separate Peace with Germany," box 172, folder 25, p. 23d, Hughes Papers.

"an extraordinary tribute . . . to the American sense of justice."[48] In reality
the German request reflected nothing more than the Wirth government's desire
to please the Harding administration so that a German-American commercial
treaty might be negotiated.

The Mixed Claims Commission, which served as a model for later
agreements with Austria and Hungary, actually functioned quite well, awarding millions of dollars to American nationals and the government.[49] Unfortunately for the claimants, Germany had no way of making immediate payment;
other arrangements would have to be made so that Americans could collect
their claims while Europeans accumulated their reparations.

WATCHFUL WAITING, REPUBLICAN STYLE

Hughes watched the situation in Europe with growing alarm in 1922.
Millions of dollars in claims against Germany gave the administration an
additional stake in the outcome of the reparations tangle, and Americans
expected reimbursement for the mounting cost of keeping an army of occupation in Germany. The secretary believed that American prosperity "largely
depends upon the economic settlements which may be made in Europe, and
the key to the future is with those who make those settlements."[50] The State
Department had been receiving a steady stream of correspondence from Berlin
indicating that everyone except the French believed Germany could not continue to fulfill its reparations obligations much longer, an opinion shared by
Boyden and Colonel James Logan, the American observers on the Reparation
Commission; Benjamin Strong, president of the Federal Reserve Bank of New
York; and Secretary of Commerce Hoover.[51]

Several factors more than offset these reasons for propelling the nation
directly into the reparations controversy. A reservation attached to the Berlin

[48]Hughes speech at mass meeting, Symphony Hall, Boston, MA, 30 October 1922, box
189, Hughes Papers.

[49]Charles P. Howland, ed., *Survey of American Foreign Relations, 1928* (New Haven,
CT: Yale University Press, 1928), pp. 471–86. For the treaties with Austria and Hungary, see
FRUS, 1924, 1:142–54.

[50]Hughes speech at Brown University, June 1921, box 189, Hughes Papers.

[51]Dresel to Castle, 8 August, 5 October, and 18 November 1921, box 6, Castle Papers;
Boyden to his cousin, 22 November 1921, box 516, Hoover Papers, HHL: "The Secret Letters
of James A. Logan, Jr.," 22 July, 22 August, 29 August, 2 September, 15 October, 3 November,
and 22 November 1921 and 9 March 1922, James A. Logan Papers, vols. 5 and 6, Hoover
Institution on War, Revolution and Peace, Stanford University, Stanford, CA (hereafter cited
as Logan Papers); Harrison to Logan, 22 October 1921, box 7, Harrison Papers; Benjamin Strong
to Montagu Norman, 25 November 1921, Benjamin Strong Papers, box 1A, Herbert Hoover
Presidential Library, West Branch, IA; Hoover to W. E. Guerin, 30 December 1921, box 236,
Hoover Papers, HHL.

Treaty forbidding American representation on the Reparation Commission without the explicit consent of Congress limited Hughes's freedom of action.[52] While most moderates in politics and the business community favored a scaling down of both reparations and war debts, Congress had set up the World War Foreign Debt Commission, a body which could not by law cancel or reduce debts.[53]

Hughes did not even have full control of the issue within the administration since Hoover believed that the Commerce Department should set reparations policy. In an effort to wrest control of the reparations issue away from Hughes, Hoover demanded to see all State Department correspondence on indemnities. He wrote to Hughes:

> The Reparations problem is essentially a commercial problem, our commercial policies greatly revolve upon it and unless this Department can be possessed of all information accessible to the Government, it cannot direct the administration of policies in those phases that of necessity lie in this Department.[54]

Castle argued that Hoover's ideas did not take into consideration the political realities in Europe. If Germany did not continue to pay reparations, France would occupy more German territory. "What appears to be necessary, therefore," he continued, "is to devise some method whereby Germany, with the consent of France, (that of England to any reasonable agreement is assured) can tide over the next three or four critical years." After this interim period, "the French presumably will have reached a more reasonable frame of mind on the general reparation question." Castle recommended giving high priority to keeping American reparations policy out of Hoover's bailiwick and within the State Department.[55] A "deeply pained" Hoover resisted for several months before lining up behind Hughes in the fall of 1922.[56]

In addition to congressional restrictions on his freedom of action and the power struggle within the administration, Hughes let the reparations question simmer during the first half of 1922 because relations with the Allies had soured. After obtaining the first annual indemnity from Germany in late 1921, the Allies divided the spoils among France, Great Britain, and Belgium for reimbursement of army occupation costs, but allotted nothing to the United

---

[52]Dexter Perkins, *Charles Evans Hughes and American Democratic Statesmanship* (Boston: Little, Brown, 1956), p. 120.

[53]Melvyn Leffler, "The Origins of Republican War Debt Policy, 1921–1923: A Case Study in the Applicability of the Open Door Interpretation," *Journal of American History* 59 (December 1972): 585–97; Richard W. Van Alstyne, "Debt Collection," in *Encyclopedia of American Foreign Policy*, p. 215.

[54]Hoover to Hughes, 6 December 1921, 462.00 R29/2171, DSNA.

[55]Castle to Hughes, 7 December 1921, 462.00 R29/2171, ibid.

[56]Hoover to Hughes, 15 December 1921, and Hughes to Hoover, 16 December 1921, 462.00 R29/2172, ibid. See also David Burner, *Herbert Hoover, A Public Life* (New York: Alfred A. Knopf, 1979), pp. 187–88.

States.[57] At the Cannes conference of January 1922, the Allies apportioned the anticipated payments for the new year along similar lines, again ignoring the Americans.[58] Two months later when the Council of Ambassadors met in Paris to confirm the distribution of reparations, Hughes instructed observer Boyden to put the Allies on notice "that this Government will insist upon payment in full" of all occupation costs.[59] The Europeans responded with a special clause in the final agreement reserving American rights, a statement which, as one British diplomat noted, meant virtually nothing.[60]

Hughes told reporters off the record at a press conference of 11 March that "it was ridiculous to suppose that we should bear our share of the expenses of occupation and then be told to whistle for our money."[61] The Allies' decision set off a wave of anti-European speeches and editorials throughout the nation.[62] On 6 April the secretary wired Ambassador Harvey in London to press the Allies further for unequivocal recognition of the American right of repayment of occupation costs.[63]

Ambassador Jusserand protested immediately against the popular outcry, charging in a telephone conversation with Castle that the American demand was like dumping vinegar into a salad bowl. The Frenchman's analogy amused Hughes, who observed that "perhaps a little more vinegar might be a good thing, as . . . the French were getting a little fond of eating all the salad themselves."[64] The United States and the Allies would discuss the matter for more than a year before coming to an agreement on reimbursement, a nagging minor question which made genuine cooperation on the much more important reparations problem all the more difficult.[65]

THE BANKERS' COMMITTEE

In early 1922, with the Allies, including France, finally coming to understand that Germany faced economic ruin, the Reparation Commission

[57]A summary by Wigram of the reparation position, 28 December 1921, *DBFP*, 16:857–60; Nelson, *Victors Divided*, p. 193.

[58]Memorandum by Wigram on the position of the reparation negotiations at the close of the Cannes Conference, 19 January 1922, *DBFP*, 20:1–3; Nelson, *Victors Divided*, pp. 194–95.

[59]The secretary of state to Boyden, American embassy, Paris, 9 March 1922, RG 59, 462.00 R294/2, DSNA. See also "Secret Letters of James Logan," 10 March 1922, vol. 6, Logan Papers.

[60]Record by Wigram of a conversation with Sir B. Blackett respecting Allied finance ministers' meeting, 16 March 1922, *DBFP*, 20:16–18.

[61]Memorandum, Division of Foreign Intelligence, 11 March 1922, 462.00 R294/2b, DSNA.

[62]Nelson, *Victors Divided*, pp. 195–97.

[63]The secretary of state to the ambassador in Britain (Harvey), 6 April 1922, 462.00 R294/63, DSNA.

[64]Castle to Sheldon Whitehouse, 18 April 1922, box 1, Castle Papers.

[65]For the occupation cost negotiations, see *FRUS, 1923*, 2:110–92.

granted the Germans a temporary reduction in indemnity payments from 31 million gold marks every ten days to an annual total of 720 million gold marks in cash, contingent on internal economic reforms.[66] On 4 April the commission created a special committee to explore the possibility of providing Germany with real stability and France a continuing source of reconstruction finances through substantial international loans. To avoid the wrath of the irreconcilables, as well as possible attempts by the Allies to link more realistic German reparations payments to reduced debts owed to the United States, the State Department resorted again to unofficial diplomacy, suggesting through Boyden and Logan the appointment of financier John Pierrepont Morgan to the Bankers' Committee.[67]

After hearing of Morgan's unofficial mission, Secretary Hoover suggested that Hughes ask Morgan to cooperate with the government by refusing to go along with any loan scheme "until the whole reparation question had been settled on a stable and possible basis." If the secretary of state did not relay this proposition to Morgan, Hoover said, then he would be forced to announce publicly that any loan floated to Germany was worthless unless coupled to a fundamental and realistic settlement of reparations.[68] The cautious Hughes refused to give Morgan any specific instructions which might compromise the unofficial nature of his mission. The secretary also knew, however, that Morgan would not loan any of his money to Germany without a scaling down of the indemnity. Besides, the department had, for some time, been urging underwriters of European loans to consult the government voluntarily for the sake of the national interest.[69] Hoover never made good on his threat, although a month later in an address before the Chamber of Commerce of the United States he called for a reparations settlement "as will create reasonable confidence that payments will be met."[70]

French leaders had no intention of giving the bankers a free hand in solving the indemnity tangle; they stipulated in advance that the committee could not tamper with German obligations under the Treaty of Versailles or the London schedule of payments hammered out in May 1921. Nevertheless observer Logan regarded the project as a great opportunity for the world financial community to make a contribution toward peace. France needs money from Germany, he reasoned, funds which the Germans would have to borrow. "The fellow who lends the money," he continued, "is the fellow who makes the conditions and states the amount, this fellow is not the politician but is

---

[66]Logan to Hoover, 17 February, 9 March, and 17 March 1922, box 12, Hoover Papers, Hoover Institution. See also Bergmann, *The History of Reparations*, pp. 114–15; and Felix, *Walter Rathenau*, p. 149.
[67]Logan to Hoover, 14 April 1922, box 12, Hoover Papers, Hoover Institution; Logan to Houghton, 17 May 1922, box 2, Logan Papers; *New York Times*, 19 April 1922, p. 3, 20 April 1922, p.2, and 25 April 1922, p. 1.
[68]Memorandum by Christian A. Herter, 22 April 1922, box 236, Hoover Papers, HHL.
[69]Leffler, *Elusive Quest*, p. 74; *New York Times*, 19 April 1922, p. 3.
[70]*New York Times*, 17 May 1922, pp. 1–2.

the banker." In the end France would have to listen to what the bankers had to say.[71] Boyden regarded Morgan's role as "simplicity itself." The American financier should, as a potential lender of money, ask the Reparation Commission how Germany could continue to pay. "I should certainly enjoy watching their faces, if he will do that," Boyden wrote to his mother, "as I mean to ask him to."[72]

The American optimism proved to be unwarranted. French Premier Poincaré refused to consider changing the current level and schedule of German payments while Morgan, following administration policy, called for reductions in reparations as he avoided any direct linkage with the debt question. Without unanimity the bankers could only agree to adjourn, promising to meet again if changes in the situation made new discussions worthwhile. The final report, which Poincaré's representative did not sign, blamed the impasse on the French for refusing to lower reparations to a reasonable amount, although the committee made no mention of the equally shortsighted declination to annul or even to lower France's huge war debt.[73] "To our mind," Logan wrote, "the main thing which has been accomplished is to bring out clearly to anyone who takes the trouble to think at all that the present policy is neither sensible nor businesslike."[74]

Morgan remained in Europe for months after the adjournment of the committee in the hope that he could be of some use. Logan tried to buoy his spirits, urging the banker at one point to "'stick by the ship' for you are badly needed in this situation."[75] A meeting with Lloyd George in August left Morgan feeling decidedly pessimistic. "I am more and more sure," he wrote to Logan, "that we outsiders can do nothing but wait and deal with the conditions as they may exist when the government people have created them."[76]

As the German economy continued to deteriorate and France and Britain became increasingly impatient with one another, Boyden came back to Washington to urge Secretary Hughes to issue a strong public statement on the reparations issue. Noting that "demands which exceed Germany's capacity defeat their own purpose," the observer recommended the appointment of a "Supreme Court of Business Judgment"—an international tribunal similar to

[71]Logan to Hoover, 15 June 1922, box 12, Hoover Papers, Hoover Institution; Logan to Houghton, 17 May 1922, box 2, Logan Papers.

[72]Boyden to A. L. Boyden, 18 May 1922, Roland W. Boyden Papers, microfilm, reel 2, Hoover Institution on War, Revolution and Peace, Stanford University, Stanford, CA (hereafter cited as Boyden Papers).

[73]*New York Times*, 28 May 1922, pp. 1 and 16, 11 June 1922, pp. 1–2, and 14 June 1922, p. 3. See also Bergmann, *History of Reparations*, pp. 133–38.

[74]"Secret Letters of James Logan," 15 June 1922, vol. 6, Logan Papers. See also Boyden to Albert Boyden, 10 June 1922, and Boyden to Augustus J. Boyden, 12 June 1922, reel 2, Boyden Papers.

[75]Logan to J. P. Morgan, 1 August 1922, box 2, Logan Papers.

[76]Morgan to Logan, 10 August 1922, box 2, ibid. See also Morgan to Logan, 25 August 1922, ibid.

the Bankers' Committee, but free from governmental interference—to study the reparations problem.[77] Before the secretary had time to act on Boyden's proposal, Arthur Balfour, manager of the Foreign Office in Lord Curzon's absence, issued a declaration that Britain would be willing to forego reparations and to reduce debts owed by France and other Allies provided that the United States decreased Britain's debts proportionally.[78] The Balfour Note, which touched off another storm of anti-European feelings in the United States, ended any possibility of Hughes undertaking a new initiative on reparations in mid-1922. The administration, Boyden wrote to Logan from Washington, "does not seem particularly courageous in regard to matters here."[79]

Hughes felt that he could not sit idle as Europe slid toward another catastrophe. If Congress and the president would not consider linking Allied debts with German indemnities, he reasoned, then the reparations question would have to be settled first. In October the secretary opened a low-key campaign to revive the Bankers' Committee, instructing Ambassador Herrick to broach the idea with Poincaré.[80] The bankers could effect a settlement, Hughes told Morgan's partner, Thomas W. Lamont, but only if the governments concerned would agree in advance to abide by the committee's decision.[81] Morgan, still bitter over his frustrating experience with the first committee of bankers, agreed to serve again reluctantly as long as the members had complete freedom to arrive at sensible recommendations. Anything less, he contended, "would be worse than useless."[82]

On 22 October Herrick explained the American proposal to Poincaré, emphasizing the need for a businesslike solution to the impasse and avoiding the question of debt reduction. The ambassador commented that he saw a parallel between the current economic plight of Europe and the situation in America after the panic of 1893. At that time a group of prominent citizens had reorganized the bankrupt Union Pacific railroad while other committees recast and refinanced other insolvent companies until good times returned. Herrick added that he had been a member of several reorganization committees which brought order—and prosperity—out of chaos. Poincaré made only

---

[77]Boyden to Hughes, August 1922, reel 4, Boyden Papers.

[78]The ambassador in Britain (Harvey) to the secretary of state, 4 August 1922, *FRUS, 1922*, 1:406–9.

[79]Boyden to Logan, 31 August 1922, box 2, Logan Papers. See also memorandum by Boyden, undated, reel 4, Boyden Papers; and Castle, "Intergovernmental Debts," unpublished manuscript, box 34, Castle Papers.

[80]The secretary of state to the ambassador in France (Herrick), 9 October 1922, and the secretary of state to the ambassador in Rome (Child), 18 October 1922, RG 59, 462.00 R296/1, DSNA. See also Beerits's memorandum, "The Dawes Plan," box 172, folder 26, p. 2, Hughes Papers; Pusey, *Charles Evans Hughes*, p. 580.

[81]Lamont to Morgan, 6 October 1922, box 211, Hoover Papers, HHL.

[82]The ambassador in France (Herrick) to the secretary of state, 13 October 1922, 462.00 R296/2 and 6, and Lamont to Hughes, 8 November 1922, 462.00 R296/7, DSNA.

noncommittal remarks about this scheme to put Europe back together again in the same way that Herrick had rebuilt a frontier railroad.[83]

In the end the ambassador found the task of bringing together two supreme egotists—Morgan and Poincaré—to be impossible. A feud had been brewing between them for months. During the summer of 1922, as Morgan awaited the call to reconvene the Bankers' Committee, Poincaré made remarks in Parliament which cast aspersions on the American financier's motives. In mid-November Louis Dubois, the former president of the Reparation Commission, finally convinced the French leader to invite Morgan to Paris for discussions. But the premier, anxious that Morgan had taken offense at his earlier Parlimentary statements, issued only an informal verbal invitation out of fear that he might be rebuffed. The American banker replied that he already had plans to leave Europe, adding that he could make himself available briefly on 22 November, provided that France agreed to accept the basic principles of the first Bankers' Committee report, along with the assurance that Germany could expect to receive a substantial moratorium on payments. After hearing of these preconditions, Poincaré suddenly remembered that he had to attend an important meeting of the cabinet that day.[84] Morgan eventually left Europe without seeing French leaders.

Meanwhile Boyden had offered "a blast of sense from the United States" to the Reparation Commission, suggesting informally that if Germany made a convincing expression of its acceptance of the Treaty of Versailles, the Allies could then adjust reparations to meet the German capacity to pay.[85] The observer hoped such a plan might strengthen British efforts to keep the French from resorting to a military solution. He and Logan also believed the proposal would have a "missionary effect" on Poincaré and moderates like Barthou, who favored exploration of a solution based on "business lines" such as the Bankers' Committee.[86]

Shortly after the Morgan-Poincaré fiasco had run its course, Boyden wired Hughes from Paris that the results of the informal American initiative had been "worse than negative." Boyden wrote, "[Poincaré] had learned nothing and forgotten nothing not from lack of intelligence but rather from definite purpose partly because he has staked his political life and reputation on his aggressive policy." If the secretary wanted results, he would have to go further than private, informal suggestions. "You must in my judgment,"

[83]The ambassador in France (Herrick) to the secretary of state, 23 and 27 October and 7 November 1922, *FRUS, 1922*, 2:175, 177–78, and 182–84.

[84]Boyden to Albert A. Boyden, 25 November 1922, reel 2, Boyden Papers; Herrick to Castle, 28 November 1922, box 1, Castle Papers; "The Secret Letters of James Logan," 24 November 1922, vol. 7, and Logan to Morgan, 16 November 1922, box 2, Logan Papers.

[85]Boyden to Charles J. Bullock, 12 February 1923, reel 2, and draft of a report to be sent by the commission to the German government, 15 November 1922, reel 4, Boyden Papers.

[86]Logan to Hoover, 16 November 1922, box 12, Hoover Papers, Hoover Institution. See also Boyden to F. S. Snyder, 8 February 1923, reel 2, Boyden Papers.

the observer noted, "make some public utterance with the idea of helping reasonable French opinion, distorted, hopelessly silent, to arrest itself [while] also stiffening Belgium, England, [and] Italy in maintaining their undoubted conviction that this policy means disaster."[87] The secretary disagreed with Boyden, suggesting to his observer that an appeal to the French people over the head of their government might make the situation even worse.[88] Within another month though, the crisis had grown acute enough for Hughes to take up Boyden's suggestion.

THE HUGHES INITIATIVE

Hughes met several times with Ambassador Jusserand in December, continuing his campaign to sell the French on the idea of an unofficial financial committee (without the troublesome Morgan) and to dissuade the Poincaré government from occupying the Ruhr Valley of Germany as punishment for nonpayment of reparations.[89] The Allied premiers met in London on 9 December to discuss the agenda and date of the forthcoming Brussels Conference on reparations, adjourning without agreement on anything except that they would meet again in early January at Paris.[90] A week later, on 16 December, British Secretary of State Lord Curzon telegraphed Ambassador Geddes that an Anglo-French understanding on future German policy seemed quite impossible. However if the United States would offer to send an observer to the Paris meeting, Curzon wrote, "it would, we think, greatly help but without American assistance the prospect is almost hopeless."[91]

When Geddes raised the question of American participation with Hughes, the secretary replied that he had heard rumors that France did not want the United States included at the meeting, one which his government could not attend in any event because the subject of inter-Allied debts might be raised. In his report on the meeting, Geddes noted that Hughes and Harding "are frightened of their own political shadows and terrified by new radical senators who whether they are [R]epublican or [D]emocratic are more strongly isolationist than the men they displaced."[92] Geddes's explanation contained a kernel of truth; Congress had already put several legal limitations on the

[87]Boyden to Hughes, 22 November 1922, 462.00 R29/2187, DSNA.
[88]Hughes to Boyden, 24 November 1922, ibid.
[89]"The Dawes Plan," box 172, folder 26, pp. 4–8, Hughes Papers; memoranda of conversations between the secretary of state and the French ambassador (Jusserand), 14, 21, and 26 December 1922, *FRUS, 1922*, 2:187–92, 195–96, and 197–98.
[90]Hughes to Lodge, undated, box 31, Hughes Papers; Curzon to Geddes, 11 December 1922, *DBFP*, 20:320–21.
[91]Curzon to Geddes, 16 December 1922, *DBFP*, 20:336.
[92]Geddes to Curzon, 18 December 1922, ibid., 20:340.

administration, including creation of a foreign debt commission and a prohibi-
tion on participation in Versailles-related bodies without prior approval,
although Hughes also had other reasons to steer clear of the European conference. The secretary still did not have complete control over reparations policy
within the administration. He believed that a political solution to the indemnities tangle in an atmosphere of high tension would be quite impossible.
Finally, the quarrels with the Allies over reimbursement for army occupation
costs and war debts had not yet been resolved. The only safe course seemed
to be continued promotion of a private, businesslike approach with a new twist.

Once again, as when the secretary of state dreamed up the Treaty of
Berlin as a marriage between the Versailles pact and the Knox-Porter resolution, Hughes would later claim that "the voice of God" gave him an idea in
the middle of the night, one not unlike Boyden's concept of a Supreme Court
of Business Judgment. He had a longstanding commitment to address the
American Historical Association on aspects of current foreign policy and his
bland remarks had been prepared and distributed to the press well in advance.
On the spur of the moment, Hughes decided to publicize the idea of a special
financial committee to solve the reparations problem.[93] On 29 December, with
Harding's warm approval, the secretary told the assembled historians that the
question of reparations had to be settled before Europe could proceed with
any other vital economic questions. The United States did not want reparations
(he said nothing about millions in claims), only reimbursement for occupation
costs. Again Hughes rejected the linking of indemnities with war debts, stating
that President Harding, like Wilson, could never agree to such a scheme.
France deserved reparations, yet Germany must not be prostrated. "There can
be no economic recuperation in Europe," he continued, "unless Germany
recuperates. There will be no permanent peace unless economic satisfactions
are enjoyed." The secretary then went on to propose the creation of a new
commission of leading international businessmen, noting that "distinguished
Americans would be willing to serve."[94]

Hughes's proposal had several flaws. First, the speech did not offer
anything new to the French; he was merely stating in public what he had been
saying in private for months. Second, the secretary spoke out, at least in part,
to appeal to European public opinion, a strategy which he rejected earlier on
the solid ground that it might do more harm than good. Third, the whole
concept of an impartial group of financiers mapping out an evenhanded plan
of European economic recovery ran counter to the postwar experience, as
most financial experts, while brothers under the skin, had been just as
nationalistic as their political leaders. Finally, not wishing to defy the public

---

[93]"The Dawes Plan," box 172, folder 26, pp. 8–9, Hughes Papers; Hyde, "Charles Evans
Hughes," p. 376; Pusey, *Charles Evans Hughes*, p. 581.
[94]Hughes, "Some Aspects of Our Foreign Policy," pp. 53–58.

mood, which demanded a divorce between debts and reparations, Hughes continued to place the burden of the problem on the Europeans. The United States might consider some debt reduction, but only after a settlement of reparations. He paid almost slavish attention to American public opinion without taking into account that European leaders had their own public opinion problems to worry about.[95]

Although the British and American publics reacted favorably to the Hughes address, France's responded negatively.[96] Poincaré went so far as to deny that the Harding administration had made any direct suggestions with regard to reparations.[97] On 5 January after Poincaré had broken off talks at the conference of premiers, Ambassador Herrick recommended against further attempts at influencing French policy. "Nothing we can say now," he wrote, "will divert the French from their present course and . . . our main advice on a future occasion will be more readily listened to by our maintaining an impartial attitude at present."[98] Two days later General Jean-Joseph-Marie Degoutte, commander of the French Army of the Rhine, informed General Henry T. Allen, commander of the American Rhineland forces, of troop concentrations in preparation for the occupation of the Ruhr.[99] Hughes confronted Ambassador Jusserand with this information, threatening to withdraw the last one thousand American troops from Germany.[100] On 10 January, following the Reparation Commission's declaration of German default on coal reparations, France announced formally that French and Belgian forces would seize German mines in the Ruhr, thereby launching a period of greatly increased tensions between the continental members of the Entente and Germany.[101]

As soon as word reached Washington of the French decision, Hughes met with President Harding and Secretary of War John L. Weeks to plan for the immediate withdrawal of American troops from the Rhine. The administration kept a token army in Germany to restrain France morally, but the

---

[95]McDougall, *France's Rhineland Diplomacy*, pp. 242–43.

[96]"Putting World Peace Up to America," *Literary Digest*, 13 January 1923, pp. 16–17. See also Castle to Houghton, 30 December 1922, box 6, Castle Papers; Glad, *Illusions of Innocence*, p. 223; McDougall, *France's Rhineland Diplomacy*, p. 243.

[97]Castle to Whitehouse, 13 January 1923, box 1, Castle Papers; memorandum of a conversation between the secretary of state and the French ambassador (Jusserand), 5 January 1923, *FRUS, 1923*, 2:46–47; Geddes to Curzon, 10 January 1923, *DBFP*, 21:19–20. See also William Phillips, *Ventures in Diplomacy* (Boston: Beacon Press, 1953), p. 114.

[98]The ambassador in France (Herrick) to the secretary of state, 5 January 1923, 462.00 R29/2320, DSNA. See also Hughes to Lodge, undated, box 31, Hughes Papers; "Secret Letters of James Logan," 5 January 1923, vol. 8, Logan Papers.

[99]Henry T. Allen, *My Rhineland Journal* (Boston: Houghton Mifflin, 1923), pp. 507–8.

[100]Memorandum of a conversation between the secretary of state and the French ambassador (Jusserand), 8 January 1923, *FRUS, 1923*, 2:47–48.

[101]Crewe to Curzon, 10 January 1923, *DBFP*, 21:20–21; Hughes to Lodge, undated, box 31, Hughes Papers; Nelson, *Victors Divided*, p. 247.

French had, in effect, called the American bluff; so Hughes had no choice other than withdrawal.[102] In the wake of growing congressional criticism of the occupation from irreconcilables and Wilsonians alike, the move proved to be a popular one on Capitol Hill since most chose to interpret it as an emphatic protest against Poincaré's resort to force.[103] As the American troops prepared to leave Coblenz, General Allen, who had been named as observer on the Rhineland High Commission, attempted to reopen negotiations on his own initiative. When France protested to the State Department, Hughes delivered a strong rebuke to the observer, prompting the general to write "that it is a deep regret for me that my humane intentions should have annoyed you."[104] On 24 January 1923 the Eighth Infantry marched to the Coblenz station and boarded a train for Antwerp, marking an end to the American military presence in Europe.[105]

Secretary Hughes made no new suggestions on how to break the reparations impasse during the Ruhr imbroglio, although the State Department did continue to monitor the situation closely. Members of the Senate Foreign Relations Committee in general and Senators Borah and Johnson in particular had not lost their fear of deepening American involvement in Europe through participation in the Reparation Commission. Johnson pressed for recall of the American observers, while Borah denounced unofficial diplomatic observation as "a sleazy, cowardly way to do business."[106] President Harding, Johnson complained, "quietly and surreptitiously, took on all the old Wilson men, and put them back into the Reparations Commission, where they have since been maintained."[107] During January of 1923 Chairman Lodge called repeatedly for the administration to make full disclosure of the observers' activities. Hughes supplied the committee with two lengthy written statements and several documents, but on 6 February, Lodge forwarded a letter from Senator Joseph T. Robinson demanding that the secretary appear before the committee in person to answer further inquiries.[108] With the president's blessing, Hughes balked at the request, noting curtly that his oral explanations

---

[102]Castle to Houghton, 12 January 1923, box 6, Castle Papers.
[103]"After the Ruhr Invasion—What?" *Literary Digest*, 20 January 1923, pp. 7–8; Nelson, *Victors Divided*, pp. 247–50; Phillips, *Ventures in Diplomacy*, pp. 114–15; Pusey, *Charles Evans Hughes*, p. 583; Trani and Wilson, *Harding*, p. 145.
[104]Allen, *My Rhineland Journal*, pp. 522–23; the unofficial observer on the Interallied Rhineland High Commission (Allen) to the secretary of state, 13 January 1923, and the secretary of state to the unofficial observer on the Interallied Rhineland High Commission (Allen), 15 January 1923, *FRUS, 1923*, 2:51–52; Royal J. Schmidt, *Versailles and the Ruhr: Seedbed of World War II* (The Hague: Martinus Nijhoff, 1968), p. 201.
[105]Nelson, *Victors Divided*, p. 251.
[106]Quoted in Maddox, *Borah and American Foreign Policy*, p. 129.
[107]Johnson to H. Johnson, Jr., 20 January 1923, box 4, part 6, Johnson Papers.
[108]Hughes to Harding, 24 January 1923; press release, 25 January 1923, reel 144, Harding Papers; Hughes to Lodge, undated, box 31, Hughes Papers.

could add nothing to the documents which he had already forwarded to the committee.[109] The secretary of state bypassed the Senate's attempts to control appointments to the Reparation Commission through his use of observers, and he refused to discuss the matter in person before the Foreign Relations Committee. But neither did he mean to deepen American involvement in the reparations question, as Boyden discovered in late January when the State Department refused to back him after he asked the Reparation Commission to reconsider his peace proposal of 15 November. "It seems to me," Boyden complained to his mother, "the Department has shown the same lack of decision and imagination in regard to all this, as they have since last summer about doing anything."[110]

In effect Hughes developed an elaborate rationale for doing nothing. The United States should not tilt toward Germany during the current crisis, he explained to Lodge, because that might offend France; on the other hand, he would not encourage France in its basically foolhardy venture in the Ruhr. Furthermore, to be successful, a new diplomatic initiative must "be sustained by overwhelming sentiment at home and abroad. The cleavage of sentiment in this country at this time is manifest and there is a similar difference of opinion in England."[111] In other words the administration had reverted to a policy of watchful waiting until the Europeans came to their senses.

THE AUSTRIAN PRECEDENT

"We are still very quiet here at the office," Boyden wrote to his family in April 1923, "partly because the Ruhr episode makes it impossible for the Commission to do much, and partly because the Department wants us to be quiet."[112] Hughes's reluctance to become involved further in the politics of reparations extended to Austria, a nation tottering on the brink of financial ruin. Between 1919 and 1921, the Austrians survived precariously on a mixture of charity and foreign loans, including over ninety million dollars in American governmental and private funds.[113] Although the Reparation Commission never

---

[109]Harding to Hughes, 8 February 1923, reel 144, Harding Papers; Hughes to Lodge, 8 February 1923, and Hughes to Lodge, undated, box 31, Hughes Papers.
[110]Boyden to A. L. Boyden, 26 January 1923, reel 2, and memorandum, undated, reel 4, Boyden Papers.
[111]Hughes to Lodge, undated, box 31, Hughes Papers. See also Geddes to Curzon, 26 February 1923, *DBFP*, 21:126–27.
[112]Boyden to A. L. Boyden, 4 April 1923, reel 2, Boyden Papers.
[113]House to Hoover, 18 December 1921, and Hoover to House, 19 December 1921, Box 212, Hoover Papers, HHL.

imposed a schedule of payments on Austria, the Allies held a general lien on all government assets as security against the eventual payment of claims.[114] To make Austria more attractive to would-be investors, Lloyd George's government appealed through the League of Nations for a suspension of Allied liens, a scheme Italy succeeded in blocking.[115]

While sympathetic to Austria's plight, the State Department opposed the postponement of claims out of fear of setting a possible precedent either for cancelling German reparations or Allied loans. "It does not seem to some," W. W. Cumberland wrote to Boyden, "to be good business to jeopardize claims running into billions, even though Austria is in a precarious situation."[116] Secretary Hughes refused also to give his support to a central bank conference on the reconstruction of Central Europe, as Strong noted, "even to the extent of expressing no objection to such a program."[117] Without State Department approval, Montagu Norman of the Bank of England saw no alternative but to drop the whole idea.[118]

In December 1921 J. P. Morgan and Company began an investigation, at the behest of the British government, into the possibility of floating an entirely private Anglo-American loan for the Austrians. Hughes declined to give Morgan his support, agreeing only not to oppose the international loan.[119] As a precautionary measure, the Morgan group dispatched British banker G. M. Young to make a thorough inquiry into Austrian finances. When Young reported conditions in Austria and Central Europe to be "so unstable as to make a public loan impossible at the present time," Morgan backed off.[120]

In desperation Austria made a renewed plea for help to Lloyd George and Poincaré, but neither was willing to do more than turn the problem back to the League.[121] The Financial Committee of the League worked out a plan calling for the Allies and other European nations to put up their liens on Austrian assets as security against a new private loan. First, however, Austria

---

[114]Harold G. Moulton and Leo Pasvolsky, *War Debts and World Prosperity*, 2 vols. (Port Washington, NY: Kennikat, 1971), pp. 235–36; Karl R. Staddler, *Austria* (London: Ernest Benn, 1971), p. 117.

[115]*DBFP*, 15:120–24, 411–39, 443–44, and 717; Hogan, *Informal Entente*, pp. 60–62.

[116]W. W. Cumberland to Boyden, 21 July 1921, RG 59, 863.51/642a, DSNA.

[117]Strong to Norman, 1 November 1921, box 1A, Strong Papers; Strong to Hughes, 24 September 1922, 863.51/366, DSNA.

[118]Norman to Strong, 11 November 1921, box 1A, Strong Papers.

[119]The secretary of state to the chargé in Austria (Frazier), 31 December 1921, 863.51/208, DSNA; Hogan, *Informal Entente*, p. 63.

[120]The ambassador in Austria (Washburn) to the secretary of state, 13 June 1922, 863.51/356, Morgan to Hughes, 5, 8, and 17 July 1922, 863.51/380 and 404, and the ambassador in Austria (Washburn) to the secretary of state, 29 July 1922, 863.51/414, DSNA; Thomas W. Lamont, "Three Examples of International Cooperation," *Atlantic Monthly*, September 1923, pp. 537–38.

[121]The American minister in Switzerland (Grew) to the secretary of state, 12 September 1922, 863.51/432, and the chargé in France (Whitehouse) to the secretary of state, 7 August 1922, RG 59, 463.00 R29/118, DSNA.

would have to effect stringent economic reforms under the watchful eye of a League commissioner to make the nation safe for foreign investors.[122]

In early 1923, with Austria on the road to a short-term recovery, a consortium of private bankers, including the House of Morgan, put together a loan package of 650 million gold crowns (130 million dollars) for the Austrians under the League plan.[123] When Morgan looked to the New York banking community for help in raising the loan, he found many financiers reluctant to lend money secured only by European promises and a lien on Austrian customs and tobacco. On 26 January Thomas Lamont sounded out Secretary Hughes on the possibility of a government guarantee for 25 percent of the first year's installment, the American share of the loan. If the plan worked in Austria, Lamont wrote, hoping to tempt Hughes, "such an example might point out the way for action in Germany."[124] This argument did not impress Arthur N. Young of the Office of the Economic Adviser, who pointed out that, with the Allies deadlocked over the Franco-Belgian invasion of the Ruhr, the outlook for success in Austria seemed problematic at best. Why should the United States bail out Austria when the Allies had not settled their war debts? Furthermore Lamont was asking the government to underwrite a Morgan loan, a prospect which "would not appeal to the baiters of Wall Street in the Senate."[125] A few weeks later, Hughes turned Lamont down, preferring to watch events in Europe from a safe distance until the Ruhr crisis simmered down.[126]

Undaunted, Lamont approached the secretary of state again in April, this time asking if Hughes "could say a word in commendation of the efforts which the Austrians have been making to get themselves out of the hole." Always the legalist, Hughes remarked that he might consider the suggestion— provided that the uniqueness of the Austrian situation was made clear.[127] But after Lamont drafted a letter of endorsement for Hughes's signature, the secretary drew back, feeling "that such action on my part would inevitably constitute an embarrassing precedent."[128] On 9 June 1923 Morgan reported to the State Department his intention of offering twenty-five million dollars in bonds as part of the international loan to Austria. Even without government endorsement, the loan was oversubscribed by 500 percent within hours.[129]

---

[122]Logan to Hughes, 30 September 1922, 863.51/445, and the American minister in Switzerland (Grew) to the secretary of state, 29 September 1922, 863.51/447, ibid.
[123]The American minister in Switzerland (Grew) to the secretary of state, 6 February 1923, 863.51/489, ibid.
[124]Memorandum A, Lamont to Hughes, 26 January 1923, 863.51/492, ibid.
[125]Arthur Young to Harrison, 3 February 1923, 863.51/493, ibid.
[126]Hughes to Lamont, 26 February 1923, 863.51/515B, ibid.
[127]Lamont to Hughes, 24 April 1923, 863.51/559, ibid.
[128]Hughes to Lamont, 26 April 1923, 863.51/559, ibid.
[129]Morgan to Hughes, 9 June 1923, Harrison to Herter, 11 June 1923, Harrison to Morgan, 11 June 1923, 863.51/583, and Harrison to Hughes, 11 June 1923, 863.51/606, ibid.

Lamont wrote an enthusiastic, and revealing, account of the Austrian loan for *Atlantic Monthly* in September 1923. While he praised the League and the Allies for their prompt and generous cooperation, Lamont saved his highest approval for

> plain men of business, who had the advantage of being able to lay out a certain definite course and then to move rapidly along that course, instead of being handicapped, as premiers are, by the necessity of constantly stopping and looking over their shoulders to see what their constituents think about it all.[130]

Morgan and his fellow international financiers had tried to settle the German reparations problem the previous year through the Bankers' Committee, but the politicians had sabotaged their efforts. To Lamont and others in the banking community, the lesson of Austria was clear: Businessmen would succeed where premiers and presidents could not. The Austrian loan showed that American bankers accepted the need for intervention in Europe. Lamont also hoped, he wrote to Hughes, that the rescue of Austria "may serve as a precedent for something in the German situation later on."[131] The bankers stood ready and willing to help; "meanwhile," as Lamont noted in *Atlantic*, "Berlin is the city of melancholy, Vienna of optimism."[132]

ANGLO-AMERICAN RAPPROCHEMENT

The Austrian loan was only one of a series of events which helped to improve Anglo-American relations during the first half of 1923. On 18 June, after six months of amicable negotiations, the British agreed to repay their debt of 4.6 billion dollars over a period of sixty-two years at an average interest rate of 3.3 percent.[133] The next month Britain and the United States ended their quarrel over Near Eastern oil with the signing of the Lausanne Treaty with Turkey. These three agreements went a long way toward bringing about an "informal entente" between the two Anglo-Saxon powers which set the stage for Britain to act as an agent for unified action on German repara-

---

[130]Lamont, "Three Examples," p. 539.
[131]Lamont to Hughes, 27 April 1923, 863.51/560, DSNA; Michael J. Hogan, "Thomas W. Lamont and European Recovery," in *U.S. Diplomats in Europe, 1919–1941*, ed. Kenneth Paul Jones (Santa Barbara, CA: ABC CLIO Press, 1981), p. 14. See also Norman to Strong, 9 April 1923, box 1A, Strong Papers.
[132]Lamont, "Three Examples," p. 540.
[133]U.S., World War Foreign Debt Commission, *Combined Annual Reports of the World War Foreign Debt Commission* (Washington: Government Printing Office, 1927), pp. 11–12 and 106–18. See also W. N. Medlicott, *British Foreign Policy Since Versailles, 1919–1963* (London: Methuen, 1968), pp. 49–50.

tions.[134] The United States, as Hughes explained to the Italian ambassador in June, "was always ready in every practicable way to use its good offices" on behalf of a reparations settlement, but the nation could go no further.[135] The French would not compromise on their position until they faced diplomatic isolation. Accordingly the British Foreign Office set out to isolate France in order to bring the United States back into the controversy, for, as Harold Nicolson noted, "her return to Europe could only be managed under the guise of 'an impartial investigation.'"[136]

While British Secretary of State Lord Curzon engaged in a diplomatic encircling movement against France, former Prime Minister Lloyd George toured North America, telling anyone who would listen that Hughes's plan of the previous December for a commission of financial experts was Europe's best hope for solving the reparations crisis.[137] These remarks prompted President Coolidge to intimate publicly that American policy still rested on Hughes's New Haven proposals.[138] Immediately, on the advice of Lord Curzon, Prime Minister Stanley Baldwin sent an aide-mémoire to Washington in the name of the British Empire designed to make the Americans reveal how far they might be willing to go in aiding a settlement.[139] On 15 October the secretary replied with an aide-mémoire of his own announcing that the United States would take part in an advisory conference on indemnities if the conferees agreed not to link debts with reparations and provided that all European governments directly concerned could participate.[140] In handing his answer to the British chargé d'affaires, the secretary emphasized that "France should not be allowed to think that there was any sort of understanding between Great Britain and the United States," a comment which indicates, at the very least, the beginnings of a new consensus on the economic future of Europe between the two Anglo-Saxon nations.[141]

France reacted positively to the British request for the formation of a

---

[134]Hogan, *Informal Entente,* pp. 50–56.

[135]Memorandum of a conversation between the secretary of state and the Italian ambassador (Caetoni), 23 June 1923, box 175, folder 84, Hughes Papers.

[136]Nicolson, *Curzon,* p. 363.

[137]Ibid., p. 367; *New York Times,* 9 October 1923, p. 1.

[138]"The Dawes Plan," box 172, folder 26, p. 15, Hughes Papers; *New York Times,* 10 October 1923, pp. 1–2.

[139]Curzon to Chilton, 12 October 1923, *DBFP,* 21:563–64; memorandum of a conversation between the secretary of state and the British chargé (Chilton), 13 October 1923, box 175, folder 77a, Hughes Papers; the British chargé (Chilton) to the secretary of state, 13 October 1923, *FRUS, 1923,* 2:68–70.

[140]The secretary of state to the British chargé (Chilton), 15 October 1923, *FRUS, 1923,* 2:70–73; memorandum of a conversation between the secretary of state and the British chargé (Chilton), 15 October 1923, box 175, folder 77a, and "The Dawes Plan," box 172, folder 26, pp. 16–17, Hughes Papers.

[141]Chilton to Curzon, 16 October 1923, *DBFP,* 21:571. See also Hogan, *Informal Entente,* pp. 66–67.

committee of financial experts to look into reparations.[142] Secretary Hughes soon discovered that Poincaré was insisting on several restrictions designed to limit the committee's inquiry, conditions which Hughes and Curzon found unacceptable.[143] Still, the British had succeeded in isolating France. The Ruhr occupation had been enough of a failure to alienate the other Allies and to hurt the French and German economies; yet Poincaré still hoped it might give him enough diplomatic leverage to obtain an acceptable revision of both reparations and war debts.[144]

During the first week in November, Sir Eyre Crowe of the British Foreign Office told Post Wheeler, the American chargé in London, that His Majesty's Government saw no point in holding an investigation burdened with French preconditions, a policy with which Hughes agreed.[145] On 9 November, after Ambassador Jusserand had insisted once again that the experts could neither inquire into French occupation policies in the Ruhr nor make recommendations regarding the German capacity to pay reparations after 1930, the secretary of state issued a statement for the press announcing that a limited investigation would be useless and futile.[146] The next day headline writers coupled the American rejection of the French terms with reports of an attempted coup d'état against the German government by Erich Ludendorff and Adolf Hitler, thereby underlining the increasingly desperate situation in Europe.[147]

Hughes's announcement created a stir in Paris. On 12 November, in an effort to scotch interpellations in the French Parliament over his unyielding stance, Poincaré launched his own initiative, authorizing his friend Barthou to request the creation of a committee of experts to study the German capacity to pay within the limits of the Reparation Commission's powers under the Treaty of Versailles.[148] The commission spent the next weeks working out details

---

[142]The secretary of state to the chargé in France (Whitehouse), 24 October 1923, 462.00 R296/49a, DSNA; memorandum of a conversation between the secretary of state and the French chargé (LaBoulaye), 26 October 1923, *FRUS, 1923,* 2:84.

[143]The American ambassador in Britain (Harvey) to the secretary of state, 1 November 1923, 462.00 R296/43, DSNA; memoranda of conversations between the secretary of state and the British chargé (Chilton), 4, 6, and 7 November 1923, box 175, folder 77a, and "The Dawes Plan," box 172, folder 26, pp. 17–20, Hughes Papers; *New York Times,* 2 November 1923, p. 1, 3 November 1923, p. 1, 5 November 1923, p. 1, 6 November 1923, p. 1, and 10 November 1923, p. 1.

[144]The ambassador in France (Herrick) to the secretary of state, 3 November 1923, 462.00 R296/50, and the chargé in Britain (Wheeler) to the secretary of state, 5 November 1923, 462.00 R296/51, DSNA.

[145]The chargé in Britain (Wheeler) to the secretary of state, 5 November 1923, 462.00 R296/52, ibid.

[146]Memorandum of a conversation between the secretary of state and the French ambassador (Jusserand), 9 November 1923, box 174, folder 74b, Hughes Papers; the secretary of state to the ambassador in France (Herrick), 10 November 1923, 462.00 R296/66, DSNA.

[147]*New York Times,* 10 November 1923, p. 1.

[148]The ambassador in France (Herrick) to the secretary of state, 12 and 13 (2) November 1923, 462.00 R296/68, 72, and 73, DSNA.

of the Barthou formula. Hughes reported to President Coolidge on 26 November that the commission proposed tentatively to set up two advisory expert committees, one to investigate the flight of German capital, the other to look into ways of stabilizing the German budget and currency.[149] The cloak of secrecy thrown around the commission's deliberations annoyed the State Department. "Other Governments or their representatives on the Reparation Commission," Acting Secretary Phillips wired Logan, "should not expect acquiescence by this Government in some vague whispered suggestion."[150] When pressed by Logan, Barthou responded with a letter defining the scope and objectives of the committee and inviting the United States to participate.[151]

On 11 December Hughes replied that while his government could not be represented formally, the administration favored unofficial American expert participation, a convenient, if rather transparent, way of circumventing senatorial confirmation of an official representative under the Treaty of Berlin. At the same time, the secretary asked Logan to suggest that the Reparation Commission extend an invitation to General Charles G. Dawes, former supply chief to the American Expeditionary Force, to participate as an expert.[152] The department also stage-managed the invitations of the other unofficial delegates as well, letting it be known that the commission should not contact any American who favored cancellation of debts.[153] Almost a year after the secretary of state's public proposal, Europe and the United States had finally agreed to take a "businesslike" approach to reparations.

THE DAWES PLAN

In December 1923 a prestigious delegation of American financial experts, including Dawes, president of the Central Trust Company of Illinois; Owen D. Young, chairman of the board of General Electric and the Radio Corporation of America; and Henry M. Robinson, president of the First National Bank of Los Angeles, prepared to leave for Paris to participate in the work of two special committees of the Reparation Commission. The

---

[149]Hughes to Coolidge, 26 November 1923, reel 115, Coolidge Papers.

[150]The acting secretary of state (Phillips) to the ambassador in France (Herrick), 30 November 1923, 462.00 R296/87, DSNA.

[151]The ambassador in France (Herrick) to the secretary of state, 3 December 1923, 462.00 R296/94, ibid.; the ambassador in France (Herrick) to the secretary of state, 6 December 1923, FRUS, 1923, 2:102–4; "The Dawes Plan," box 172, folder 26, p. 25, Hughes Papers.

[152]The secretary of state to the ambassador in France (Herrick), 11 December 1923, 462.00 R296/95, DSNA; the secretary of state to the ambassador in France (Herrick), 11 December 1923, FRUS, 1923, 2:105–6.

[153]The secretary of state to the ambassador in France (Herrick), 13 and 14 December 1923, 462.00 R296/100 and 106, DSNA.

government did not have to give instructions to these experts; they shared with the administration a belief that America would benefit from a reparations settlement which stabilized the German economy and promoted general European economic reconstruction.[154] The secretary of state met with the three delegates, discussing the events leading up to the creation of the expert committees "in his usual masterful and clear way," according to the general.[155] In addition Hughes provided them with documents and statistics as well as the services of economic adviser Arthur N. Young, with the understanding that Young would not sit on any committees.[156] Eager as ever to influence the administration's reparations policy, Hoover also courted Dawes, Robinson, and Owen Young, furnishing them with information and a staff of experts, including Alan Goldsmith, the chief of the Western European Division of the Department of Commerce.[157] When Dawes asked the president if he had any instructions for the delegation, Coolidge replied enigmatically, "Just remember you are Americans."[158]

Owen Young emerged as the real leader of the mission even as the businessmen steamed toward Europe on board the *America*. While Dawes puffed on his pipe and interjected anecdotes, Young formulated the outline of a plan to rescue Europe from the reparations tangle. Germany should be allowed to recover, but not to the point where it dominated the continent; so Young proposed to put a tax burden on the Germans proportionate to that of the Allies. The German government would deposit the taxes in a special bank of issue to the accounts of reparation creditors. To eliminate Germany's hitherto impossible task of transforming credits into massive amounts of foreign exchange, Young stipulated that the Allies would have to buy German goods to obtain their reparation credits. "It doesn't differ very much from other plans," Ambassador Houghton wrote after Young submitted his ideas to the conference, "but it differs enough to make it acceptable."[159]

Acting as a team, Young and Dawes dominated the first committee on

---

[154]Costigliola, "Reconstruction of Germany," pp. 485–86; Hogan, *Informal Entente*, p. 68.
[155]Charles G. Dawes, *A Journal of Reparations* (London: Macmillan, 1939), p. 1.
[156]Diary of Arthur N. Young, 29 December 1923, Arthur N. Young Papers, box 1, p. 2, Hoover Institution on War, Revolution and Peace, Stanford University, Stanford, CA (hereafter cited as Young Papers).
[157]Hoover to Owen Young, 20 December 1923, box 516, and Herter to Logan, 27 December 1923, box 12, Hoover Papers, HHL; Hoover to Henry M. Robinson, 27 December 1923, Henry M. Robinson Papers, box 8, Hoover Institution on War, Revolution and Peace, Stanford University, Stanford, CA (hereafter cited as Robinson Papers).
[158]Quoted in Costigliola, "Reconstruction of Germany," p. 486.
[159]The ambassador in Germany (Houghton) to the secretary of state, 19 February 1924, box 31, Hughes Papers. See also Stuart M. Crocker to Gerald Swope, 26 January 1924, box 178, Hoover Papers, HHL; Alan Goldsmith to Herter, 20 and 28 January 1924, Leonard P. Ayres Papers, box 4, Library of Congress, Manuscript Division, Washington (hereafter cited as Ayres Papers); Arthur Young Diary, 26 January 1924, pp. 13–14, Young Papers; the ambassador in France (Herrick) to the secretary of state, 18 February 1924, 462.00 R296/176, DSNA.

German currency and budget reforms; Young provided the ideas while Dawes, as chairman, guided the discussions. Young compared his approach to the making of a picture puzzle in which each separate piece was carefully presorted before facing the problem of putting them all together. By avoiding potentially explosive subjects such as the French occupation of the Ruhr and the total amount of German indemnities, the committee made substantial progress on German economic problems during the first weeks of the conference.[160] "Young is a peach!" Logan wrote enthusiastically, "and one of the best citizens I have seen anywhere."[161]

Although Dawes and Young impressed many observers both inside and outside of the conference, they also had their critics. Cleveland banker Colonel Leonard P. Ayres, former chief of statistics for the American Expeditionary Force and an adviser to both committees, complained soon after arriving in Paris that Dawes and Young all but ignored other members of the mission, including Robinson, the American delegate to the second committee on the flight of German capital.[162] Ayres and Goldsmith criticized Dawes's brother Rufus, chief of the technical experts, for failing to act as an effective liaison between the delegates and the staff, a state of affairs which deprived Young of badly needed information while leaving the technical men bored and frustrated. "We were shooting memoranda into the air," Goldsmith later wrote, "hoping that they would hit the mark."[163] Young's failure to consult the experts more frequently, coupled with his experience at General Electric as a competitor with the excellent German electrical industry, led him to overestimate Germany's power to recuperate consistently.[164]

As the conference wore on, the American technical advisers, dissatisfied with their lack of contact with Dawes and Young and convinced that the American position was too pro-French, became more and more friendly with their British counterparts. Hoover's commercial attachés even made up a song:

Yes, we have no memoranda to-day.
We get our information

---

[160]A. Young to Phillips, 30 January 1924, box 1, Young Papers; Goldsmith to Herter, 20 and 28 January 1924, box 4, Ayres Papers; Logan to Hoover, 1 February 1924, box 3, Logan Papers; the ambassador in Germany (Houghton) to the secretary of state, 4 February 1924, 462.00 R296/159, DSNA.

[161]Logan to Boyden, 7 February 1924, box 3, Logan Papers; Dawes, *A Journal of Reparations*, p. 65.

[162]Ayres Diary, 20 January 1924, Leonard P. Ayres Papers, Hoover Institution on War, Revolution and Peace, Stanford University, Stanford, CA (hereafter cited as Ayres Diary).

[163]Goldsmith to Richard S. Emmett, 26 March 1924, box 4, Ayres Papers; Goldsmith to Edward E. Hunt, 17 December 1924, box 516, Hoover Papers, HHL; Ayres Diary, 21 January 1924, p. 11; Arthur Young Diary, 18 March 1924, p. 46, Young Papers.

[164]Ayres Diary, 26 January, 4, 10, and 11 February 1924, pp. 20, 35, 45, and 46; Goldsmith to Herter, 3 March 1924, and Goldsmith to Emmett, 26 March 1924, box 4, Ayres Papers.

From the British delegation
For we have no memoranda to-day.[165]

Sir Josiah Stamp, the British representative on the Dawes committee, felt close enough to the Americans to confide to Robinson in a moment of pique that Young "has a mind that delights to operate in a vacuum, without facts, without figures, and without principles."[166] As for Dawes, some of the Americans believed that he was not up to the job. He stopped attending meetings of the subcommittee on the budget and taxation, claiming he did not understand the discussions. "He said," Arthur Young wrote in his diary, "the committee was made up of 'J. P. Morgans and Herbert Spencers' and that it was too deep for him."[167] Ayres complained that Dawes wandered in and out of conferences, paying little attention when present. "This whole conference," he concluded, "seems increasingly to be Mr. [Owen] Young's party."[168]

Young tried to keep the conference his "party" by taking a middle ground between Britain, which advocated Franco-Belgian evacuation of the Ruhr along with scaled down reparations, and France, Belgium, and Italy, nations insisting on high German indemnities and a continued foreign military presence in the Ruhr. Most of the American technical experts, with backgrounds in finance, did not appreciate Young's considerable skills as a mediator. "Young is a negotiator, and a lawyer," Goldsmith wrote. "You never know whether he means something or is using it as a crow–bar."[169] He had to use both sincerity and a crowbar to accomplish the difficult task of setting up a workable reparations plan acceptable to France, Germany, Britain, and the United States.

To win over the trust of the French, Young courted them early in the conference, letting it be known that the Americans did not oppose a strictly military occupation of the Ruhr; he did not regard the occupation issue as important enough to risk alienating the French. "We are businessmen," he said while in Germany. "We do not see soldiers anywhere. If the French want to continue armed forces in the occupied regions, well and good; but they must not interfere with production, and France must pay for them."[170] Privately, however, the American industrialist fretted that a continued foreign military presence might retard German economic recovery, especially after the Francophile Dawes told the French secretly that they could have a free hand in

---

[165]Ayres Diary, 16 February 1924, p. 52.
[166]Ibid., 23 February 1924, p. 62.
[167]Arthur Young Diary, 5 February 1924, p. 24, Young Papers.
[168]Ayres Diary, 26 January 1924, p. 18.
[169]Goldsmith to Herter, 24 February 1924, box 4, Ayres Papers.
[170]The ambassador in Germany (Houghton) to the secretary of state, 19 February 1924, box 31, Hughes Papers; the ambassador in France (Herrick) to the secretary of state, 22 February 1924, 462.00 R296/182, DSNA.

the Ruhr and announced publicly that the occupation had brought about positive results.[171] In the end the Americans did not insist on evacuation of the Ruhr because American bankers assured Young that French withdrawal was not a precondition for the loans needed to get the plan going.[172]

In late February, as the committees began work on their final reports, Dawes believed that the crisis had already passed. "From this time on," he wrote on 29 February, "I cease to worry."[173] But back in Washington, Secretary Hughes was very worried about the effective protection of American interests. After studying expert analysis of the Dawes Committee's preliminary report, Hughes wired observer Logan that Dawes and Young had not pressed hard enough for recognition of American rights of reimbursement for occupation costs and wartime claims against Germany.[174] Logan and Arthur Young found the secretary's timing "very unfortunate" considering the complications, and bad feelings, these issues could raise after the delegates had worked so hard to engender a new spirit of cooperation between "Uncle Shylock" and Europe. On 7 March after receiving a second despatch from Hughes, the diplomats raised the question with Owen Young, who did not want to be put into the awkward position of taking orders from the State Department.[175] Two weeks later Logan wrote Young that the first committee's report, as it stood, "would embarrass me somewhat" because he would have to file a protest with the Reparation Commission unless American claims were left unprejudiced.[176] Young, Dawes, and Robinson finally acceded to Hughes's wishes, slipping in the necessary language at the last minute. The final report of the second committee protected American occupation costs while a catchall clause in the first committee's report papered over differences between the United States and Britain on claims.[177]

Owen Young chose to take a middle ground between "the Latins" (France, Belgium, and Italy) and Britain and Germany on the amount of reparations due the victors. In February, much to the chagrin of his technical advisers and Sir Josiah Stamp—all of whom insisted that Germany could pay, at most, about two billion gold marks annually beginning in five years—Young seemed to back the French insistence on four and a half billion a year.[178] By

---

[171]Goldsmith to Herter, 3 March 1924, box 4, Ayres Papers; Arthur Young Diary, 18 March 1924, pp. 45–46, Young Papers; *New York Times*, 25 February 1924, p. 3.

[172]Arthur Young Diary, 9 April 1924, p. 58, Young Papers.

[173]Dawes, *A Journal of Reparations*, p. 135.

[174]Memoranda, Office of the Economic Adviser, 19 and 20 February 1924, 462.00 R296/176, DSNA; Hughes to Logan, 23 February 1924, *FRUS, 1924*, 2:1–2.

[175]Arthur Young Diary, 25 and 28 February and 7 March 1924, pp. 34–37, Young Papers.

[176]Logan to Young, 21 March 1924, and Logan to Robinson, 27 March 1924, box 8, Robinson Papers.

[177]The ambassador in France (Herrick) to the secretary of state, 22 March 1924, *FRUS, 1924*, 2:10–11.

[178]Ayres Diary, 11 February 1924, p. 46; Goldsmith to Herter, 24 January 1924, box 4, Ayres Papers.

March when the serious bargaining began, Young had patiently talked the French into accepting a payment schedule which began at one billion marks the first year and gradually increased to a standard annuity of two and a half billion after five years, plus a sum based on a sliding prosperity index worked out by Stamp and Ayres.[179]

On 26 March, as the first committee prepared to finalize the annuity figures, E. W. Kemmerer and Joseph S. Davis of the American technical staff tried to convince Young that the figures were still too high, emphasizing that an unrealistic plan might break German morale while scaring off potential foreign investors.[180] With the technical advisers in revolt against the compromise, Young telegraphed Ambassador Houghton for help. The ambassador rushed to Paris, where he found Young "pretty much broken down nervously and physically" and unable to cope with threats by Kemmerer and Ayres to denounce the whole plan to the press. Although Houghton also found the figures to be beyond Germany's capacity to pay, he worked to heal the breach, rationalizing that the actual figures meant less than nations agreeing on a sum "which bears some relation to reality."[181] Everyone in the American delegation, with the exception of General Dawes, found the final standard annuity to be too high; they also understood the importance of leaving Paris with a plan all parties could live with.[182] Many delegates began to speak openly of adjustments even before the public release of the reparations proposal.[183] But revisions could wait, for now the Americans had a blueprint which might guide Germany back into limited prosperity while preserving world peace. "I think," Logan wrote, "we have caught the psychological moment."[184]

On 9 April the two expert committees made their recommendations public. The second committee, chaired by London banker Reginald McKenna, which had been assigned the tasks of appraising the sum of exported German capital and devising ways to return it to Germany, could only guess at figures while concluding, unremarkably, that Reich capital would stop flowing abroad once the capitalists had faith in German currency.[185] Insiders paid little attention

[179]Goldsmith to Herter, 9, 17, and 24 March 1924, box 4, Ayres Papers; Arthur Young Diary, 21 and 24 March 1924, pp. 47–49, Young Papers.

[180]J. S. Davis and E. W. Kemmerer to Dawes, 26 March 1924, box 14, Robinson Papers; Arthur Young Diary, 26 March 1924, p. 50, Young Papers; Goldsmith to Herter, 26 March 1924, box 4, Ayres Papers.

[181]Houghton to Castle, 6 April 1924, box 6, Castle Papers; Arthur Young Diary, 30 March 1924, p. 51, Young Papers.

[182]A. Young to Harrison, 11 April 1924, box 1, Young Papers; Herring and Goldsmith to Hoover, 14 April 1924, box 516, Hoover Papers, HHL.

[183]Goldsmith to Herter, 31 March 1924, box 4, Ayres Papers; Ayres Diary, 30 March, 2 and 4 April 1924, pp. 103–15; Arthur Young Diary, 8 April 1924, p. 56, Young Papers.

[184]Logan to Boyden, 28 April 1924, box 3, Logan Papers; Houghton to Castle, 24 April 1924, box 4, Castle Papers.

[185]Reginald McKenna to Robinson, 6 March 1924, box 8, Robinson Papers. See also Bergmann, The History of Reparations, pp. 254–56; and Schuker, The End of French Predominance, p. 181.

to McKenna's report because, from the outset, it had been a smokescreen devised by Logan to divert the French. "By creating a separate Committee to consider export of capital," Logan wrote to Boyden, "our French friends were given a chance of shooting off as much as they wanted to, but in such a manner as not to prejudice the possible constructive results of the operations of the First Committee."[186]

In the report of the first committee, or the Dawes Report as the press called it, most of Young's ideas survived the British protests. The report neatly sidestepped the all-important question of the total German reparations obligation, recommending instead a rising scale of payments for the first five years and use thereafter of a prosperity index which would tie yearly installments to the strength of the German economy. The German budget was to provide half the annual payment with the balance coming from interest on mortgage bonds of Germany's excellent railroad network and various German industries. Under the Dawes Plan, Germany paid reparations to an agent general, who, along with a Transfer Committee, would decide how best to employ the funds without upsetting the stability of the German economy. The experts recommended a further bracing of German currency through a foreign loan of 800 million gold marks (about 200 million American dollars). The loan would rebuild the German Reichsbank's badly depleted gold reserves while upgrading Germany's international credit rating. With foreign loans to prime the pump and built-in safeguards against destabilization of the German economy, the experts hoped to make reparations the basis for recovery of the German economic power plant.[187]

If the American delegation and Ambassador Houghton had real doubts about the feasibility of the Dawes Plan as it stood, officials in Washington did not. As the conference wound up its work, Hughes advised the president that the world was about to enter "a new era."[188] "It is difficult, as a matter of fact, to restrain our rejoicing," Phillips observed, "but to the press at least we are holding our horses and trying not to express too much jubilation."[189] Castle wrote to Houghton of the general feeling in Washington that the experts would not have made unrealistic recommendations.[190] The ambassador did his best to disabuse Castle of such optimism, noting that in "plain truth," the plan was only an experiment which "might need to be changed in details,

---

[186]Logan to Boyden, 7 February 1924, box 3, Logan Papers. See Logan to Hoover, 1 February 1924, ibid.

[187]Bergmann, *The History of Reparations*, pp. 230–54; Stephen V. O. Clarke, *Central Bank Cooperation, 1924–31* (New York: Federal Reserve Bank, 1967), pp. 45–50; *New York Times*, 10 April 1924, pp. 1 and 9–16; Schuker, *The End of French Predominance*, pp. 181–86; U.S., Federal Reserve Board, "Report of Committees of Experts to the Reparation Commission," *Federal Reserve Bulletin* 10 (May 1924): 351–417.

[188]Hughes to Coolidge, 20 March 1924, reel 140, Coolidge Papers.

[189]Phillips to Logan, 10 April 1924, 462.00 R296/275a, DSNA.

[190]Castle to Houghton, 5 April 1924, box 6, Castle Papers.

and perhaps in total."[191] In his correspondence with Coolidge, Ambassador Herrick emphasized American economic leverage as the prime mover behind the settlement, "a power that we can use with care and discretion for the benefit of mankind generally."[192]

Dawes noted that the experts' plan had to be two different things to two very different groups. First, he said, "it must partake of the nature of a business prospectus appealing to the conservative judgment of individuals expected to invest in a preferred loan." In other words, the plan had to make sense to bankers such as J. P. Morgan, who would float the German reconstruction loans. Second, the recommendations "must take into consideration the interests of the fathers and mothers and friends of the millions of Allied soldiers who lost their lives in the war."[193] The Illinois banker realized that the plan would also have to appeal to Allied public opinion to meet with success. The experts had to convince one more group as well, for their reports constituted only a series of suggestions to the Reparation Commission. Hughes had come up with the idea of taking reparations out of the politicians' hands, but in the end there would be no Dawes Plan until the political leaders of the victorious nations and Germany chose to accept the experts' recommendations.

THE LONDON CONFERENCE

Within a few days of the release of the reports, the Reparation Commission and the governments of Belgium and Italy approved the Dawes Plan.[194] The British added their endorsement, but, in the words of one official, "without enthusiasm as a means of getting the French out of the Ruhr and tiding over the next 18 months."[195] On 22 April President Coolidge publicly commended the experts and gave sanction to American participation in the German reconstruction loans, thus giving the reports an important additional boost.[196] More than a month earlier, even as the delegates were writing their final draft, Morgan had committed the French unofficially to the Dawes Plan by granting their government 100 million dollars worth of credit to halt the fall of the franc. "England and America have the franc in their control," Houghton explained, "and can probably do with it what they want."[197] Nevertheless

---

[191]Houghton to Castle, 24 April 1924, ibid.
[192]Herrick to Coolidge, 3 April 1924, reel 38, Coolidge Papers.
[193]Dawes, *A Journal of Reparations*, p. 138.
[194]Logan to Hughes, 25 April 1924, 462.00 R296/287, DSNA.
[195]"Excerpts From a Personal Letter of One of the Leading Members of the British Economic Staff with the Reparations Commission," 30 April 1924, box 516, Hoover Papers, HHL.
[196]*New York Times*, 23 April 1924, p. 1.
[197]Quoted in Costigliola, "Reconstruction of Germany," p. 490.

Poincaré refused to endorse the experts' plan, holding out stubbornly until mid-May when the Chamber of Deputies defeated him on an unrelated issue.[198] The new premier, left-center Radical Socialist Edouard Herriot, gave his government's approval to the Dawes Plan, joining British Prime Minister Ramsay MacDonald in calling for a conference in London to put the reports into effect.[199]

Kellogg, the American ambassador to Britain, cabled Hughes in mid-June that the Allies would invite the United States to the London Conference.[200] On 24 June the secretary instructed Kellogg to let the British know that the administration did not desire a formal invitation and that Colonel Logan would instead make himself available for informational purposes only.[201] Before the ambassador could carry out his assignment, Prime Minister MacDonald invited the United States, forcing the administration to accept in order to avoid the appearance of remaining aloof from the implementation process after taking credit for originating the idea of the Dawes Plan. On 25 June, just one day after President Coolidge told a press conference that the nation would not be represented, the administration announced its acceptance of the British invitation "for the purpose of dealing with such matters as affect the interests of the United States and otherwise for purposes of information."[202] The administration did not acknowledge that acceptance meant formal American participation in a European diplomatic conference for the first time since Wilson left Paris.

The British and the Americans wanted to take away from France the legal authority to invade Germany in case of a default in reparations while the French wanted to retain that option as a controlling device. London financiers, led by Montagu Norman, governor of the Bank of England, also wished to exercise as much influence as possible over reparations policy to ensure Britain of a healthy share of German trade. In order to keep the crucial post of agent general out of the reach of French and American politicians (and in the hands of the Anglo-American banking community), British Treasury officials pressed for the candidacy of Dwight Morrow, a partner in J. P. Morgan

---

[198]Logan to Hughes, 24 April 1924, 462.00 R296/285, DSNA; Logan to Hughes, 15 May 1924, box 5, Logan Papers.

[199]Clarke, *Central Bank Cooperation*, p. 51; *New York Times*, 4 May 1924, p. 1, 7 May 1924, p. 3, 14 May 1924, p. 18, and 16 June 1924, p. 1; Schuker, *The End of French Predominance*, pp. 55 and 232–35.

[200]The ambassador in Britain (Kellogg) to the secretary of state, 18 June 1924, *FRUS, 1924*, 2:24.

[201]The secretary of state to the ambassador in Britain (Kellogg), 24 June 1924, ibid., 2:27.

[202]Howard H. Quint and Robert H. Ferrell, eds., *The Talkative President: The Off-the-Record Press Conferences of Calvin Coolidge* (Amherst: University of Massachusetts Press, 1964), p. 185. See also David Bryn-Jones, *Frank B. Kellogg, A Biography* (New York: G. P. Putnam's Sons, 1937), p. 145; statement for the press, 25 June 1924, reel 140, Coolidge Papers; the secretary of state to the ambassador in Britain (Kellogg), 27 June 1924, *FRUS, 1924*, 2:32–35; Schuker, *The End of French Predominance*, p. 295.

and Company. At first Coolidge supported the idea, but dropped Morrow when his political advisers warned that Progressive Party presidential candidate Robert LaFollette might use the appointment to whip up support in the Middle and Far West, where resentment already ran high against Morgan and other eastern bankers. Morgan and his partners were equally determined to block the candidacy of Logan, whom they regarded as too close to Hughes and Hoover. With Owen Young eager to return to General Electric and willing to serve only temporarily, the administration and the bankers went into the conference divided over the agent general nomination.[203]

On 5 July the French chargé in Washington told Secretary Hughes that on the eve of the conference France and Britain still had several minor differences regarding implementation of the Dawes Plan. Without taking sides, Hughes emphasized the importance of putting the experts' report into practice as quickly as possible.[204] To make sure that the process would not break down, Hughes decided to go to Europe himself. The State Department billed the trip as unofficial because the secretary was going in his capacity as president of the American Bar Association, which just happened to be meeting in London concurrently with the diplomatic conference. Other Americans, including Owen Young, Secretary of the Treasury Andrew W. Mellon, Ambassador Houghton, and several State Department officials also put in appearances during the conference.[205]

Morgan and Lamont represented the considerable interests of American bankers at the London discussions. Like so many of the Americans involved with the committees of experts, the moneylenders had serious reservations about the Dawes Plan. Before risking a loan to Germany of 200 million dollars, Dwight Morrow wrote to Hughes, the international banking community had to weigh not only the economic questions involved, but the political situation as well. "In reality," he observed, "the successful initiating of the plan depends upon France really accepting the view that the payment of reparations is desired. Heretofore the reparations have been balanced against security, as though the two things are contradictory." The bankers wanted the principal European powers committed to a policy of noninterference with Germany's servicing of the loan. In regard to security for their money, Morrow made it clear that the bankers expected repayment to be a higher priority than reparations. To keep the agent general and his associates from becoming

---

[203]Logan to Hoover, 27 June 1924, box 5, Logan Papers; Costigliola, "Reconstruction of Germany," p. 491; Glad, *Illusions of Innocence*, p. 225; Kenneth Paul Jones, "Discord and Collaboration: Choosing an Agent General for Reparations," *Diplomatic History* 1 (Spring 1977): 118–39; Schuker, *The End of French Predominance*, pp. 284–89.

[204]Memorandum of a conversation between the secretary of state and the French chargé (LaBoulaye), 5 July 1924, box 174, folder 74, Hughes Papers.

[205]Castle to Houghton, 10 May 1924, box 6, Castle Papers; "The Dawes Plan," box 172, folder 26, pp. 26–27, Hughes Papers; Hughes, *Autobiographical Notes*, p. 260; Pusey, *Charles Evans Hughes*, pp. 587–88; Schuker, *The End of French Predominance*, p. 296.

creatures of the Reparation Commission, the financiers demanded clarification of the Transfer Committee's independence. The loan, they felt, should be used primarily to finance German currency, not to pay for reparations. As a further protection for potential investors, the bankers proposed that a fourth of the loan be raised in Britain and a fourth in France and the rest of Europe.[206] Hughes and his official representatives, Ambassador Kellogg and Logan, faced a difficult task at London. To implement the Dawes report, they would have to bring the Allies together while treating with the Germans on an equal basis for the first time in the postwar era. They also had to placate a vital third force: the financiers whose capital would move Europe off dead center.

While Kellogg and Logan tried to play the role of peacemakers in the conference, Secretary Hughes met informally with European leaders. On 28 July, after less than two weeks of meetings, the conference came to the brink of collapse as British and French delegates argued bitterly over Britain's insistence on some form of arbitration in the event of conflicting interpretations of the Versailles Treaty's reparations clauses.[207] In Washington President Coolidge became concerned enough to consider sending the chief justice to arbitrate the dispute, just as Wilson had dispatched Chief Justice Edward D. White to umpire the Costa Rican-Panamanian border controversy ten years earlier.[208] Over lunch at Crewe House, the American ambassador's official residence, Hughes urged Herriot to implement the Dawes plan immediately. When the premier claimed that his government might fall if he agreed to the plan, Hughes replied dryly that Herriot would fall if he did not carry it out. The secretary of state also visited Paris, where he talked with the still powerful Poincaré, noting that if the French turned down the Dawes Plan, they could not expect further economic or diplomatic help from the United States.[209]

Herriot could not afford to hold out for long because the French needed another large foreign loan for currency stabilization. "We feel," Kellogg wired Hughes, "that Herriot has a full appreciation of the possible French financial difficulties which would follow [the] failure to reach agreement at this conference." On 30 July, in a desperate bid to break the deadlock, Herriot proposed

---

[206]Morrow to Hughes, 12 July 1924, box 56, Hughes Papers; Morgan, Grenfell, and Company to J. P. Morgan and Company, 1 July 1924, J. P. Morgan and Company to Morgan, Grenfell, and Company, 3 and 10 July 1924, and Lamont to Kellogg, 17 July 1924, Frank B. Kellogg Papers, microfilm, reels 12 and 13, Minnesota Historical Society, St. Paul, MN (hereafter cited as Kellogg Papers). See also Hogan, "Lamont," pp. 15–16; and Leffler, *Elusive Quest*, pp. 101–4.
[207]The ambassador in Britain (Kellogg) to the secretary of state, 28 July 1924, 462.00 R296/458, DSNA; Kellogg to Henry White, 31 July 1924, reel 13, Kellogg Papers.
[208]The acting secretary of state (Grew) to the ambassador in Britain (Kellogg), 29 July 1924, 462.00 R296/460a, DSNA. See also Bryn-Jones, *Kellogg*, pp. 154–55; and Grew, *Turbulent Era*, pp. 626–30.
[209]"The Dawes Plan," box 172, folder 26, p. 27, Hughes Papers; Pusey, *Charles Evans Hughes*, p. 591.

that if the Reparation Commission did not agree on a charge of default unanimously the minority could appeal to an American-chaired arbitral panel.[210] The British and the bankers, still smarting over the rejection of Morrow as agent general, viewed the French attempt at compromise as only a first step toward depoliticizing the reparations issue. Morgan and Lamont met with George Theunis, the premier and finance minister of Belgium, on 9 August to explain their prerequisites for a German loan. The next day Lamont handed a letter to the Belgian demanding, among other things, a more solid guarantee that the commission would be stripped of the power to declare Germany in default, an end to French and Belgian control over German railways, military evacuation of the Ruhr, and a plan for future withdrawal from the Rhineland.[211] Kellogg, who believed that this "rather inconsiderate letter" might "blow up the whole thing," convinced Lamont to telegraph Theunis and the French that he was not making an ultimatum, just a series of private suggestions.[212]

As Kellogg tried to keep the bankers in check, he also worked to bring the French and Germans together. Secretary Hughes had talked with German leaders in Berlin just before their departure for London in early August, stressing, as he had with the French, that Europe must accept the Dawes Plan as America would not help again.[213] Once the Germans had arrived at the conference, Kellogg invited Herriot and Gustav Stresemann, Germany's foreign minister, to Crewe House. The ambassador convinced the French premier that the Germans would not come to a final agreement until France had set a date for evacuating the Ruhr. After a quick trip to Paris, Herriot offered to withdraw within a year after the implementation of the Dawes Plan, an overture which the Germans rejected, hoping for an even earlier date. But once Herriot had persuaded Kellogg that he could make no more concessions and Hughes had wired from Berlin that Germany would settle for the one year delay, the American representative pushed hard for Herriot's proposal. Stresemann, with a weak diplomatic hand strengthened by the demands of the bankers, resisted until he had wrung a few more concessions out of the French at the urging of the Americans.[214]

As the conference wound down in mid-August, the bankers continued to campaign for an agent general who would answer to them first and the

---

[210]The ambassador in Britain (Kellogg) to the secretary of state, 30 July 1924, 462.00 R296/463, DSNA; Kellogg to Hughes, 1 August 1924, reel 13, Kellogg Papers.

[211]Lamont to Theunis, 9 August 1924, and Lamont to Kellogg, 10 August 1924, reel 13, Kellogg Papers.

[212]Kellogg to Cordenio A. Severance, 18 August 1924, ibid.

[213]Beerits's memorandum, "The European Trip of 1924," box 173, folder 54, pp. 41–42, and "The Dawes Plan," box 172, folder 26, p. 27, Hughes Papers.

[214]Kellogg to Hughes, 18 August 1924, reel 13, and Kellogg to White, 19 September 1924, reel 14, Kellogg Papers. See also Bergmann, *The History of Reparations*, pp. 263–64; Bryn-Jones, *Kellogg*, pp. 149–51; and Schuker, *The End of French Predominance*, pp. 374–82. For the final agreement see the ambassador in Britain (Kellogg) to the secretary of state, 16 August 1924, 462.00 R296/505–507, DSNA; and memorandum, undated, box 1, Young Papers.

Coolidge administration second. Knowing full well that family matters prevented Owen Young from making a long-term commitment, Montagu Norman and Lamont offered Young the job for a minimum term of three years. When, as expected, Young turned the position down, the bankers began to push Norman Davis, a choice unacceptable to Coolidge and Hughes because of his activism in the Democratic party. The bankers and the administration settled eventually on S. Parker Gilbert, a young former undersecretary in the Treasury Department employed most recently as a liaison between Morgan and the government. Logan, whose candidacy had also been ruled out, sniffed that "the whole affair was ridiculous and petty in the extreme."[215]

The bankers' role in the conference had been anything but petty. Their demand that the German loan be safeguarded through a series of French concessions strengthened the positions of Britain and Germany, nations advocating a policy of *Gleichberechtigung*, or political equality, for the Germans. The hard line of the British and the bankers made the American government's task more difficult; yet the State Department also wanted a revitalized Germany to help promote European—and ultimately American—prosperity. "The bankers were fighting the German battles better than they could do it themselves," Kellogg wrote to Houghton after the conference, "and of course you know we were."[216] The Americans worked diligently for the banking interests, getting for them most of what they required to safeguard the German loan. Still, the House of Morgan came away from London with misgivings.

American officials on both sides of the Atlantic tried to convince Morgan and Montagu Norman that the Dawes Plan and the London Conference had created a new spirit of cooperation in Europe, one providing ample security for their money. On 10 October bankers from the United States and the Allied countries signed an agreement with Germany for a 200 million dollar loan which would make the experts' report a reality.[217] With Morgan's prestige behind the bond issue, the German loan, as Kellogg noted, "went like wildfire."[218] Even Morgan admitted he was "very happy to have been so closely associated with it."[219] Now Europeans could finally leave the bitterness of the Great War behind them and proceed with reconstruction for the benefit of all—or so it seemed.

---

[215]Logan to Hoover, 5 September 1924, box 516, Hoover Papers, HHL; Jones, "Discord and Collaboration," pp. 132–35; Leffler, *The Elusive Quest*, pp. 109–10.

[216]Kellogg to Houghton, 18 August 1924, reel 13, Kellogg Papers.

[217]Kellogg to Hughes, 1 October 1924, and Kellogg to John Callan O'Laughlin, 14 October 1924, reel 14, Kellogg Papers. See also Clarke, *Central Bank Cooperation*, pp. 54–70; Costigliola, "Reconstruction of Germany," pp. 494–95; Feis, *Diplomacy of the Dollar*, pp. 39–43; and Hogan, *Informal Entente*, pp. 70–71.

[218]Kellogg to Severance, 17 October 1924, reel 14, Kellogg Papers.

[219]Morgan to Kellogg, 16 October 1924, ibid.

RENEWED ANGLO-AMERICAN FRICTION

Hughes had involved the administration and Wall Street deeply in the reparations negotiations in order to help create a stable political and economic order in Europe conducive to the prosperity of the United States and to ensure that the nation could collect on American Army of Occupation costs and claims against the former Central Powers. During the London Conference, when the Allies agreed to hold a meeting of finance ministers in Paris to divide German payments collected since January 1923, Hughes made it known immediately that the United States would be represented.[220] However British Chancellor of the Exchequer Philip Snowden announced that his ministry opposed American participation and all American damage claims against Germany.[221] Acting Secretary of State Grew cabled Kellogg that he should block any attempts at adjournment until Hughes returned to Washington. Failing that, he was to press the Allies for specific recognition of the American right to participate in payments from Germany.[222] Kellogg refused, claiming that Grew's order might disrupt the conference needlessly at a critical time, a position which Hughes supported subsequently, although he did share Grew's apprehension about the British attitude.[223] The secretary of state preferred to wait for a more auspicious moment to lodge a protest.

In early 1925, as part of his bitter campaign against the Turkish-American treaty, Senator King introduced a resolution calling on the president to protest to the Allies over the disposition of large amounts of Turkish gold seized from the Berlin Reichsbank after the war. In response to a request from Foreign Relations Committee Chairman Borah, Hughes explained that, at the time of the Lausanne Conference, the department concluded that the United States had no proper claim on the gold and did not sign the instrument by which the Turks relinquished their rights to the bullion. "The Department has not, therefore," Hughes wrote, "raised objection to the disposition of this gold by the parties having legal title thereto."[224] The secretary of state's statement to the committee was deceptive in the extreme; a few months earlier, he had used the Turkish gold in an attempt to extract a quid pro quo from the British Treasury for American damage claims against Germany. On 21 October 1924 Hughes instructed Ambassador Kellogg to let the British know

---

[220]The ambassador in Britain (Kellogg) to the secretary of state, 5 and 8 August 1924, *FRUS, 1924*, 2:54–55; "The Dawes Plan," box 172, folder 26, p. 28, Hughes Papers.

[221]The ambassador in Britain (Kellogg) to the secretary of state, 13 August 1924, *FRUS, 1924*, 2:56–57; Kellogg to Hughes, 22 September 1924, reel 14, Kellogg Papers.

[222]The acting secretary of state (Grew) to the ambassador in Britain (Kellogg), 13 August 1924, *FRUS, 1924*, 2:57.

[223]Bryn-Jones, *Kellogg*, pp. 153–54; the ambassador in Britain (Kellogg) to the secretary of state, 14 August 1924, *FRUS, 1924*, 2:58; "The Dawes Plan," box 172, folder 26, p. 28, Hughes Papers.

[224]Hughes to Borah, 21 February 1925, box 763, Borah Papers.

that while the administration did not wish to link the gold to the claims issue directly, the United States had no intention of helping countries which did not treat America fairly, a message which left the Foreign Office distinctly unmoved.[225] Ambassador Kellogg spent the next two months discussing Allied recognition of American war claims with British Secretary of State Sir Austen Chamberlain and Under Secretary Crowe.[226] Meanwhile Hughes maneuvered to isolate Britain from the other Allies, wiring observer Logan on 11 November that Morgan had consulted the department in regard to a 100 million dollar loan to France. Without offending the French, Hughes wrote, let them know that the administration would block the loan if France did not support America's right to participate in the Dawes annuities.[227] Ten days later Logan sent to the department notes from France and Belgium assuring Hughes of their support.[228] On 1 December the Italian Foreign Office informed the American chargé that his nation would also uphold the American claims.[229]

Hughes's demand for an American share of reparations payments infuriated British officials on two counts. First, they believed that the American claims settlement had been much more harsh on Germany than the Allied adjustment, proportionate to the actual amounts of damage suffered. Second, the American application came at a time when the Treasury felt trapped between the United States, which clamored loudly for repayment of English war debts, and France, which worked just as hard to avoid repaying its debt to Britain. "If Great Britain," the new chancellor of the exchequer, Winston Churchill, wrote, "remains a sort of spongy, squeezable mass on which these two conflicting wills may imprint their stamp, our fundamental interests will suffer."[230] Churchill, Chamberlain, and other British officials hoped to use the Paris finance conference as a forum to promote a comprehensive inter-Allied debt settlement whereby Britain would only have to pay the United

---

[225]The secretary of state to the ambassador in Britain (Kellogg), 21 October 1924, *FRUS, 1924*, 2:64–65.
[226]The ambassador in Britain (Kellogg) to the secretary of state, 28 October 1924, 2:68–69, ibid.; Kellogg to Elliot Wadsworth, 16 October 1924, Kellogg to Hughes, 3 November 1924, and Kellogg to Frederic Dolbeare, 1 December 1924, reel 14, Kellogg Papers.
[227]The secretary of state to the ambassador in France (Herrick), 11 November 1924, *FRUS, 1924*, 2:72–73. See also memorandum of a conversation between Harrison and Hoover, 20 November 1924, box 212, Hoover Papers, HHL.
[228]The unofficial representative at the Reparation Conference (Logan) to the secretary of state, 21 November 1924, *FRUS, 1924*, 2:80–84; the secretary of state to the ambassador in France (Herrick), 24 November 1924, 462.00 R296/721, DSNA.
[229]The chargé in Italy (Summerlin) to the secretary of state, 1 December 1924, *FRUS, 1924*, 2:95.
[230]Quoted in Martin Gilbert, *Winston S. Churchill*, vol. 5, *The Prophet of Truth, 1922–1939* (Boston: Houghton Mifflin, 1977), p. 71. See also Winston S. Churchill, *The Second World War*, vol. 1, *The Gathering Storm* (Boston: Houghton Mifflin, 1977), pp. 22–23; and Kellogg to Hughes, 5 December 1924, reel 14, Kellogg Papers.

States in proportion to money received from France.[231] The British hoped that they might be able to lure the United States into such a settlement in return for their recognition of American damage claims against Germany. At the very least, they expected that the United States would reduce its claims to a more reasonable figure.

On 4 December 1924 Chamberlain sent Ambassador Kellogg a memorandum spelling out in detail Britain's objections to the American damage claims. After quoting Hughes as saying in 1922 that the United States did not seek reparations, Chamberlain noted that "the intimation that they [the Americans] now claim a share in the Dawes annuities in respect of reparations, and apart from the cost of the army of occupation, came upon his Majesty's Government as a complete surprise."[232] In responding Hughes used arguments similar to those he put forth during the mandates controversy with Japan. America's failure to ratify the Treaty of Versailles did not impair any rights gained as one of the victorious powers in the Great War. Furthermore, "by its voluntary action in not pressing large categories of claims for general reparations," Hughes concluded, "my Government has greatly limited, to the benefit of the Allied Powers, the extent of its participation in Germany's payments."[233] To put additional pressure on the British government, Kellogg asked Agent General Gilbert to talk to Montagu Norman, who promised "to soften the Treasury down to a reasonable spirit."[234]

While Hughes and Chamberlain continued to trade lengthy legalistic memoranda on the subject of American claims, Colonel Logan and Frederick Leith-Ross of the British Treasury talked at preliminary meetings of the finance conference in Paris. Hughes authorized Logan to offer the British a compromise: The United States would be willing to extend the period of the Wadsworth Army Costs Agreement in order to reduce the annual installment for past occupation costs if the Allies would use the savings to provide America with 2 percent of the reparations payments for claims.[235] Without replying officially to the American offer, Churchill, the chief British delegate to the Paris gathering, discussed the situation informally with Kellogg, his American

---

[231]Kellogg to Severance, 10 December 1924, and Kellogg to White, 15 December 1924, reel 15, Kellogg Papers. See also Gilbert, *The Prophet of Truth*, pp. 79–80.

[232]The secretary of state for foreign affairs (Chamberlain) to the American ambassador (Kellogg), 3 December 1924, *American War Claims Against Germany*, S. Doc. 173, 69th Cong., 2nd sess., pp. 50–54.

[233]The American ambassador (Kellogg) to the secretary of state for foreign affairs (Chamberlain), 10 December 1924, pp. 54–59, ibid.; "The Dawes Plan," box 172, folder 26, pp. 29–30, Hughes Papers; Hughes, *Autobiographical Notes*, p. 61; Hyde, "Charles Evans Hughes," pp. 387–92.

[234]Kellogg to Hughes, 16 December 1924, reel 14, Kellogg Papers.

[235]Leith-Ross to Logan, 23 December 1924, and memorandum given to Leith-Ross by the American ambassador, 3 January 1925, *American War Claims Against Germany*, pp. 71–73.

counterpart. The ambassador and Churchill continued talking even as they walked to the Quai d'Orsay for the first plenary session. The chancellor of the exchequer, realizing that Hughes had succeeded in isolating Britain, remarked that the two Anglo-Saxon powers should not air their differences in public.[236] After the session Churchill agreed to the American proposal, although it took three more days to work out the final figures.[237]

On 13 January 1925 the American delegation telegraphed Washington that the conference report provided for reimbursement to the United States of occupation costs amounting to 255 million dollars. America would also receive annual payments to the Mixed Claims Commission in an amount not to exceed a cumulative total of 350 million.[238] Immediately Acting Secretary of State Grew wired back that the clause limiting American claims to 350 million dollars had to be eliminated because final claims totals could run well above that sum.[239] An hour later Grew instructed the delegates to make sure that nothing in the agreement precluded the United States from recovering damage claims from the other former Central Powers.[240] Then Grew sent off yet another wire directing that the Americans read into the text a statement denying any formal American obligations in regard to the agreement.[241] Logan and Ambassadors Herrick and Kellogg did succeed in eliminating the claims limitation clause, but the diplomats, at Kellogg's insistence, ignored the last telegram and signed the agreement. Kellogg, who labeled Grew's instructions "unnecessary" and "embarrassing," may have understood better than the career diplomat that the public—and the Senate—would accept and even applaud economic entanglements with Europe as long as the administration maintained the illusion that the agreement did not include political considerations.[242]

---

[236]Kellogg to Hughes, 5 January 1925, reel 14, Kellogg Papers. See also Bryn-Jones, *Kellogg*, p. 156.

[237]Bryn-Jones, *Kellogg*, pp. 156–57; the ambassador in France (Herrick) to the secretary of state, 7, 9, and 10 January 1925, and the secretary of state to the ambassador in France (Herrick), 9 and 10 January 1925, *FRUS: 1925*, 2:134–39.

[238]The ambassador in France (Herrick) to the secretary of state, 13 January 1925, *FRUS, 1925*, 2:140–42; Kellogg to Severance, 21 January 1925, and Kellogg to Walter Sanborn, 23 January 1925, reel 115, Kellogg Papers.

[239]The acting secretary of state (Grew) to the ambassador in France (Herrick), 13 January 1925, *FRUS, 1925*, 2:142.

[240]The acting secretary of state (Grew) to the ambassador in France (Herrick), 13 January 1925, ibid.

[241]The acting secretary of state (Grew) to the ambassador in France (Herrick), 13 January 1925, ibid., 2:143–44.

[242]The ambassador in France (Herrick) to the secretary of state, 14 January 1925, ibid., 2:144–45. See also Bryn-Jones, *Kellogg*, p. 157; and Castle to Kellogg, 19 January 1925, box 3, Castle Papers. This was the second time in six months that Kellogg had disregarded instructions from Acting Secretary Grew, incidents which certainly must have contributed to the growing enmity between the two men. After Kellogg became secretary of state, he took the first opportunity to exile Grew to Ankara as ambassador to Turkey.

RESULTS OF REPUBLICAN REPARATIONS POLICY

The Paris agreement represented the climax of several years of official and unofficial diplomatic activity designed to gain recognition of American economic rights as one of the victors in the Great War. The Republicans, in their own way, imposed an American solution to the reparations problem on Europe not unlike that which Wilson had advocated six years earlier before finally bowing to Allied pressure. At Paris President Wilson fought for a limited reparations settlement based on Germany's capacity to pay, the same basic idea behind the Dawes Plan. American and British bankers primed the pump of the Dawes machinery with 200 million dollars in loans to expand German industry so that Germany could afford to resume payments. For a time, everything went according to plan. German production increased as American money poured into the Reich creating prosperity and reparations. The Allies made debt settlements with the United States which required relatively low installments for the first five years, payments more than offset by private American loans. While France pulled out of the Ruhr, the Europeans attempted to lay a new foundation of security through the Locarno pact. As German reparations flowed to the Allies, the Western Europeans began to repay their war debts to America.[243]

In 1927, once German industry had been reconstructed, cracks started to appear in the Dawes system. Germany needed new markets in order to insure continued expansion, markets which did not exist yet. Rather than responding to Germany's changing economic needs, American bankers invested surplus dollars in increasingly wasteful projects such as parks, hotels, and swimming pools. "As a matter of fact," an alarmed Lamont wrote to Hoover, "the manner in which certain American bankers have been scrambling for all sorts of loans in Europe is little less than scandalous, just because the bond market happens to be so excellent here just now that people can sell almost anything."[244] When Germany requested a revision of the Dawes Plan, the Allies and American bankers responded in early 1929 with the Young Plan, which reduced German obligations and set up new collection machinery. But with world trade shrinking and American capital investments in Germany going under, the Young Plan never got off the ground before the Great Depression caused the entire reparations system to collapse.[245]

---

[243]Adler, *Isolationist Impulse*, pp. 163–64; Costigliola, "Reconstruction of Germany," pp. 494–98; Ellis, *Republican Foreign Policy*, pp. 201–2; Eyck, *Weimar Republic*, pp. 324–26; John Kenneth Galbraith, *The Great Crash, 1929* (Boston: Houghton Mifflin, 1961), p. 186; Glad, *Illusions of Innocence*, pp. 230–31; Moulton and Pasvolsky, *War Debts and World Prosperity*, pp. 420–21; Parrini, "Reparations," pp. 896–97.
[244]Lamont to Hoover, 5 May 1927, box 363, Hoover Papers, HHL.
[245]Costigliola, "Reconstruction of Germany," pp. 499–500; Ellis, *Republican Foreign Policy*, pp. 202–5; Feis, *Diplomacy of the Dollar*, pp. 44–46; Parrini, "Reparations," pp. 896–97.

For too long writers have been content to emphasize the absurdity of triangular payments—America loaned money to Germany, Germany paid the Allies reparations, and the Allies paid the United States their war debts—while ridiculing Hughes and other Republicans for refusing to link reparations and debts, a policy which blocked cancellationist schemes.[246] Yet Hughes and his confederates, like the Wilsonians before them, saw compelling reasons for following this seemingly shortsighted policy. Wilson and Hughes advocated priority reconstruction of Germany, the industrial power plant of Europe, as the best way of ensuring rapid expansion of the world economy in a wide open system of equal opportunity for all. This plan for an Open Door world would have benefited the United States chiefly while foiling the Allied system of closed trade doors in their colonial empires. "England and France," Wilson wrote to House in 1917, "have not the same views with regard to peace that we have by any means. When the war is over we can force them to our way of thinking, because by that time they will, among other things, be financially in our hands."[247] When the Allies did not capitulate, Wilson, and then Hughes, held out promises of private loans and a debt settlement to persuade the Europeans to adopt the American plan, one which would, after all, benefit the capitalist West as a whole.[248]

In agreeing to the Dawes Plan, the Allies finally recognized the necessity of following the American lead. Hughes, Young, and other Americans involved in implementing the plan understood that it represented only a beginning point in the revitalization of Europe. "The Dawes Plan," one American wrote at the time, "is a poultice with a sprinkling of red pepper, the whole laid upon several running sores. These require something more for cure than such a poultice, soothing as it may be now."[249] Hughes and his successors, however, faced severe constraints on their freedom of action owing to the American mood of disillusionment with Europe. At a dinner in London in 1924, the secretary of state explained candidly why businessmen had helped to put the Dawes Plan together as unofficial representatives instead of the State Department:

> I may give it as my conviction that had we attempted to make America's contribution to the recent plan of adjustment a governmental matter, we should have been involved in a hopeless debate, and there would have

---

[246]See for example Leuchtenburg, *The Perils of Prosperity*, pp. 109–11; and Hicks, *Republican Ascendency*, pp. 138–44.

[247]Wilson to House, 21 July 1917, in Ray Stannard Baker, *Woodrow Wilson: Life and Letters*, vol. 7: *War Leader, 1917–1918* (New York: Charles Scribner's Sons, 1946), pp. 180–81. See also Seymour, *Colonel House*, 3:51.

[248]Levin, *Wilson and World Politics*, pp. 141–47; Parrini, "Reparations," pp. 894–96.

[249]Oscar T. Crosby, "The Dawes Plan: A Temporary Basis for Reparations Payments," *The Annals of the American Academy of Political and Social Science* 120 (July 1925): 15. See also Hyde, "Charles Evans Hughes," p. 385; and Ida M. Tarbell, *Owen D. Young, A New Type of Industrial Leader* (New York: Macmillan, 1932), p. 178.

been no adequate action. We should have been beset with demands, objections, instructions. That is not the way to make an American contribution to economic revival.[250]

Unfortunately diplomacy by well-intentioned capitalists—which Norman Davis labeled "inadequate, undignified and cowardly" (when the Republicans used it)—had its limitations.[251] To gain their ultimate objective of an Open Door world, the Republicans would have had to foster a coordinated European economic and political settlement based on the lessons learned in a rapidly changing postwar era, the one thing they could not do because of the prevailing American mood. Hughes did not admit to the connection between American economic and political involvement in Europe. Instead he plunged ahead, erecting a new system of trade based on the third of Wilson's Fourteen Points, which he hoped would open the door to American commerce around the world without concomitant political entanglements.

---

[250]Hughes, "A Better Understanding—Support of the Dawes Plan," *The Pathway to Peace*, p. 108. See also Hughes, *Autobiographical Notes,* p. 260.

[251]Norman Davis, "American Foreign Policy: A Democratic View," *Foreign Affairs* 3 (September 1924): 32.

6

THE CULMINATION OF PEACE
Renewing Commercial Relations Between
the United States and Germany, Austria, and Hungary

The World War greatly accelerated America's already changing position in the international economy. The United States had always been a net debtor, but it emerged after the conflict as the world's leading active creditor. Furthermore, in 1900 the sale of agricultural products and raw materials accounted for 65.1 percent of American exports while finished goods and semimanufactures totaled 34.2 percent. Twenty years later America exported more manufactured goods than farm products and raw materials for the first time, 51.6 to 48.4 percent.[1] The shift to the sale of factory goods overseas made American exports more vulnerable to restrictive and discriminatory measures than ever before due to competition with industrial Western Europe. Americans found this discrimination especially objectionable because of their increasing dependence on foreign markets. Internationalists in the business community and government realized that America's altered world economic position dictated a reexamination of traditional commercial policies, including use of the tariff and the conditional form of most-favored-nation status.[2]

Even before the war, some American leaders (including Wilson) foresaw the need to overhaul the nation's commercial policies. During his first administration, Wilson supported tariff, currency, and banking reforms to correct structural defects in the economy which hindered the continued expansion of exports. The third part of Wilson's blueprint for the postwar world, the Fourteen Points, called for the "removal, so far as possible, of all economic barriers and the establishment of an equality of trade conditions among all

---

[1]U.S., Department of Commerce, Bureau of Foreign and Domestic Commerce, *Statistical Abstracts of the United States, 1922* (Washington: Government Printing Office, 1923), pp. 354–55.

[2]William B. Kelly, Jr., "Antecedents of Present Commercial Policy, 1922–1934," in *Studies in United States Commercial Policy*, ed. William B. Kelly, Jr. (Chapel Hill: University of North Carolina Press, 1963), pp. 44–46; Jim Potter, *The American Economy Between The World Wars* (New York: John Wiley and Sons, 1974), pp. 25–26; Wilson, *American Business*, p. 75.

154 INTERNATIONAL NORMALCY

nations consenting to the peace and associating themselves for its maintenance."[3] These lofty ideals complimented the president's desire to further
American commercial interests since an Open Door world would benefit the
strongest competitor, the United States. President Wilson succeeded in writing
the freer trade principle into the Treaty of Versailles, albeit in a more ambiguous form, but the Senate's rejection of the pact and the nation's repudiation
of the Democrats left Wilson's work on behalf of American trade reform
unfinished.[4]

Unlike Wilson, Harding came into office with little knowledge of complicated economic problems. He astounded Bruce Bliven of the *New Republic*
with the observation that "the United States should adopt a protective tariff
of such a character as will best help the struggling industries of Europe to
get on their feet."[5] Understandably Harding relied on the experts, especially
Secretary of State Hughes and William S. Culbertson, a progressive Republican and vice-chairman of the Tariff Commission appointed under Wilson,
who convinced the Senate to pass a tariff with flexible provisions. Once that
had been accomplished, the two men decided to revise the whole American
commercial treaty structure, scrapping the old conditional most-favored-nation
clause giving trade privileges to third-party nations only in return for special
compensations. They hoped to use the unconditional most-favored-nation
clause as the best means of implementing the Open Door policy by automatically granting, and receiving, all third-party privileges given to any particular
state.[6]

The secretary negotiated a commercial treaty with Germany based on
the new ideas only to see the Senate balk at granting full equality of treatment.
The German-American commercial treaty and similar pacts with Austria and
Hungary were meant to serve as models for other bilateral agreements, as
well as being the final steps in the restoration of normal relations between
the United States and its former wartime enemies. These model treaties yielded
disappointing results; they did not lead to the Open Door world which both
the Wilsonians and internationalist Republicans envisioned as the formula for
peace and prosperity. Instead they illustrated the frustrations which American
policymakers faced in the 1920s in their pursuit of expanding trade possibilities
at a time when Congress was intent on building high tariff walls around the
nation.

---

[3]Wilson, *State Papers and Addresses*, p. 468. For the evolution of Wilson's tariff
philosophy, see William Diamond, *The Economic Thought of Woodrow Wilson* (Baltimore: Johns
Hopkins University Press, 1943), pp. 25–26, 54–55, 66–67, 97–98, 134, and 166.

[4]John M. Dobson, *Two Centuries of Tariffs: The Background and Emergence of the U.S.
International Tariff Commission* (Washington: Government Printing Office, 1976), p. 31; Levin,
Wilson and World Politics, pp. 13–15.

[5]Quoted in Ellis, *Republican Foreign Policy*, p. 19.

[6]Justus D. Doenecke, "The Most-Favored-Nation Principle," in *Encyclopedia of American
Foreign Policy*, pp. 603–9.

THE OPEN DOOR TARIFF

During the 1912 election campaign, Wilson put heavy emphasis on the traditional Democratic promise to lower the tariff, an idea he had championed for many years as a political scientist. "The tariff," he told the Democratic National Convention, "was once a bulwark; now it is a dam—and you can spell the word either way you want to."[7] The next year President Wilson signed the Underwood Act, providing the United States with its first real tariff reductions in a half century. The Democratic triumph proved to be short-lived, as the outbreak of the Great War in 1914 disrupted normal trade patterns and rendered the new tariff virtually inoperative.[8] Slowly the president began to move toward the progressive Republican argument that protectionism was justified under certain circumstances, rationalizing that the tariff might encourage national development. He became interested in the idea of a flexible tariff, one which Congress and the administration could adjust after they received the recommendations of a bipartisan committee, thus "employing to the utmost the resources of the country in a vast development of our business enterprise."[9] In September 1916 Congress created the United States Tariff Commission to collect and analyze trade data and to advise the government on commercial policy.[10]

Momentum toward further tariff reforms continued after the war when the Allies threw up roadblocks in the way of the American drive for new world markets, including pursuit of a punitive policy in the mandates, and preliminary steps to monopolize petroleum in the underdeveloped regions.[11] The change in administrations in 1921 did not alter basic tariff planning. Culbertson, vice-chairman and ranking member of the Tariff Commission,

---

[7]Quoted in Lloyd Gardner, "A Progressive Foreign Policy," in *From Colony to Empire: Essays in the History of American Foreign Policy*, ed. William A. Williams (New York: John Wiley and Sons, 1972), p. 225. See also Arthur S. Link, *Wilson, The Road to the White House* (Princeton, NJ: Princeton University Press, 1947), pp. 3, 7–9, 26–27, and 128; and Harley Notter, *The Origins of the Foreign Policy of Woodrow Wilson* (Baltimore: Johns Hopkins University Press, 1937), pp. 181–82.

[8]William C. Redfield to Wilson, 24 May 1916, and memorandum, Louis Dombratzy, Department of Commerce, "Commercial Treaties and Economic Preparedness," [May 1916], 611.0031/84, DSNA. See also memorandum, R. H. Patchin, secretary of the National Foreign Trade Council, [May 1916], Redfield to Wilson, 2 June 1916, 611.0031/85, ibid.; and Link, *Wilson, The New Freedom*, pp. 177–97.

[9]Quoted in Parrini, *Heir to Empire*, p. 214. See also Dobson, *Two Centuries of Tariffs*, p. 87; Arthur Link, *Wilson: Confusions and Crises, 1915–1916* (Princeton, NJ: Princeton University Press, 1964), pp. 341–44; and J. Richard Snyder, "William S. Culbertson and the Formation of Modern American Commercial Policy, 1917–1925," *Kansas Historical Quarterly* 35 (Winter 1969): 400.

[10]Dobson, *Two Centuries of Tariffs*, pp. 87–91.

[11]Fletcher to Lansing, 13 November 1916, 611.0031/138, DSNA; Lloyd C. Gardner, "American Foreign Policy, 1900–1921: A Second Look at the Realist Critique of American Diplomacy," in *Towards a New Past*, p. 213; Parrini, *Heir to Empire*, pp. 212–23.

continued to enlarge on tariff reform ideas first put forth under Wilson. In May 1921 Congress passed the Emergency Tariff Act which temporarily raised rates on meat, corn, sugar, and wool to pre-Underwood Act levels as a response to the minor postwar economic depression.[12] Meanwhile officials at the Department of State worked with Culbertson to coordinate recommendations to Congress for permanent tariff reforms.

Culbertson, one of the forces behind the Tariff Commission's report of 1918 arguing for the adoption of equality of treatment as the primary goal of American tariff policy, believed that the administration should oppose the movement in Congress to return to the use of bargaining tariff clauses as in the 1890s. Such reciprocity clauses would countenance special bargaining for tariff favors and clash with Secretary Hughes's attempt to implement the Open Door. The vice-chairman recommended instead that the department urge Congress to reinstate a modified version of the maximum-and-minimum clause of the 1909 Payne-Aldrich Act, a provision enforcing maximum rates against nations discriminating against American goods and minimum rates against those not discriminating, with a view toward obtaining nondiscriminatory treatment through the threat of penalty duties. In 1911 Secretary of State Knox asked Congress for additional executive authority to raise rates against nations discriminating against American goods, a move which Culbertson had applauded. Department of State officials decided to follow the vice-chairman's advice to push for equality of treatment through an improved version of Knox's flexible tariff idea.[13]

As expected the House Ways and Means Committee drafted the new tariff with the intent of reducing foreign rates through reciprocity rather than making equality of treatment the ultimate goal. The State Department went to work on key senators while Culbertson convinced President Harding to give the effort on behalf of the Open Door his support.[14] In his first annual State of the Union message, Harding discussed the tariff at some length. "I hope a way will be found," he noted, "to make for flexibility and elasticity, so that rates may be adjusted to meet unusual and changing conditions which cannot be accurately anticipated."[15]

---

[12]Ellis, *Republican Foreign Policy*, pp. 19–20.
[13]Diary of William S. Culbertson, 9 June–8 October 1921, William S. Culbertson Papers, box 4, pp. 13–31, Library of Congress, Manuscript Division, Washington (hereafter cited as Culbertson Papers). See also William S. Culbertson, *Reciprocity: A National Policy for Foreign Trade* (New York: McGraw-Hill, 1937), pp. 154–64; Dobson, *Two Centuries of Tariffs*, pp. 24–27; Parrini, *Heir to Empire*, pp. 226–28; U.S., Tariff Commission, *Second Annual Report* (Washington: Government Printing Office, 1918), pp. 27–28; and U.S., Tariff Commission, *Third Annual Report* (Washington: Government Printing Office, 1919), pp. 12–16.
[14]Culbertson Diary, 12 October–4 December 1921, box 4, pp. 32–47, Culbertson Papers; Thomas Walker Page to Harding, 1 December 1921, box 594, Hoover Papers, HHL.
[15]Fred L. Israel, ed., *The State of the Union Messages of the Presidents, 1790–1966*, 3 vols. (New York: Chelsea House, 1966), 3:2620. See also Culbertson Diary, 7 December 1921,

On 24 April 1922 Senator Reed Smoot of Utah, chairman of the Finance Committee, introduced amendments to the Fordney tariff bill as Sections 315–317 to replace the offending reciprocity clauses. The senator explained that Section 317 merely improved upon Knox's proposal for an effective maximum-and-minimum clause, although he did not mention that the Tariff Commission had actually drafted the equality of treatment sections.[16] In August, however, when the amendments came up for debate briefly, some senators, including Irvine L. Lenroot of Wisconsin, charged that Section 317 appeared to be inconsistent with the traditional American use of the conditional form of most-favored-nation treatment because of a provision which penalized nongeneralized tariff reductions in reciprocity agreements made by other countries.[17] In defending the amendments, Senator Lodge denied the validity of that interpretation while, at the same time, suggesting a rewording of Section 317 to affirm the principles of reciprocity and conditional most-favored-nation treatment, advice which the Senate took before passing the "open door tariff" a month later in its final form.[18] Most senators did not realize it, but Lenroot's suspicions had been correct: The Smoot amendments shifted the emphasis away from reducing the tariffs of other nations to acquiring equality of treatment for American goods in competition with exports of third nations. The changes had far-reaching implications for America's traditional commercial policies, at least in the minds of the original authors, members of the nonpolitical (but nonetheless internationalist) U.S. Tariff Commission.[19]

FROM CONDITIONAL TO UNCONDITIONAL
MOST-FAVORED-NATION POLICY

Culbertson did not wait for final passage of the Fordney-McCumber Tariff Act to make recommendations to Secretary Hughes on further changes in American commercial policy. In a letter of 31 May 1922, the vice-chairman summarized several recent reports of the Tariff Commission calling for continued pursuit of equality of treatment in commercial relations. The best way

---

box 4, p. 49, Culbertson Papers; Culbertson, *Reciprocity*, pp. 207–13; John Day Larkin, *The President's Control of the Tariff* (Cambridge, MA: Harvard University Press, 1936), p. 21, note 20; Murray, *Harding Era*, pp. 273–74; Snyder, "Culbertson," p. 402.

[16]*Congressional Record*, 67th Cong., 2nd sess., p. 5879. See also Culbertson Diary, 10 December 1921, box 4, p. 50, Culbertson Papers; Kelly, "Antecedents," pp. 39–40; Parrini, *Heir to Empire*, p. 233; Wilson, *American Business*, p. 81.

[17]*Congressional Record*, 67th Cong., 2nd sess., p. 11245. For Lenroot's part in the debate, see Margulies, *Senator Lenroot of Wisconsin*, pp. 352–59.

[18]*Congressional Record*, 67th Cong., 2nd sess., p. 11247; Kelly, "Antecedents," pp. 41–42; Murray, *Harding Era*, pp. 276–77.

[19]Culbertson Diary, 28 May–20 September 1922, box 4, pp. 61–84, Culbertson Papers.

to move toward this goal would entail conversion to use of the unconditional most-favored-nation clause in bilateral trade agreements while forcing the Allies to accept "the open door in economically backward areas of the earth, including colonies." In effect the progressive Republican proposed revision of the entire American commercial treaty structure. Use of the unconditional form of most-favored-nation status would establish a solid base from which to demand equal treatment in forcing open new markets. The unconditional form, he continued, "is simply an application to commercial intercourse between nations of the other equality-of-treatment principle—the open door— adopted by western powers to regulate their competitive commercial activities in certain third countries." Culbertson also recommended that the State Department undertake field studies of the colonial policies of Britain, France, the Netherlands, and Japan so that the United States could more effectively open the door to underdeveloped areas. He concluded that the nation had to continue the push for the Open Door in the mandates because certain nations used "concealed methods" to shut out American trade and deny access to vital raw materials as they made cosmetic concessions on customs and trade regulations.[20]

Hughes agreed with much of Culbertson's analysis. The more the secretary studied America's commercial treaties, the more he realized that most should be renegotiated. Many had been signed between the War of 1812 and the Civil War, reflecting policies long since abandoned and conditions which no longer existed. The United States did not even have commercial treaties with the new nations carved from the Central Powers at the Paris Peace Conference. Furthermore, trade treaties between the United States and former wartime enemies needed to be renegotiated, especially the German-American pact, for the sake of U.S. trade interests and to counter Allied attempts at keeping the economic power plant of Europe in a permanent state of artificial inferiority. As a lawyer, the idea of creating a standard treaty that the United States could submit to any nation on earth, at least as a starting point for negotiation, appealed to Hughes.[21] In 1922 he began to think in terms of creating such a model treaty as a prelude to implementing sweeping changes in the commercial treaty structure.

Stanley K. Hornbeck and Wallace M. McClure of the Office of the Economic Adviser also responded enthusiastically to Culbertson's ideas. Hornbeck suggested that the department give full attention to changes in the

---

[20]Culbertson to Hughes, 31 May 1922, 611.0031/155, DSNA. See also memorandum, Stanley K. Hornbeck, 17 March 1922. box 303, and Hornbeck to Culbertson, 20 May 1922, box 136, Stanley K. Hornbeck Papers, Hoover Institution on War, Revolution and Peace, Stanford University, Stanford, CA (hereafter cited as Hornbeck Papers).

[21]Castle, "Commercial Treaties," unpublished manuscript, box 33, p. 3, Castle Papers; Beerits's memorandum, "The Commercial Treaty with Germany," box 172, folder 31, pp. 1–2, Hughes Papers; Hyde, "Charles Evans Hughes," pp. 309–10.

most-favored-nation clause in new commercial treaties. Because American commerce is expanding more rapidly than any other nation on earth, McClure wrote, "it is probably the nation which has most to gain by extending the policy of the Open Door to include equality of treatment in all matters of commerce."[22]

Once Congress had passed the Fordney-McCumber Act, State Department officials began a study of the new tariff. On 16 October McClure reported that language in Section 317 gave the executive branch an "apparent mandate" to make the conversion from the conditional to the unconditional form of the most-favored-nation clause as the best means of preventing discrimination against American products.[23] If the department negotiated a series of new treaties with the unconditional clause, McClure noted a month later, it would "accomplish among fully-sovereign states what the policy of the Open Door aims to do in the markets of weak and dependent states."[24] Meanwhile, in their *Annual Report* to the House, members of the Tariff Commission had to come to similar conclusions:

> Section 317, as finally enacted with certain House amendments, provides, in effect, that the President shall endeavor to secure the removal of all discriminations which foreign countries may inflict upon the commerce of the United States . . . . [E]very country which "discriminates in fact . . . in such manner as to place the commerce of the United States at a disadvantage compared with the commerce of any foreign country" is liable to discrimination against its commerce by the United States. The law itself thus defines discrimination and makes it clear that the point to be regarded is the effect upon American commerce and not the nature or intent of the foreign country in adopting its legislation or in adjusting its rates.[25]

The commission, which wrote the original version of 317 for Senator Smoot, interpreted the section as applying to all cases of discrimination, including the differential treatments resulting, almost inevitably, from the use of reciprocity agreements.[26]

This new concept of what constituted discrimination was not consistent

---

[22]Hornbeck and McClure to Millspaugh, 18, 19, and 26 May 1922, box 303, Hornbeck Papers.

[23]McClure to Harrison, 16 October 1922, box 406, ibid. See also Castle, "Commercial Treaties," box 33, p. 4, Castle Papers.

[24]McClure to A. Young, 11 November 1922, and McClure to A. Young, 14 November 1922, box 303, Hornbeck Papers.

[25]U.S., Tariff Commission, *Sixth Annual Report* (Washington: Government Printing Office, 1923), pp. 5–6.

[26]A. Young to Hughes, 21 October 1922, 611.0031/179, and memorandum, Culbertson, "Proposed Policy of the Tariff Commission for the First Six Months of 1923," 28 December 1922, 611.031/182, DSNA.

with conditional most-favored-nation policy. Therefore, the commission concluded, Congress must have mandated a change to the unconditional form. But if Congress had intended for the executive branch to scrap an economic policy which the nation had followed since the Treaty of Amity and Commerce with France during the American Revolution, surely some mention of it would have been made during the debates.[27] Senators had, in fact, reworded parts of Section 317 at the suggestion of Lodge so as not to imply that penalty duties applied to reciprocity treaties based on the use of the unconditional most-favored-nation treatment clause. Nevertheless, State Department and Tariff Commission officials were so eager to convert to the unconditional form that they chose to ignore the congressional mandate against change.

The Department of State also failed to take into account the fundamental split in the business community over government economic policy. Generally small- and medium-sized manufacturing interests favored a course of action which protected the home market at all costs. These businessmen and their national spokesmen in the American Protective Tariff League, who distrusted the internationalist Tariff Commission's ideas for promoting the Open Door, demanded that Congress pass high tariffs for total protection. In contrast, the chief lobby organization of the larger industries, the National Foreign Trade Council, desired to acquire vast new markets for American goods, even at the expense of some home industries. Most congressmen, ever solicitous of small- and medium-sized manufacturers in their home districts, supported the raising of rates as part of the congressional logrolling process. Unable to match the local clout of small business, the big companies concentrated their lobbying efforts in the executive branch, where they supported the policies of Hughes and Culbertson. Thus, Congress and the State Department consistently tugged in opposite directions throughout the decade. In the end this dichotomy of purpose would frustrate Republican internationalists in their attempts to respond to the nation's changing economic needs.[28]

Regardless of whether or not Congress intended that the State Department shift American commercial policy to the unconditional most-favored-nation principle, there could be little argument that the conditional form had long since outlived its usefulness. It had worked well through much of the previous century when the United States exported mostly raw materials and agricultural items while importing European manufactured goods. As the nation industrialized, American products came into direct competition with exports from Europe, forcing both sides to make temporary tariff arrangements because the United States refused to convert to unconditional most-favored-nation treatment. Administration officials, including Hughes, Culbertson, Hornbeck,

[27]Kelly, "Antecedents," p. 42. See also Robert Freeman Smith, "Reciprocity," in *Encyclopedia of American Foreign Policy*, pp. 867–81; and Snyder, "Culbertson," pp. 405–6.
[28]Parrini, *Heir to Empire*, pp. 234–35; Wilson, *American Business*, pp. 81–82.

and McClure, realized that there could be no return to normalcy in American trade. The Great War had greatly accelerated long-term trends militating against further use of the conditional policy as a means of receiving immunity from discrimination.[29]

On 14 December, after a series of meetings with Hughes, Culbertson once again put his thoughts concerning future American commercial policy in a memorandum for the secretary. He argued against using the "sterile . . . . quiescent and ineffective" conditional principle which "has hindered more than it has helped the development of our foreign trade." Now that Congress had endorsed the idea of equality of treatment, the administration should seize the opportunity to make the switchover. "The adoption of the unconditional most-favored-nation policy with certain safeguards," he concluded, "can be made to support an open door policy not only in the Far East but throughout the world."[30] The secretary of state forwarded this forceful letter to Senator Lodge, who found it "very convincing and very well put."[31] Then Hughes went to work on the president, noting that there was "an opinion among many" that the nation should adopt the unconditional form of the most-favored-nation clause in American treaties of commerce and navigation.[32] Harding quickly gave his approval to the project, while expressing the hope that Cuba could be exempted from the policy change.[33] With the support of Lodge and the president behind him, Hughes proceeded with the drafting of a model commercial treaty which would ensure, in theory, the continued expansion of trade for years to come.

"NEGOTIATING" WITH GERMANY

Secretary Hughes formed a special task force made up of experts from the State, Treasury, and Commerce departments to prepare the model treaty of amity, commerce, and consular rights, a job the committee finished in June 1923.[34] At first the secretary had no particular preferences as to which

---

[29]Doenecke, "The Most Favored Nation Principle," pp. 603–8; Kelly, "Antecedents," pp. 44–47.

[30]Culbertson to Hughes, 14 December 1922, *FRUS, 1923*, 1:121–26. See also Culbertson Diary, 27 November 1922, box 4, p. 95, Culbertson Papers.

[31]Lodge to Hughes, 8 January 1923, *FRUS, 1923*, 1:126–27. See also Culbertson Diary, 30 January 1923, box 4, pp. 5–6, Culbertson Papers.

[32]Hughes to Harding, 15 January 1923, *FRUS, 1923*, 1:127–28.

[33]Culbertson Diary, 28 February 1923, box 4, pp. 11–12, Culbertson Papers; Harding to Hughes, 27 February and 5 March 1923, *FRUS, 1923*, 1:128–30.

[34]"The Commercial Treaty," box 172, folder 31, p. 2, Hughes Papers.

country the department opened negotiations with first.[35] However the former
Central Powers seemed especially anxious to resume commercial relations
and the secretary had promised Germany during negotiation of the separate
peace, and the claims settlement, that the reestablishment of formal trade ties
would follow shortly. The Office of the Economic Adviser had just completed
a review of a Tariff Commission study on discriminatory trade practices of
foreign nations. The new French two-column tariff, which put all agreements
on a reciprocity basis, seemed to present the greatest threat to the principle
of equality of treatment. McClure of the Treaty Division recommended a
strategy of negotiating unconditional most-favored-nation treaties with as many
European nations as possible and then pressing the French to scrap reciprocity.[36] Therefore, the secretary decided to begin with nations surrounding
France, including Germany, Austria, and Hungary.

On 19 July Assistant Secretary of State Harrison suggested that "all
other factors being equal, it would be to our advantage to have these treaties
negotiated in Washington" so that Secretary Hughes and other State Department officials could supervise the talks.[37] Less than a week later, Hughes sent
a draft of the proposed treaty to Otto Weidfeldt, the German ambassador in
Washington, pointing out "that Article VII makes full provision for the enjoyment of the most favored nation clause in its unconditional form, as applied
to persons, vessels and cargoes."[38] This was important for two reasons: Not
only did it mark the first time that the Americans had offered the unconditional
form to another industrial power, but the terms also stood in contrast to the
Allied policy of restricting Germany's ability to recover through denial of
most-favored-nation treatment while forcing the Germans to grant that status
to them.[39] Hughes felt confident that, in this case, the Germans, famous for
their endless haggling over small details, would jump at the pact, for as he
noted to Ambassador Houghton, "it may be said with entire candor that this
treaty embodies no attempt whatever to attain by sharp bargaining any undue
advantage over a friendly state, or to request any peculiar favor which the
United States is not itself ready to offer in return."[40] Once the Germans had
assented to what Castle called "a wonderfully fair document," other states

[35]Castle, "Commercial Treaties," box 33, p. 5, Castle Papers; Hyde, "Charles Evans
Hughes," p. 311.
    [36]Enclosure, A. Young to Phillips, 21 October 1922, 611.0031/189, DSNA; Graham H.
Stuart, "Tariff Making in France," in *Tariff Problems of the United States*, ed. Harry T. Collins.
(Philadelphia: American Academy of Political and Social Science, 1928), pp. 241–42.
    [37]Harrison to Castle, 19 July 1923, 711.622/21, and Castle to Hyde, 19 July 1923,
611.0031/194, DSNA.
    [38]The secretary of state to the German ambassador (Weidfeldt), 25 July 1923, *FRUS,
1923*, 2:22.
    [39]See the Treaty of Versailles, Articles 264–270, in *Treaties of Peace*, pp. 158–61.
    [40]The secretary of state to the ambassador in Germany (Houghton), 3 August 1923,
711.622/23A, DSNA.

would follow rapidly, so ending the threat to American trade and prosperity.[41]

Although Germany needed the new American commercial treaty desperately, Hughes had picked a poor time to offer his model pact. In the summer of 1923, Germany's currency had, for all intents and purposes, ceased to exist. In the wake of a wild inflationary spiral, one American dollar equalled over one million marks. For several months France and Belgium had occupied the Ruhr, where they supported several separatist movements. On 11 August the government of Chancellor Wilhelm Cuno collapsed. Stresemann struggled to form a solid coalition amidst endless interparty feuds, only to fall himself three months later. In the interim the right-wing Austrian fanatic Adolf Hitler led an unsuccessful putsch in Munich. In this atmosphere of almost total confusion, which the normally eloquent British Ambassador to Berlin, Lord D'Abernon, could only label as "indescribable," the German Foreign Office acted slowly on Secretary Hughes's offer to negotiate a new commercial treaty, at least until an embarrassing incident forced the Wilhelmstrasse and Washington to take quick action.[42]

Ever since the time of the great Reich Chancellor Otto von Bismarck, the German Foreign Office had followed the practice of consulting with leading German corporations on important matters of commercial policy. The idea had worked well for a half century, until late November 1923, when a legal counsel to a local organization in Berlin gave a verbatim copy of Hughes's model treaty to the German-American Chamber of Commerce in New York, which released the text to the press.[43] On 28 November Ambassador Weidfeldt expressed his great regret to Secretary Hughes over the incident, noting further that as "only a few points of difference" seemed to separate the two sides, early agreement seemed possible. An angry Hughes replied that because the Germans had embarrassed his government, the United States might withdraw the treaty unless Berlin consented to immediate signature as a way of ending the American discomfiture.[44]

Two days later, on 30 November, Weidfeldt and his counselor met with Castle, McClure, Solicitor Charles C. Hyde, and his assistants. The Germans made "numerous inquiries and proposed numerous changes," but after two days of American explanations, Ambassador Weidfeldt agreed to sign after

---

[41]Castle to Houghton, 25 July 1923, box 6, Castle Papers; the secretary of state to American diplomatic officers, 18 August 1923, 611.0031/-, DSNA.

[42]Eyck, *Weimar Republic*, pp. 246–83.

[43]Phillips to Lodge, 27 November 1923, 711.622/30A, DSNA; the acting secretary of state to the ambassador in Germany (Houghton), 30 November 1923, *FRUS, 1923*, 2:23; the ambassador in Germany (Houghton) to the secretary of state, 2 December 1923, 711.622/29, DSNA.

[44]Memorandum of a conversation between the secretary of state and the German ambassador (Weidfeldt), 28 November 1923, box 175, folder 75b, Hughes Papers. See also Castle, "Commercial Treaties," box 33, p. 6, Castle Papers.

the department authorized textual changes Solicitor Hyde described as "for the most part . . . of slight consequence."[45] On 8 December 1923 Secretary Hughes and the German ambassador signed the Treaty of Friendship, Commerce and Consular Rights, thus returning the former enemies to full diplomatic and economic relations for the first time since President Wilson broke ties over six and one-half years earlier.[46] The first six articles detailed the rights of nationals of each party living in the other's territory. Article 7 committed the two nations to unconditional most-favored-nation treatment for trade passing between them while Article 9 provided for reciprocal national treatment of shipping. Other articles dealt with the status, rights, and immunities of diplomats.[47] Prompt German signature of the model treaty, as Hughes confided to President Coolidge a few days in advance of the event, relieved much of the embarrassment of the leak to the press.[48] The secretary of state had already taken the precaution of securing Lodge's blessing for the pact, in order to ease its passage through the Senate. However, much to the State Department's dismay, the treaty made it out of the Foreign Relations Committee only over the dead body of the chairman.

THE MODEL TREATY AND THE SENATE

Secretary Hughes hoped that the Senate would ratify the treaty as quickly as possible so that the department's overhaul of the commercial treaty framework could proceed smoothly. On 14 January 1924 the Foreign Relations Committee began to study the model pact. After the session Senator Lodge wrote a letter asking Secretary Hughes to provide the committee with information on prewar consular and commercial arrangements between Germany and the United States. Almost as an afterthought, he noted that there "are indications that we are going to have some difficulty over the favored-nation clause."[49] That news probably did not come as a surprise to Hughes; back in November, shortly after the Germans leaked the draft treaty to the press, the *New York Times* had reported that the most-favored-nation articles would give the Senate the opportunity to stand by or ignore the discriminatory duty provisions of the Jones Merchant Marine Act of 1920. Section 34 of the act

[45]Memorandum regarding a conference held in the State Department, 1 December 1923, and Hyde to Hughes, 5 December 1923, *FRUS, 1923*, 2: 24–29. See also Houghton to Castle, 3 December 1923, box 6, Castle Papers; and Hyde, "Charles Evans Hughes," p. 311.

[46]*New York Times*, 9 December 1923, p. 2.

[47]Treaty between the United States and Germany, 8 December 1923, *FRUS, 1923*, 2:29–45; the secretary of state to the ambassador in Germany (Houghton), 3 August 1923, 711.622/23A, DSNA.

[48]Hughes to Coolidge, 4 December 1923, 711.622/30B, DSNA.

[49]Lodge to Hughes, 14 January 1924, 711.622/36, ibid.

instructed the president to notify foreign nations of the unilateral abrogation of any and all commercial agreements with the United States in conflict with the American right to give preferential treatment to its shipping vessels. Although President Wilson had signed the bill, he refused to carry out Section 34 when advisers informed him that thirty-two treaties would have to be cancelled, a policy which Presidents Harding and Coolidge also followed.[50] In 1923 when the administration gave Germany national treatment, that is, levying the same charges against foreign ships entering the United States as those imposed on American bottoms, certain elements in the Senate decided on a showdown.[51]

Republican Senator Wesley L. Jones of Washington, author of the Merchant Marine Act, testified before the committee during the first day of hearings on 25 January that the national treatment of shipping clause would cripple the American merchant marine by preventing the United States from levying higher duties on goods imported in foreign vessels than in American ships.[52] On 31 January and again on 7 February, Vice-Chairman Culbertson defended the treaty at committee hearings, emphasizing that the pact symbolized the beginning of an active new commercial policy designed to safeguard American interests abroad and assure continued access to vital foreign sources of raw materials. He justified the conversion to the unconditional form of most-favored-nation status as "entirely in line with America's well known attitude toward the 'open door' in certain [F]ar [E]astern countries and in mandated areas, a policy which has been generally recognized as a distant [sic] contribution to commercial stability and to peace."[53]

After testifying Culbertson told Hughes that Commissioner E. C. Plummer of the United States Shipping Board, the agency which supervised the merchant marine, would appear before the committee to argue for elimination from the pact of clauses granting national treatment to shipping. This deletion, Culbertson reminded Hughes, would give the United States the freedom of action which the Senate desired, but it also freed other nations to adopt discriminatory policies. "Something should be done," Culbertson concluded, "to make the Committee realize the far-reaching effect of the elimination of the national-treatment provisions."[54] The vice-chairman understood that there could be no real Open Door without national treatment and that if the Senate yielded to the pressures of American shipping interests by amending the model

---

[50]Memorandum, Office of the Solicitor, 6 September 1920, and Fred K. Nielsen to N. Davis, 6 September 1920, 611.0031/151, ibid.; Jeffrey J. Safford, *Wilsonian Maritime Diplomacy, 1913–1921* (New Brunswick, NJ: Rutgers University Press, 1978), pp. 222–23 and 227–29.

[51]*New York Times*, 27 November 1923, p. 5.

[52]U.S., Congress, Senate, Committee on Foreign Relations, *Hearings on the German Commerce Treaty*, 68th Cong., 1st sess., 25 January 1924, p. 5.

[53]Ibid., 7 February 1924, p. 82.

[54]Culbertson to Hughes, 12 February 1924, 711.622/53, DSNA. See also Castle, "Commercial Treaties," box 33, pp. 9–10, Castle Papers.

treaty with Germany, it would deal a crippling blow to hopes for a breakthrough against the preferential tariff systems of the Allies.

On 13 March 1924 Secretary Hughes wrote a long letter to Senator Lodge justifying ratification of the German-American treaty without reservations. The nation needed freedom from trade discrimination in order to assure the continued peaceful expansion of trade. "The way to assure this freedom," he noted, "is by agreement and, of course, what the United States asks it must give." If the United States discriminates in favor of national shipping, the British will inevitably retaliate and "reprisal would follow reprisal," resulting in ruinous commercial warfare. In the long run, national treatment could be the best means to assure the prosperity of American shipping. The secretary went on to explain the necessity of switching from the conditional to the unconditional most-favored-nation principle. As the United States grew to great power status, in defense of vital interests, it became the leading champion of the Open Door without practicing that policy uniformly. "To be consistent with our professions, and to conserve our interests," Hughes continued, "it has become important that we make our commercial practice square in fact with the theory upon which our policy has been based."[55] In spite of Hughes's explanation, Lodge elected to keep the treaty bottled up in committee indefinitely.

The secretary did what he could on behalf of the model pact. When he came across criticisms in the *Congressional Record* or newspapers, he would fire off a letter to Chairman Lodge answering the charges in his unyieldingly legalistic style. As months went by without action, Hughes suspended negotiation of the other commercial treaties based on the German-American agreement. After Lodge died on 9 November 1924, Hughes learned from Borah, the new chairman, that Lodge had not presented any of the secretary's letters to the committee in defense of the treaty. The new chairman and the secretary agreed that Hughes would go before the committee personally in an attempt to get the treaty onto the floor of the Senate.[56]

In January 1925 Virginia Democrat Swanson, a leading critic of the Turkish-American pact also pending before the Senate, offered the administration a compromise on the model treaty: He proposed to eliminate the clause specifically guaranteeing national treatment of shipping. However the most-favored-nation provisions would still guarantee national treatment to German shipping because of the existence of national treatment clauses in other treaties. Opponents of national treatment could then vote for the treaty, as it no longer directly contravened terms of the Jones Merchant Marine Act.[57]

[55]Hughes to Lodge, 13 March 1924, *FRUS, 1924*, 2:183–92. See also Culbertson Diary, 13 March 1924, box 4, pp. 111–12, Culbertson Papers.

[56]"The Commercial Treaty with Germany," box 172, folder 31, pp. 6–7, Hughes Papers.

[57]Memorandum, Arthur Young, "The Department's Course of Action Regarding the Pending German Treaty," 26 January 1925, 711.622/61, DSNA; *New York Times*, 18 December 1924, p. 6, 11 January 1925, section 9, p. 6, and 17 January 1925, p. 3.

On 26 January Economic Adviser Arthur N. Young weighed the pros and cons of accepting the compromise in a lengthy memorandum. If the department approved Swanson's amendment, the Senate would, by giving its endorsement to the policy of unconditional most-favored-nation treatment, be fulfilling a major goal of the ambitious commercial treaty reform program without actually giving up national treatment of shipping. On the other hand, this compromise meant abandonment of a historic policy, followed for over one hundred years, of granting national treatment. Every time the department renegotiated one of the older commercial treaties, it would be eroding the basis for continued adherence to national treatment. Finally, Young noted, "To give up national treatment of shipping would be inconsistent with our present policy of equality of treatment which is manifested in our contention for the open door." The economic adviser recommended rejection of the compromise, offering instead another arrangement whereby provisions for national treatment could be terminated by either nation on twelve months notice.[58]

Secretary Hughes agreed with Young's idea, adopting it as departmental policy as he prepared to testify in person before the Senate Foreign Relations Committee. On 2 February 1925 the secretary of state argued his case to the senators, after a careful rehearsal with subordinates the day before at his home, stressing that the treaty with national treatment clauses would prevent Germany from discriminating against American vessels while a policy of discrimination in favor of U.S. bottoms could serve only to invite injurious retaliation. The nation would not win such a commercial war because it exported more than it imported. Again the secretary made the distinctly Wilsonian argument that the United States should work toward ending economic reprisals rather than increasing them as a contribution to world peace. Although he argued for passage of the treaty without amendments, the secretary called the committee's attention to the economic adviser's reservation idea that the shipping clauses could be denounced on a year's notice.[59] The next day the Foreign Relations Committee reported favorably on the treaty with two reservations, one of which gave the president the right to cancel national treatment. The other reservation specified that nothing in the agreement could be construed to conflict in any way with immigration restrictions which Congress had recently passed.[60]

---

[58]Young, "The Department's Course," 711.622/61, Dorsey Richardson to Grew, 1 November 1924, 711.622/90, and memorandum, McClure, "What the Opponents of the National Treatment of Shipping Clauses in the Treaty with Germany Say They Want," 31 January 1925, 711.622/65, DSNA.

[59]Abstract of statement of Hughes before the Committee on Foreign Relations, 2 February 1925, box 172, folder 30, and "The Commercial Treaty with Germany," box 172, folder 31, pp. 7–8, Hughes Papers.

[60]*New York Times*, 4 February 1925, p. 12.

Many senators objected to the State Department approved reservation since it left implementation of possible cancellation procedures to the executive branch. Senator Jones led a movement to change the amendment so that Congress would decide on the termination of national treatment.[61] On 10 February the Senate passed the treaty with the Jones amendment, a compromise the *New York Times* reported to be "not wholly acceptable to the State Department," although an administration spokesman called the vote "very gratifying" to the president and secretary of state.[62] On the whole the Senate's action did please Hughes, who believed that the amended version at least respected the theory behind the change from conditional to unconditional most-favored-nation status.[63] In late April, speaking before the New York Chamber of Commerce, the secretary praised the model treaty as an instrument of peace and prosperity. "I trust the time will not come when we shall change our policy," he said in reference to the Jones amendment. "Such a change, I believe, instead of helping our commerce would be a disaster."[64] The Senate had finally passed the reform treaty, but in doing so, it had also incorporated into the pact, at the behest of shipping interests, a provision which threatened to undo the equality of treatment philosophy at the base of the new commercial treaty superstructure. Hughes could do nothing but proceed with negotiation of the other treaties.

THE HUNGARIAN TREATY

American business and government leaders waited anxiously for the opportunity to open the door to new markets in Eastern Europe after the Great War. In March 1921 Ulysses Grant-Smith, the American commissioner in Hungary, sent a letter to the Hungarian foreign minister, stating that the United States had taken the "unusual and altruistic course" of relinquishing its right to reparations and indemnities from the Central Powers. He felt impelled to state, however,

> that one of the returns which it is confidently expected that Hungary will make for this act of generosity, not to speak of the measures of relief which have been and are still being carried on by the American people

[61]Ibid., 8 February 1925, p. 23. See also George Wharton Pepper, *In the Senate* (Philadelphia: University of Pennsylvania Press, 1930), p. 87.
[62]*New York Times*, 11 February 1925, section 9, p. 6, and 12 February 1925, p. 9.
[63]"The Commercial Treaty with Germany," box 172, folder 31, p. 10, Hughes Papers; Hyde, "Charles Evans Hughes," p. 316. See also Coolidge to Borah, 11 February 1925, box 138, and Hughes to Borah, 11 February 1925, box 763, Borah Papers; and Hughes to Wadsworth, 28 February 1925, 611.0031/227, DSNA.
[64]*New York Times*, 29 April 1925, p. 23.

in Hungary, will be not only a continuation of the fair treatment which American owned property, investments, and bank deposits have thus far enjoyed at your Government's hands, but also the maintenance of the open door for American financial and industrial activities throughout Hungary, that no concessions may be granted which will exclude their participation in similar ventures.[65]

When the letter came to the attention of Castle and Secretary Hughes, the department rebuked the American commissioner, not for his arrogant demand for the Open Door in Hungary, but because he had stated that the United States definitely relinquished reparations.[66] Grant-Smith retracted the statement on indemnities and promised to continue pressuring Hungarian authorities to keep the door open for American trade.[67]

Hungary, with the threat of American reparations hanging over it and saddled with repayment of loans to the United States at high interest rates, proved quite receptive to American overtures for a new commercial pact based on the model treaty with Germany.[68] On 23 October 1923 the counselor of the Hungarian legation in Washington wrote to Secretary Hughes that "as a token of its readiness and its cordial spirit of cooperation, my Government does not even suggest minor changes by the United States Government in the wording of the transmitted draft." At the same time, the Hungarian diplomat reported that his nation could not accept Article 6 because it conflicted with two sections of the Treaty of Trianon.[69] Article 6 provided that in the event of war between the United States or Hungary and a third nation, either party could conscript nationals of the other residing in the warring country for military service.[70] In the Treaty of Trianon, Article 103 banned the draft in Hungary, while in Article 142, the Hungarian government promised to prevent its nationals from enlisting in the armed forces of foreign powers.[71] Castle believed that the Hungarians were sincere, noting that "[Prime Minister] Count Bethlen is doing his utmost to have the Hungarian Government live up very strictly to the terms of the Treaty to avoid any just criticism on the part of

---

[65]Enclosure, the American commissioner in Hungary (Grant-Smith) to the secretary of state, 19 March 1921, 711.64/3, DSNA.
[66]Castle to Fletcher, 14 April 1921, and the secretary of state to the American commissioner in Hungary (Grant-Smith), 15 April 1921, 711.64/3, ibid.
[67]The American commissioner in Hungary (Grant-Smith) to the secretary of state, 19 April 1921, 711.64/4, ibid.
[68]Iván T. Berend and György Ránki, "The Horthy Regime," in *A History of Hungary*, ed. Ervin Pamlényi (London: Collet's, 1975), p. 475; Howland, *American Foreign Relations, 1928*, pp. 424 and 437.
[69]The Hungarian legation to the secretary of state, 23 October 1923, 711.642/3, DSNA.
[70]Treaty of Friendship, Commerce, and Consular Rights Between the United States and Hungary. Enclosure in the secretary of state to the minister in Hungary (Brentano), 3 August 1923, 711.642/A, DSNA.
[71]*Treaties of Peace*, pp. 497 and 511.

the surrounding states."[72] After corresponding for several months with Count László Széchényi, the Hungarian minister at Washington, Hughes finally convinced the Hungarians to overlook the conflict between Article 6 and the Trianon treaty.[73] The secretary then suspended the negotiations until the Senate passed the model treaty with Germany.

On 27 March 1925 Solicitor Hyde called Secretary of State Kellogg's attention to the Hungarian-American treaty, which had been shelved for more than a year. As the first in a number of treaties based on the German model, Hyde noted, the department should carefully consider how to proceed in view of the Senate's amendments to the German-American pact. The department could go ahead with the signing of the treaty while making it clear to the Hungarians that they could expect reservations regarding the right of either party to revoke national treatment and harmonizing the pact with American immigration restrictions. Other alternatives included redrafting the two relevant articles to meet the views of the Senate or making the reservations part of the treaty itself.[74] On 24 June Kellogg and Count Széchényi signed the Treaty of Friendship, Commerce, and Consular Rights as originally negotiated the previous year.[75] The two diplomats then exchanged notes to the effect that they anticipated, and agreed in advance to, Senate reservations identical to those appended to the model German-American treaty.[76] Ten months later, on 26 March 1926, the Senate consented unanimously to ratification of the treaty with the two expected reservations.[77] That took care of only part of the old Austro-Hungarian state, as the department also wished to treat with Austria, a process which took somewhat longer to complete and illustrated that Hughes's vaunted model treaty program had become a failure.

THE AUSTRIAN TREATY

Austrian authorities wanted a commercial treaty with the United States at least as much as their counterparts in Budapest; throughout the year 1923,

---

[72]Castle to Hyde, 2 January 1924, 711.642/3, DSNA.

[73]The secretary of state to the Hungarian minister (Széchényi), 9 November 1923 and 3 January 1924, ibid.

[74]Hyde to Kellogg, 27 March 1925, 711.642/9, ibid.

[75]The secretary of state to the minister in Hungary (Brentano), 24 June 1925, 711.642/9A, ibid.; the Treaty of Friendship, Commerce, and Consular Rights Between the United States and Hungary, 24 June 1925, *FRUS, 1925*, 2:341–54.

[76]The secretary of state to the Hungarian minister (Széchényi), 24 June 1925, and the Hungarian minister (Széchényi) to the secretary of state, 24 June 1925, *FRUS, 1925*, 2:354–56.

[77]U.S., Congress, Senate, *Journal of the Executive Proceedings of the Senate of the United States of America*, 69th Cong., special session, and 69th Cong., 1st sess., pp. 175, 756, and 802–3.

the Austrian chargé urged Secretary Hughes to open negotiations repeatedly.[78] On 5 August Hughes sent a copy of the model treaty to Minister Albert H. Washburn, presuming that the Austrians would be eager to sign.[79] A month later Washburn reported that both the foreign minister and his top assistant "have not attempted to conceal their satisfaction with the tenor of the draft as proposed. They state definitely that they gladly accept it in general and are prepared to conclude a treaty on this basis." The American minister predicted optimistically that he could have the whole treaty-making process wrapped up within another month.[80] In December Washburn sent to the department a detailed report of conferences and negotiations with the Austrian Foreign Office over trade matters and the rights of foreign nationals and diplomats which the American minister characterized as "rather formidable at first glance."[81] On 8 March and 17 September 1924, he forwarded more treaty counterproposals from the Vienna government, propositions the department studied for more than a year before replying.[82]

When the State Department finally did reopen talks with Austria in May 1926, Secretary of State Kellogg offered to incorporate only the minor changes the department had accepted during the brief German-American negotiations almost three years earlier. The department could not possibly approve the dozens of small changes the Austrians wanted because "uniformity in every particular in which it is possible is essential in all the treaties of the series which it is negotiating." Kellogg addressed the Austrian request for the right of its nationals to lease agricultural lands in the United States on a most-favored-nation basis, pointing out that "leasing of agricultural lands by Japanese [has] been regarded as a menace in California and possibly one other Pacific Coast State." The United States could not allow Austria to lease farmlands without discriminating against Japan, whose nationals had been denied the right to rent such property in an earlier treaty. The secretary also noted that Austrians could not have the most-favored-nation right to own American real estate because an 1853 treaty conferred that right on Argentinians. This meant that ownership rights would become available automatically to the nationals of countries with most-favored-nation treaty clauses with respect to acquiring real estate. In closing Secretary Kellogg asked Washburn

---

[78]The secretary of state to the minister in Austria (Washburn), 19 July 1923, 711.632/7A, DSNA.

[79]The secretary of state to the minister in Austria (Washburn), 3 August 1923, *FRUS, 1923,* 1:399–413.

[80]The minister in Austria (Washburn) to the secretary of state, 7 September 1923, 711.632/9, DSNA.

[81]The minister in Austria (Washburn) to the secretary of state, 18 December 1923, *FRUS, 1923,* 1:413–30.

[82]The minister in Austria (Washburn) to the secretary of state, 8 March and 17 September 1924, 711.632/15, the secretary of state to the minister in Austria (Washburn), 25 June 1925, and Prentis B. Gilbert to Grew, 15 June 1925, 711.632/17, DSNA.

to write the Senate's now-standard reservation on immigration into the first article of the treaty to avoid any possible misunderstanding later.[83]

On 20 July 1926 Minister Washburn reported that "we have reached an understanding on practically all the matters in controversy, one provision only remaining unsettled." Although the foreign minister admitted that few Austrian nationals would actually lease American farmland, he continued to insist on obtaining that right through the treaty. He also requested most-favored-nation treatment in regard to acquisition of land because Austrian law required reciprocity in regard to the owning of real property.[84] The two sides finally solved this problem in early 1927, when the Austrians agreed that existing American laws at the state level which permitted aliens to own land would satisfy the reciprocity requirements of Austrian law.[85] By that time, however, the treaty no longer satisfied the State Department.

Kellogg sent Minister Washburn instructions in early 1927 to tighten up arrangements implementing unconditional most-favored-nation status owing to continuing discrimination against American commerce in Europe. The department desired a clause stipulating specifically that American products would receive equality of treatment even when the goods were shipped from third countries. Another new provision called for equal treatment with regard to licenses, quotas, and contingents. These and other changes would be written into all subsequent Open Door treaties.[86] On 30 June at the suggestion of the Commerce Department, Kellogg forwarded another clause to be included in the treaty, this one stipulating most-favored-nation treatment for commercial travelers.[87] The Austrians agreed to many, but not all, of the changes. "The Austrian negotiators," Washburn wrote, "feel that they have receded on most of their conditions, as indeed they have, and if the Department can see its way clear to do so, I trust it will speedily meet the Austrian views . . . and express its preference for the various alternatives suggested."[88] Ignoring the minister's advice, the department continued to quibble over details for almost another full year before finally signing the pact on 19 June 1928.[89]

Secretary Kellogg decided on one final change after the treaty went to the printer. The department wanted to have a showdown with the Senate over

[83]The secretary of state to the minister in Austria (Washburn), 12 May 1926, 711.632/15, ibid.

[84]The minister in Austria (Washburn) to the secretary of state, 20 July 1926, *FRUS, 1928,* 1:932–37.

[85]Memorandum, Green Hackworth, 12 February 1927, 711.632/21, DSNA; the acting secretary of state to the minister in Austria (Washburn), 24 February 1927, *FRUS, 1928,* 1:956–60.

[86]The secretary of state to the minister in Austria (Washburn), 2 April 1927, *FRUS, 1928,* 1:960–64.

[87]Castle to Hoover, 30 June 1927, 711.632/24, DSNA; the secretary of state to the minister in Austria (Washburn), 30 June 1927, *FRUS, 1928,* 1:972–74.

[88]The minister in Austria (Washburn) to the secretary of state, 11 July 1927, 1:974–84.

[89]The minister in Austria (Washburn) to the secretary of state, 19 June 1928, 711.632/46, DSNA; the Treaty Between the United States and Austria, 19 June 1928, *FRUS, 1928,* 1:995–1006.

the standard reservation which gave Congress the right to terminate national treatment of shipping provisions since most of the large American shipping interests no longer favored the amendment.[90] On 30 January 1929, shortly before leaving office, Kellogg testified before the Senate Foreign Relations Committee that the Shipping Board, the Department of Commerce, and the National Chamber of Commerce all viewed the national treatment reservation as counterproductive to American interests. The secretary also defended the many minor differences between the model treaty and the Austro-American commercial pact, noting that the latter was actually superior to the German agreement because of new provisions designed to insure equality of treatment for American goods in light of European attempts at restricting imports.[91] The Senate ratified the treaty with the standard reservation on national treatment.[92]

President Hoover's secretary of state, Henry L. Stimson, carried on the fight against the Senate's reservation, calling it "a renewed statement to the world that the United States may abandon its century-old policy of reciprocal national treatment of shipping." The nation's trading partners, Stimson noted, have been quite critical of America's commercial policy for demanding the Open Door abroad while maintaining a protectionist stand at home. Revocation of the Senate reservation in the Austrian treaty and its omission in future commercial pacts might help to allay the criticisms and consequently benefit American exporters. He returned the treaty to Hoover, requesting resubmission to the Senate for ratification without the reservation.[93] The Senate refused to retreat from its original position, forcing the administration to accept the reservation.[94] By the time Hoover and Stimson gave up their challenge to the Senate in early 1931, the normal flow of commerce had been interrupted almost completely and along with it went America's last hopes for a new Open Door commercial order based on the unconditional most-favored-nation clause.

ANATOMY OF A FAILURE

In his study of American economic foreign policy published in 1929, Benjamin H. Williams observed that "in building a worldwide commercial

[90]Unsigned memorandum, Treaty Division, 4 June 1928, 711.632/42, DSNA; the secretary of state to the minister in Austria (Washburn), 5 June 1928, *FRUS, 1928,* 1:994.

[91]Memorandum for the Foreign Relations Committee, undated, 711.632/50, and unsigned memorandum, Office of the Economic Adviser, 6 February 1929, 711.632/51, DSNA.

[92]The secretary of state to the minister in Austria (Washburn), 12 February 1929, 711.632/51a, ibid.

[93]Stimson to Hoover, undated, no index number, but in the 711.632 file, ibid. See also Castle to Washburn, 28 August 1929, 711.632/57, and McClure to Stimson, 19 August 1929, 711.632/60 1/2, ibid.

[94]The minister in Austria (Stockton) to the Austrian vice-chancellor and the federal minister for foreign affairs, 20 January 1931, *FRUS, 1928,* 1:1006–7.

treaty system incorporating unconditional most-favored-nation treatment the Department of State has encountered a formidable task."[95] The author's observation was, if anything, understated, for Hughes and his successors tried to create an Open Door commercial treaty system at a time when Congress was following a high tariff policy. Shortly after the Great War, members of the Tariff Commission, most of whom were Wilson appointees, and experts in the Department of State recommended that the administration base the nation's commercial treaty system on the unconditional most-favored-nation clause in order to open new markets for American manufactured goods. The first breakthrough came in 1922, when the administration induced Congress to accept Section 317 of the Tariff Act, granting the president power to retaliate against the discriminatory commercial practices of foreign nations. Internationalists in the executive branch regarded Section 317 as inconsistent with the traditional American use of the conditional most-favored-nation principle because the tariff clause sought to secure equality of treatment for American goods rather than reducing foreign tariffs through reciprocity selectively. Many members of Congress, however, including most of the Republican leadership, acted in response to the efforts of small- and medium-sized manufacturers interested in protectionism, giving every indication that they did not share the administration's interpretation, clear signs which Hughes, Culbertson, and others ignored in their haste to erect an Open Door system.

McClure of the Department of State's Treaty Division briefed Secretary of State Stimson on American commercial policy in March 1929. "The progress of this program," McClure observed, "has been painfully slow." In seven years the department had been able to negotiate eight Open Door treaties, only five of which were actually in effect, and a dozen executive agreements utilizing the unconditional form of most-favored-nation treatment in customs matters. The assistant chief of the Treaty Division blamed the lack of progress on a shortage of qualified personnel. He also acknowledged that "serious opposition has been encountered in a number of quarters." The idea of a new commercial treaty with the United States had "been cooly received and in a number of instances . . . flatly turned down" in Latin America.[96] In Europe the department had made Open Door agreements with the prostrated Central Powers, but the two leading nations with discriminatory systems, Britain and France, had rejected the American overtures for an Open Door.

France, the department's number-one target for an unconditional most-favored-nation agreement, would not come to terms since high American duties obstructed the import of French goods more than France's tariff did to other countries. McClure had not lost faith in the most-favored-nation clause, observing that it was "from almost every point of view the fairest commercial policy that a country can maintain and the one that is best calculated to

[95]Benjamin H. Williams, *Economic Foreign Policy of the United States* (New York: McGraw-Hill, 1929), p. 302.

[96]McClure to Stimson, 30 March 1929, *FRUS, 1929*, 1:988–93.

promote peace and good will among nations." Yet Europe, the key to world trade, would not join the American economic peace movement because of the high tariff of the United States. "It would be impossible to maintain that such an attitude is wholly unreasonable," McClure wrote of the Europeans. "Obviously, the advantages of most-favored-nation treatment are greater where a tariff is moderate than where it is extremely high."[97] Even a bitter administration critic could not have written a better epitaph for the Open Door commercial treaty system than that.

Just before leaving office, Secretary of State Kellogg wrote a letter to Willis C. Hawley, chairman of the House Ways and Means Committee, regarding the movement in Congress to revise the tariff. The inconsistencies between high duties and other protective devices on the one hand and the general equality of treatment policy envisaged in Section 317 of the Fordney-McCumber Act of 1922 on the other, Kellogg observed, "have in fact proved to be a source of embarrassment to this Department in important negotiations having in view the removal of discriminations against American trade."[98] Congress chose to ignore the secretary's statement, passing instead, in a repeat performance of the protectionist logrolling of 1922, the Smoot-Hawley Tariff which raised rates on imported industrial goods even higher than they had been earlier.[99]

Once Congress had erected higher tariff walls, further attempts to create an Open Door commercial system had no real chance of success. From the outset Hughes and his advisers deluded themselves in the belief that Congress supported the attempt to implement a Republican version of the third of Wilson's Fourteen Points, a call for equality of trade conditions as a means of ensuring eternal peace, when, in fact, the two branches of government were responding to two different groups of manufacturing interests. The price for making this liberal internationalist goal a reality was concomitant acceptance of a high tariff. Congress further undermined administration attempts to obtain equal treatment through the use of a reservation advertising that the United States did not wish even to grant national treatment to shipping on a permanent basis. Surveying the wreckage of Republican commercial policy from the perspective of the 1930s, Castle could conclude only that "no system or principle is either fool-proof or knave–proof."[100] Hughes had hoped that the commercial treaties with Germany, Austria, and Hungary would be both the climax of efforts to restore relations with America's wartime enemies—a job Wilson had begun many years earlier at Paris—and the beginning of an Open Door world. Instead he met with a defeat which hurt American economic interests every bit as much as Wilson's downfall had harmed the cause of internationalism.

---

[97]Ibid.
[98]Kellogg to Hawley, 26 February 1929, ibid., 1:985–88.
[99]Dobson, *Two Centuries of Tariffs*, pp. 33–35.
[100]Castle, "Commercial Treaties," box 33, p. 13, Castle Papers.

CONCLUSION
Continuities in Ideals and Policies

Shortly after Harding's landslide victory in 1920, Wilson asked rhetorically, "How can he lead when he does not know where he is going?"[1] Harding may not have known exactly where he was headed, any more than Wilson had eight years earlier, but he did know the general direction. President Harding and his cabinet should be viewed as caretakers of policies and programs already in place, not innovators; indeed the armistice of November 1918 provides a more meaningful watershed in foreign affairs than the change in administrations of March 1921.[2] In making peace with the former Central Powers, Secretary of State Hughes carried forward many of Wilson's basic ideas while reshaping others to fit changed circumstances and the philosophy of his political party. Continuity rather than transformation is the key to understanding this important phase of diplomatic "normalcy."

Hughes faced many foreign policy problems growing out of the late war in Europe when he came into office. Senate rejection of the Treaty of Versailles meant that the secretary either had to resubmit the pact for ratification or renegotiate another set of treaties from scratch. During the great debate over the Versailles pact, Hughes had favored ratification with mild reservations designed to provide for maximum flexibility in foreign policy. As secretary of state, he advocated returning the treaty to the Senate with a new set of reservations, dropping the idea only when the irreconcilables threatened to block the administration's domestic program. Congress then passed the Knox-Porter bill which declared the state of war between the United States and the Central Powers to be over while reserving all American rights as a victorious power. Realizing that the congressional peace did not provide an adequate framework for the comprehensive settlement he envisaged, the secretary created a unique set of "index" treaties with Germany, Austria, and Hungary weaving together the Knox-Porter bill and references to sections of the original treaties granting rights and privileges to the United States.

Former President Wilson broke his self-imposed public silence to denounce the treaties as iniquitous, just as he had scorned the Treaty of Versailles with reservations and even though the only other viable alternative, the Knox-Porter bill as originally passed by Congress, would have been even

---

[1] Quoted in Baker, *American Chronicle*, p. 485.

[2] Burl Noggle, *Into the Twenties: The United States From Armistice To Normalcy* (Urbana: University of Illinois Press, 1974), pp. viii and 31.

more one-sided. Wilson found an unlikely ally in the fight against the separate peace in his old foe, Senator Borah. Although poles apart in regard to international relations, Wilson and Borah shared a penchant for moral righteousness which led to a reluctant mutual admiration. Each regarded the other as misguided yet honorable and moral. Borah opposed the separate peace because it retained the worst features of Wilsonian internationalism—American involvement in European politics and the unfair peace imposed upon the vanquished Central Powers—while shunning the nation's moral obligations. Wilson damned the treaties as dishonorable because they referred only to rights and not responsibilities. Both men based their opposition to Hughes's practical efforts on moral grounds.

Wilson and Borah could also be very pragmatic in matters of policy. After Versailles, disillusioned British liberals grumbled that "Wilson talks like Jesus Christ, but he acts like Lloyd George," meaning that the president had compromised as much as anyone at the peace conference.[3] H. L. Mencken observed the same phenomenon in Wilson's moral successor, Borah, writing that "he has curled up on so many noble causes that no one trusts him any more."[4] When it came to economic foreign policy, it turned out, Wilson and Borah were every bit as practical as Hughes. All three envisioned the United States as the commercial leader of a new Open Door world, even if they disagreed strongly over specifics.

Borah's economic internationalism infuriated his fellow political isolationists. Journalist William Hard wrote Johnson:

> Bill Borah is against political plunging into Europe but he still seems to think that one can plunge into Europe's economics without getting politically drowned. He seems to divide life into the political compartment and the economic compartment and does not seem to see that there is only a gauze partition between the two. Consequently, although he is invaluable at all other times, he goes off watch as soon as the State Department says that its purpose in Europe is economic only.[5]

Borah became a critic of Hughes's foreign policy only when the secretary of state ventured into the international "political compartment" and proved indispensable in his support of piecemeal efforts at reestablishing diplomatic and economic relations with the former Central Powers. Wilson did not live long enough to pass judgment on most of the separate peace effort, but Hughes based much of it on policies the former president had inaugurated.

In the Yap controversy, Secretary Hughes carried on with Wilson's demand for recognition of American rights both to stop Japanese expansionism and to establish a policy of equal economic opportunity for all in the mandates.

---

[3]Gilbert, *The Mirrors of Washington*, p. 34.

[4]H.L. Mencken, *A Carnival of Buncombe*, ed. Malcolm Moos (Baltimore: Johns Hopkins University Press, 1956), p. 296.

[5]William Hard to Johnson, 2 November 1923, part 3, box 42, Johnson Papers.

However Hughes the legalist far outdistanced Wilson the professor in securing those rights effectively, bypassing Wilson's pedantic argument based on what had allegedly been said in Paris, noting instead that the Allies had proceeded illegally in not making formal arrangements with the United States before dividing up the trust territories. To weaken Japan's diplomatic and military position, the secretary also escalated Wilson's campaign against the Anglo-Japanese alliance, an initiative which culminated at the Washington Conference, where he linked the Four Power Pact with a compromise Japanese-American settlement on North Pacific mandates.

Hughes took a cue from the former president's wartime pragmatism as embodied in the Lansing-Ishii Agreement, when Wilson shelved the Open Door in practice while reaffirming the principle on paper. In the Yap negotiations, the Republican secretary of state called for Japanese recognition of the Open Door in its mandate, but settled as a matter of practical policy for less than full equality of treatment because of the low trade potential of the area. Hughes did not have any more success than Wilson in implementing the Open Door in Asia; still he used the Yap settlement as a precedent for demanding equal treatment in French African and Near Eastern mandates, Belgian East Africa, and, eventually, in British trusts after a bitter Anglo-American confrontation over the future of Western enterprise in Turkey.

The United States never declared war on Turkey, although that did not stop either Wilson or Hughes from immersing the nation in the long and involved Near Eastern peace process. At Paris Wilson blocked Allied attempts to implement secret wartime treaties calling for the partition of the Ottoman Empire among the victors. At San Remo in 1920, the Allies distributed mandates from Turkish territories among themselves, an action which brought an immediate written protest from the Wilson administration. Even after the crushing Democratic defeat in the 1920 election, Secretary of State Colby continued to object to the Allied carving of spheres, reiterating President Wilson's faith in an Open Door world as the surest path to peace and prosperity. When Hughes became secretary of state, he carried on the acrimonious correspondence with Whitehall out of a belief, as Wilson had once confided to Frank Polk, that Britain might be "capable of as great commercial savagery as Germany."[6] Two and one half years later, Hughes sent a team of diplomatic observers to the Lausanne Conference, in spite of President Harding's misgivings, to counter the British-led movement for a closed door in the Near East.

America also sent observers to Lausanne to protect the interests of Near Eastern Christians, especially the Armenians, against the resurgent Turks. In the days after the Great War, Hughes had worked diligently on behalf of an Armenian homeland, surpassing even Wilson in his determination to see the establishment of a Christian state. But by 1922, with Armenia overrun and American troops demobilized, Hughes saw little point in antagonizing the

---

[6]Quoted in Smith, *Aftermath of War*, pp. 46–47.

Turks over a dead issue. Early in the Lausanne Conference, when Lord Curzon traded away Armenia's last hope for independence, the observers could do little, for Hughes had put them on a short leash to avoid stirring up the irreconcilables. As the conference wore on and public opinion seemed to favor American participation, the secretary gave his diplomats more freedom of action.

At the resumed conference, Grew blocked British attempts to confirm monopolistic Allied prewar petroleum concessions, an Open Door victory which turned out to be quite hollow. In the end, as with Yap, Hughes scrapped the Open Door, approving an American oil cartel's entrance into the Allied oil monopoly. In his enthusiastic—if futile—pursuit of the idealistic Open Door policy inherited from the previous administration, Hughes laid the State Department open to charges of trading blood for oil which led to the defeat of the Turkish-American treaty in the Senate. Wilson's and Hughes's Near Eastern policies both must be judged net failures because they did not balance their concerns for human rights and the Open Door. President Wilson crusaded for the lost cause of Armenia while confining himself to written protests of the Allied closed-door scheme. Hughes chased economics principles too relentlessly at a time when American influence and power might have been brought effectively to bear on behalf of humanitarian concerns.

Early in the Harding administration, Secretary Hughes sent unofficial diplomatic observers to the Reparation Commission, the Supreme Council, and the Council of Ambassadors just as Wilson and Colby had in 1919. The German-American claims settlement of 1922 made the secretary even more interested in the outcome of the ongoing crisis over reparations which kept Germany perpetually broke and unable to meet claims obligations and army occupation costs owed to the United States. When the Allies told Americans "to whistle for our money," as Hughes put it, by failing to allocate a cut of German payments to the United States, the secretary called, first privately and then publicly, for a committee of businessmen to recommend revisions in the reparations settlement made in the aftermath of Versailles. While the diplomatic initiative did not prevent France from invading the Ruhr, the administration, with the help of Britain, finally pressured the French into accepting a "businesslike" approach to the problem. When it appeared that there might be delays in implementing the resulting Dawes Plan, Hughes went to Europe to gain final British and French agreement.

Unlike Wilson, who went to Paris just after the war with passions still running high, Hughes used time as an ally, waiting until the harsh policies of the victors against Germany had brought Europe to the brink of financial ruin and war. As a final incentive, Hughes, taking another cue from Wilson, held the Allies accountable for their debts and, as time wore on, the pressure became irresistible. Thus the secretary of state triumphed where the former president had failed in imposing on Europe a limited reparations settlement based on Germany's capacity to pay. Both men favored moderate reparations

as a means of making Germany a great industrial power again while recon-
structing France and Belgium, a policy which would help to expand the world
economy on the basis of equal opportunity, not the Allied system of the closed
door. Hughes finally succeeded in carrying out an American solution to the
reparations tangle remarkably like the one Wilson first proposed several years
earlier.

The Senate rejected American entrance into the League of Nations, an
organization Wilson hoped to use, among other things, to help remove national
economic barriers to the flow of trade and to provide equal access to all world
markets. Secretary Hughes could not use that avenue; instead he approached
the challenge of creating an Open Door world through a series of bilateral
treaties. The Harding administration faced yet another handicap in that Congress insisted upon raising the tariff. Although economic internationalists such
as Hughes and Culbertson regarded the rates in the Fordney-McCumber bill
as excessive, they chose to view the new tariff as a triumph for the Open
Door because of flexibility provisions and language implying a changeover
to the use of the unconditional most-favored-nation principle. In 1923 Hughes
set out with hopes high to align the American commercial treaty system with
the Open Door policy. Beginning with the former Central Powers, the secretary
of state negotiated a series of pacts using the unconditional clause to automatically give and receive all third-party privileges granted to another nation.
The high tariff, congressional reservations demanding the right to revoke
national treatment, and continuing European evasions of equal treatment provisions frustrated Hughes (and then Kellogg and Stimson) in their Republican
approach to a Wilsonian ideal.

Wilson was an idealist with a lofty vision of a new world of peace and
prosperity and of America's role in this new order. The president's idealism
also coincided in great measure with the national interest of the United States;
his insistence on a modified free trade system based on the Open Door was
designed to assure the continuing expansion of American exports, a condition
Wilson and his advisers perceived as vital for the maintenance of prosperity
at home in the coming years. This practical side of the New Diplomacy
appealed to business-oriented internationalist Republicans led by Hughes and
Hoover. Consequently they adopted much of the Democratic president's program for economic expansion as their own in the 1920s.

Secretary Hughes had, in the words of Clinton Wallace Gilbert, "an
analytical, not a synthetical mind, a lawyer's mind, not a creator's like Wilson's, with, perhaps it may turn out, a fatal habit of oversimplification."[7] The
cautious corporate lawyer seldom plunged into foreign policy problems the
way Wilson did. These differences in style and temperament led each man
to be somewhat contemptuous of the other. "A greatly overestimated man,"
Wilson said of the secretary in early 1923, ". . . he has certain qualities of

---

[7]Gilbert, *The Mirrors of Washington*, p. 73.

industry in a prepared course, but goes to the core of nothing."[8] In his *Autobiographical Notes*, Hughes recalled meeting Wilson for the first time in 1907, when the future president recited a favorite limerick:

> There was a young man of Siberia
> Whose life grew drearier and drearier,
> So he burst from his cell
> With a hell of a yell
> And eloped with the Mother Superior.

Hughes later interpreted the rhyme "in a figurative sense, to be autobiographical," meaning, perhaps, that after many dreary years in sheltered academia Wilson yearned even then to burst upon the world stage in an incautious bid for immortality.[9]

Changing times and circumstances also have to be considered when comparing the foreign policies of these two very different individuals. In the 1920s American foreign policymakers faced a Congress eager to establish popular control over foreign affairs, a factor which made the already cautious Hughes even more so. He had witnessed Wilson's tragic confrontation with the Senate and acted accordingly. When necessary, the secretary of state retreated from showdowns only to develop resourceful ways and means of circumventing the irreconcilables. For all his cleverness in dealing with a series of recalcitrant Congresses, Hughes still had to work within a narrow domestic political framework which often left him frustrated. The Democratic *Brooklyn Eagle* summed up the frustration which the internationalists felt during the era of political isolationism, commenting after the defeat of the Turkish-American treaty, "Here is another illustration of how the absence of accurate information and ill-founded prejudice hamper American interests abroad. We are imperial in pretension but provincial in understanding."[10]

Senator Borah's idea that American foreign policy could be separated into distinct political and economic compartments was not inherently contradictory. While he believed that the nation had to find foreign markets for farm goods, he also stressed—just as rural leaders had since the days of Thomas Jefferson—that international political involvement did not inevitably follow. Nevertheless the Lion of Idaho failed to consider that the realities of the modern industrial age and America's emergence as a great power made this traditional ideal of American foreign policy more and more elusive. Hughes understood the nation's changing role in the world better than Borah did, yet he also failed to face up to the correlation between enhanced economic and political power. Political entanglement with Europe could be avoided, Hughes believed, if the United States used its enormous economic power wisely. The

---

[8]Quoted in Baker, *American Chronicle*, p. 501.
[9]Hughes, *Autobiographical Notes*, pp. 153–56.
[10]Quoted in *American Public Opinion*, 711.672/568, DSNA.

secretary chose to play an international political role primarily through economics—and more often than not Borah approved. When Hughes saw that vital American political interests were at stake, he dealt with Europe, but only through unofficial observers, even playing that role himself during the implementation of the Dawes Plan.

Wilson and Hughes both understood the need of the American economic system for expansion. The two also coupled practical economic requirements to more altruistic ideas of disarmament and freer trade. President Wilson wanted to use the League while Hughes advocated a series of piecemeal initiatives, but they had the same ends in mind. The ideology of Wilson left much less room for the admission that the United States would still be following a policy of enlightened self-interest. However he did not remain in office long enough after the war to face the contradictions caused by the pursuit of world and national interests simultaneously.

Hughes was the more candid of the two in admitting that America came first even as he continued to espouse his brand of idealism, a style Lord Hankey described as "that strange mixture of high moral purpose and practical bargaining, which I had always thought peculiar to President Wilson."[11] Hughes reminded the British diplomat of Wilson because the continuities in the two administrations in foreign policy, especially in peacemaking activities, far outweighed the discontinuities. In that sense many of Wilson's ideas survived the president's losing battle with the Senate and outlived Wilson himself and even Hughes, who lived long enough to observe another set of American leaders, Franklin D. Roosevelt and Harry S. Truman, wrestling with the same ideals and contradictions in the aftermath of another crusade to make the world safe for democracy.

[11]Hankey (Washington delegation) to Lloyd George, undated, *DBFP*, 14:572.

BIBLIOGRAPHY

MANUSCRIPTS

Ayres, Leonard P. Hoover Institution on War, Revolution and Peace, Stanford University, Stanford, CA.
——. Library of Congress, Washington.
Borah, William E. Library of Congress, Washington.
Boyden, Roland W. Hoover Institution on War, Revolution and Peace, Stanford University, Stanford, CA. Microfilm.
Bristol, Mark L. Library of Congress, Washington.
Castle, William R., Jr. Herbert Hoover Presidential Library, West Branch, IA.
Child, Richard W. Library of Congress, Washington.
Coolidge, Calvin. National Archives and Records Service, Washington. Microfilm.
Culbertson, William S. Library of Congress, Washington.
Davis, Norman H. Library of Congress, Washington.
Dresel, Ellis L. Houghton Library, Harvard University, Cambridge, MA.
Grew, Joseph C. Houghton Library, Harvard University, Cambridge, MA.
Harding, Warren G. Ohio State Historical Society, Columbus, OH. Microfilm.
Hoover, Herbert C. Herbert Hoover Presidential Library, West Branch, IA.
——. Hoover Institution on War, Revolution and Peace, Stanford University, Stanford, CA.
Hornbeck, Stanley K. Hoover Institution on War, Revolution and Peace, Stanford University, Stanford, CA.
Hughes, Charles Evans. Library of Congress, Washington.
Johnson, Hiram. Bancroft Library, University of California (Berkeley).
Kellogg, Frank B. Minnesota State Historical Society, Minneapolis, MN. Microfilm.
Knox, Philander C. Library of Congress, Washington.
Logan, James A., Jr. Hoover Institution on War, Revolution and Peace, Stanford University, Stanford, CA.
Robinson, Henry M. Hoover Institution on War, Revolution and Peace, Stanford University, Stanford, CA.
Strong, Benjamin. Herbert Hoover Presidential Library, West Branch, IA.
Wilson, Woodrow. National Archives and Records Service, Washington. Microfilm.
Young, Arthur N. Hoover Institution on War, Revolution and Peace, Stanford University, Stanford, CA.

DEPARTMENT OF STATE RECORDS

Papers Relating to the Foreign Relations of the United States. Volumes for
   1920–29 and the Paris Peace Conference. Washington: Government
   Printing Office, 1935–46.

General Records of the Department of State, Record Group 59. Washington:
   National Archives and Records Service.
   462.00 R29   Reparation from Germany in Accordance with the Treaty
                  of Versailles.
   462.00 R294   Army Costs To Be Paid by Germany.
   462.00 R296   Germany, Financial and Businessmen's Commission.
   463.00 R29   Reparation from Austria in Accordance with the Treaty
                  of St. Germain-En-Laye.
   464.00 R29   Reparation from Hungary in Accordance with the Treaty
                  of Trianon.
   611.0031   Trade Relations, Tariff Treaties, Arrangements, etc.
                  Between the United States and Foreign Countries.

General Records of the Department of State, Record Group 59. Washington:
   National Archives and Records Service. Microfilm.
   M336   Internal Affairs of Germany, 1910–1929, 182 rolls.
   M353   Internal Affairs of Turkey, 1910–1929, 88 rolls.
   M355   Political Relations Between the United States and Germany,
           1910–1929, 4 rolls.
   M363   Political Relations Between Turkey and Other States, 1910–
           1929, 29 rolls.
   M365   Political Relations Between the United States and Turkey,
           1910–1929, 8 rolls.
   M695   Internal Affairs of Austria–Hungary and Austria, 1910–1929,
           69 rolls.
   M696   Political Relations Between the United States and Austria–
           Hungary and Austria, 1910–1929, 4 rolls.
   M709   Political Relations Between the United States and Austria–
           Hungary and Hungary, 1921–1929, 1 roll.

OTHER DOCUMENTS AND OFFICIAL SOURCES

Great Britain. Foreign Office. *Documents on British Foreign Policy, 1919–
   1939.* Rohan Butler, J.P.T. Bury, and M.E. Lambert, eds. First Series.
   21 vols. London: Her Majesty's Stationery Office, 1947–78.

Hurewitz, Jacob C., ed. *Diplomacy in the Near and Middle East: A Documentary Record, 1535–1956*. 2 vols. Princeton, NJ: D. Van Nostrand, 1956.

Israel, Fred L., ed. *The Chief Executive: Inaugural Addresses of the Presidents of the United States from George Washington to Lyndon B. Johnson*. New York: Crown, 1965.

———, ed. *The State of the Union Messages of the Presidents, 1790–1966*. 3 vols. New York: Chelsea House, 1966.

Mantoux, Paul. *Les Délibérations Du Conseil Des Quatres (24 Mars–28 Juin)*. Paris: Editions du Centre National de la Recherche Scientifique, 1955.

Porter, Kirk H., and Johnson, Donald Bruce, eds. *National Party Platforms, 1840–1960*. Urbana: University of Illinois Press, 1969.

The Treaties of Peace, 1919–1923. 2 vols. New York: Carnegie Endowment for International Peace, 1924.

U.S., Congress. *Congressional Record* containing proceedings and debates from the following sessions: 67th Cong, 1st sess.; 67th Cong., 2nd sess.; 68th Cong., 1st sess.; 69th Cong., 1st sess.; and 69th Cong., 2nd sess. Washington: Government Printing Office, 1921–27.

———. Senate. Committee on Foreign Relations. *Hearings on the German Commerce Treaty*. 68th Cong., 1st sess. Washington: Government Printing Office, 1924.

———. Senate. *American War Claims Against Germany*. Senate Document 173. 69th Cong., 2nd sess. Washington: Government Printing Office, 1927.

U.S., Department of Commerce. Bureau of Foreign and Domestic Commerce. *Statistical Abstracts of the United States, 1922*. Washington: Government Printing Office, 1922.

U.S., Federal Reserve Board. "Report of Committees of Experts to the Reparation Commission." *Federal Reserve Bulletin* 10 (May 1924):351–417.

U.S., Tariff Commission. *Second Annual Report*. Washington: Government Printing Office, 1918.

———. *Third Annual Report*. Washington: Government Printing Office, 1919.

———. *Sixth Annual Report*. Washington: Government Printing Office, 1923.

U.S., World War Foreign Debt Commission. *Combined Annual Reports of the World War Foreign Debt Commission*. Washington: Government Printing Office, 1927.

AUTOBIOGRAPHIES, DIARIES, MEMOIRS, PERSONAL ACCOUNTS, AND PUBLISHED LETTERS

Allen, Henry T. *My Rhineland Journal*. Boston: Houghton Mifflin, 1923.

Baker, Ray Stannard. *American Chronicle*. New York: Charles Scribner's Sons, 1935.

——, and Dodd, William E., eds. *The Public Papers of Woodrow Wilson.* 6 vols. New York: Harper and Brothers, 1925–27.

Child, Richard Washburn. *A Diplomat Looks at Europe.* New York: Duffield, 1925.

Churchill, Winston S. *The Second World War.* Vol. 1, *The Gathering Storm.* Boston: Houghton Mifflin, 1977.

Culbertson, William S. *Reciprocity: A National Policy for Foreign Trade.* New York: McGraw-Hill, 1937.

Dawes, Charles G. *A Journal of Reparations.* London: Macmillan, 1939.

[Gilbert, Clinton Wallace]. *The Mirrors of Washington.* New York: G. P. Putnam's Sons, 1921.

Grew, Joseph C. *Turbulent Era: A Diplomatic Record of Forty Years, 1904–1945.* Ed. Walter Johnson. 2 vols. Boston: Houghton Mifflin, 1952.

Hoover, Herbert C. *The Memoirs of Herbert Hoover.* Vol. 2, *The Cabinet and the Presidency.* New York: Macmillan, 1952.

Houston, David F. *Eight Years with Wilson's Cabinet.* 2 vols. New York: Doubleday, Page, 1926.

Hughes, Charles Evans. *The Autobiographical Notes of Charles Evans Hughes.* Ed. David J. Danelski and Joseph S. Tulchin. Cambridge, MA: Harvard University Press, 1973.

——. *The Pathway of Peace.* New York: Harper and Brothers, 1925.

Hull, Cordell. *The Memoirs of Cordell Hull.* 2 vols. New York: Macmillan, 1948.

Lamont, Thomas W. *Across World Frontiers.* New York: Harcourt, Brace, 1951.

Lansing, Robert. *The Peace Negotiations: A Personal Narrative.* Boston: Houghton Mifflin, 1921.

Mencken, H. L. *A Carnival of Buncombe.* Ed. Malcolm Moos. Baltimore: Johns Hopkins University Press, 1956.

Norris, George. *Fighting Liberal: The Autobiography of George W. Norris.* New York: Macmillan, 1945.

Phillips, William. *Ventures in Diplomacy.* Boston: Beacon Press, 1953.

Quint, Howard H., and Ferrell, Robert H., eds. *The Talkative President: The Off-the-Record Press Conferences of Calvin Coolidge.* Amherst: University of Massachusetts Press, 1964.

Seymour, Charles, ed. *The Intimate Papers of Colonel House, III.* 4 vols. Boston: Houghton Mifflin, 1928.

Wilson, Woodrow. *President Wilson's State Papers and Addresses.* New York: George H. Doran, 1918.

BIOGRAPHIES

Ashby, LeRoy. *The Spearless Leader: Senator Borah and the Progressive Movement in the 1920's.* Urbana: University of Illinois Press, 1972.

Bryn-Jones, David. *Frank B. Kellogg: A Biography*. New York: G. P. Putnam's Sons, 1937.

Burner, David. *Herbert Hoover: A Public Life*. New York: Alfred A. Knopf, 1979.

DeWitt, Howard A. "Hiram Johnson and American Foreign Policy, 1917–1941." Ph.D. diss., University of Arizona, 1972.

Garraty, John A. *Henry Cabot Lodge: A Biography*. New York: Alfred A. Knopf, 1953.

Gilbert, Martin. *Sir Horace Rumbold: Portrait of a Diplomat*. London: Heinemann, 1973.

———. *Winston S. Churchill*. Vol. 5, *The Prophet of Truth, 1922–1939*. Boston: Houghton Mifflin, 1977.

Glad, Betty. *Charles Evans Hughes and the Illusions of Innocence: A Study in American Diplomacy*. Urbana: University of Illinois Press, 1966.

Heinrichs, Waldo H., Jr. *American Ambassador: Joseph C. Grew and the Development of the United States Diplomatic Tradition*. Boston: Little Brown, 1966.

Johnson, Claudius O. *Borah of Idaho*. Seattle: University of Washington Press, 1967.

Johnson, Evans C. *Oscar W. Underwood: A Political Biography*. Baton Rouge: Louisiana State University Press, 1980.

Kinross, Lord. *Ataturk: A Biography of Mustapha Kemal*. New York: William Morrow, 1965.

Link, Arthur S. *Wilson: Confusions and Crises, 1915–1916*. Princeton, NJ: Princeton University Press, 1964.

———. *Wilson the Diplomatist: A Look at His Major Foreign Policies*. Chicago: Quadrangle, 1965.

———. *Wilson: The New Freedom*. Princeton, NJ: Princeton University Press, 1967.

———. *Wilson: The Road to the White House*. Princeton, NJ: Princeton University Press, 1947.

Lowitt, Richard. *George W. Norris: The Persistence of a Progressive, 1918–1933*. Urbana: University of Illinois Press, 1971.

Maddox, Robert J. *William E. Borah and American Foreign Policy*. Baton Rouge: Louisiana State University Press, 1969.

Margulies, Herbert F. *Senator Lenroot of Wisconsin: A Political Biography, 1900–1929*. Columbia: University of Missouri Press, 1977.

Mott, T. Bentley. *Myron T. Herrick, Friend of France*. Garden City, NY: Doubleday, Doran, 1929.

Murray, Robert K. *The Harding Era: Warren G. Harding and His Administration*. Minneapolis: University of Minnesota Press, 1969.

Nicolson, Harold. *Curzon: The Last Phase, 1919–1925*. New York: Harcourt, Brace, 1939.

Osborn, George Coleman. *John Sharp Williams, Planter-Statesman of the Deep South*. Baton Rouge: Louisiana State University Press, 1943.

Perkins, Dexter. *Charles Evans Hughes and American Democratic Statesman-
ship*. Boston: Little, Brown, 1956.
Pusey, Merlo. *Charles Evans Hughes*. 2 vols. New York: Macmillan, 1951.
Rowland, Peter. *Lloyd George*. London: Barris and Jenkins, 1975.
Russell, Francis. *The Shadow of Blooming Grove: Warren G. Harding in His
Times*. New York: McGraw-Hill, 1968.
Tarbell, Ida M. *Owen D. Young, A New Type of Industrial Leader*. New
York: Macmillan, 1932.
Trani, Eugene P., and Wilson, David L. *The Presidency of Warren G. Hard-
ing*. Lawrence: Regents of Kansas, American Presidency Series, 1977.
Woodward, C. Vann. *Tom Watson, Agrarian Rebel*. New York: Oxford Uni-
versity Press, 1963.

MONOGRAPHS AND GENERAL HISTORICAL WORKS

Adler, Selig. *The Isolationist Impulse: Its Twentieth Century Reaction*. New
York: Collier, 1961.
———. *The Uncertain Giant: 1921–1941*. London: Collier, 1965.
Anderson, M. S. *The Eastern Question, 1774–1923*. London: St. Martin's
Press, 1966.
Bagby, Wesley M. *The Road to Normalcy: The Presidential Campaign and
Election of 1920*. Johns Hopkins University Studies in Historical and
Political Science. Vol. 80. Baltimore: Johns Hopkins University Press,
1962.
Bailey, Thomas A. *Woodrow Wilson and the Great Betrayal*. Chicago: Quad-
rangle, 1963.
Barker, Elisabeth. *Austria, 1918–1972*. Coral Gables, FL: University of Miami
Press, 1973.
Beers, Burton F. *Vain Endeavor: Robert Lansing's Attempts to End the
American-Japanese Rivalry*. Durham, NC: Duke University Press, 1962.
Bemis, Samuel Flagg. *The United States as a World Power: A Diplomatic
History, 1900–1955*. New York: Henry Holt, 1955.
Bergmann, Carl. *The History of Reparations*. Boston: Houghton Mifflin, 1927.
Bernstein, Barton J., ed. *Towards a New Past: Dissenting Essays in American
History*. New York: Random House, 1968.
Brandes, Joseph. *Herbert Hoover and Economic Diplomacy*. Pittsburgh: Uni-
versity of Pittsburgh Press, 1962.
Buckley, Thomas H. *The United States and the Washington Conference,
1921–1922*. Knoxville: University of Tennessee Press, 1970.
Burns, Richard Dean, and Bennett, Edward M., eds. *Diplomats in Crisis:
United States–Chinese–Japanese, 1919–1941*. Santa Barbara, CA: Clio
Press, 1974.

Busch, Briton Cooper. *Mudros to Lausanne: Britain's Frontier in West Asia, 1918–1923*. Albany: State University of New York Press, 1976.

Carr, Edward H. *A History of Soviet Russia*. Vol 3, *The Bolshevik Revolution*. New York: Harper and Row, 1966.

———. *International Relations Between the Two World Wars, 1919–1939*. New York: Harper and Row, 1966.

Churchill, Winston S. *The Aftermath, 1918–1923*. New York: Charles Scribner's Sons, 1929.

Clarke, Stephen V. O. *Central Bank Cooperation, 1924–1931*. New York: Federal Reserve Bank, 1967.

Clyde, Paul H. *Japan's Pacific Mandate*. New York: Macmillan, 1935.

Collins, Harry T., ed. *Tariff Problems of the United States*. Philadelphia: American Academy of Political and Social Science, 1928.

Craig, Gordon A. *Germany, 1866–1945*. New York: Oxford University Press, 1978.

Curry, Roy Watson. *Woodrow Wilson and Far Eastern Policy, 1913–1921*. New York: Octagon, 1968.

Daniel, Robert L. *American Philanthropy in the Near East, 1820–1960*. Athens, OH: Ohio State University Press, 1970.

DeConde, Alexander, ed. *Encyclopedia of American Foreign Policy: Studies of the Principal Movements and Ideas*. 3 vols. New York: Charles Scribner's Sons, 1978.

DeNovo, John A. *American Interests and Policies in the Middle East, 1900–1939*. Minneapolis: University of Minnesota Press, 1963.

Diamond, William. *The Economic Thought of Woodrow Wilson*. Baltimore: Johns Hopkins University Press, 1943.

Dobson, John M. *Two Centuries of Tariffs: The Background and Emergence of the U.S. International Tariff Commission*. Washington: Government Printing Office, 1976.

Dudden, Arthur P., ed. *Woodrow Wilson and the World of Today*. Philadelphia: University of Pennsylvania Press, 1957.

Duroselle, Jean-Baptiste. *From Wilson to Roosevelt: Foreign Policy of the United States, 1913–1945*, trans. Nancy Lyman Roelker. Cambridge, MA: Harvard University Press, 1968.

Ellis, L. Ethan. *Republican Foreign Policy, 1921–1933*. New Brunswick, NJ: Rutgers University Press, 1968.

Evans, Laurence. *United States Policy and the Partition of Turkey, 1914–1924*. Baltimore: Johns Hopkins University Press, 1965.

Eyck, Erich. *A History of the Weimar Republic*. 2 vols. New York: Atheneum, 1970.

Feis, Herbert. *The Diplomacy of the Dollar: The First Era, 1919–1932*. Baltimore: Johns Hopkins University Press, 1950.

Felix, David. *Walter Rathenau and the Weimar Republic: The Politics of Reparations*. Baltimore: Johns Hopkins University Press, 1971.

Ferrell, Robert H. *American Diplomacy in the Great Depression: Hoover–Stimson Foreign Policy, 1929–1933.* New Haven, CT: Yale University Press, 1957.

Fleming, Denna Frank. *The United States and World Organization, 1920–1933.* New York: Columbia University Press, 1938.

Fry, Michael G. *Illusions of Security: North Atlantic Diplomacy, 1918–1922.* Toronto: University of Toronto Press, 1972.

Galbraith, John Kenneth. *The Great Crash, 1929.* Boston: Houghton Mifflin, 1961.

Garraty, John A., ed. *A Treasury of American Heritage: A Selection from the First Five Years of the Magazine of History.* New York: Simon and Schuster, 1960.

Gibb, George S., and Knowlton, Evelyn H. *History of Standard Oil Company (New Jersey).* Vol. 2, *The Resurgent Years, 1911–1927.* New York: Harper and Brothers, 1956.

Grabill, Joseph L. *Protestant Diplomacy in the Near East.* Minneapolis: University of Minnesota Press, 1971.

Graebner, Norman A., ed. *An Uncertain Tradition: American Secretaries of State in the Twentieth Century.* New York: McGraw-Hill, 1961.

Graham, Malbone W., Jr. *New Governments of Central Europe.* New York: Henry Holt, 1924.

Griswold, A. Whitney. *The Far Eastern Policy of the United States.* New Haven, CT: Yale University Press, 1966.

Gulick, Charles A. *Austria from Hapsburg to Hitler.* 2 vols. Berkeley: University of California Press, 1948.

Haines, C. Grove, and Hoffman, Ross S. J. *The Origins and Background of the Second World War.* New York: Oxford University Press, 1947.

Helmreich, Paul C. *From Paris to Sèvres: The Partition of the Ottoman Empire at the Peace Conference of 1919–1920.* Columbus: Ohio State University Press, 1974.

Hicks, John D. *Republican Ascendancy, 1921–1933.* New York: Harper and Row, 1963.

Hogan, Michael J. *Informal Entente: The Private Structure of Cooperation in Anglo–American Economic Diplomacy, 1918–1928.* Columbia: University of Missouri Press, 1977.

Howard, Harry N. *The Partition of Turkey: A Diplomatic History.* Norman: University of Oklahoma Press, 1931.

———. *Turkey, the Straits, and U.S. Policy.* Baltimore: Johns Hopkins University Press, 1974.

Howland, Charles P., ed. *Survey of American Foreign Relations, 1928.* New Haven, CT: Yale University Press, 1928.

Hulen, Bertram D. *Inside the Department of State.* York: Maple Press, 1939.

Isle, John. *The United States Oil Policy.* New Haven, CT: Yale University Press, 1926.

Jervis, Robert. *Perception and Misperception in International Politics*. Princeton, NJ: Princeton University Press, 1976.

Jones, Kenneth Paul, ed. *U.S. Diplomats in Europe, 1919–1941*. Santa Barbara, CA: Clio Press, 1981.

Kelly, William B., Jr., ed. *Studies in United States Commercial Policy*. Chapel Hill: University of North Carolina Press, 1963.

Kennan, George F. *Russia and the West Under Lenin and Stalin*. Boston: Mentor Books, 1962.

King, Clyde, ed. *American Policy and International Security*. Philadelphia: American Academy of Political and Social Science, 1925.

Larkin, John Day. *The President's Control of the Tariff*. Cambridge, MA: Harvard University Press, 1936.

Leffler, Melvyn P. *The Elusive Quest: America's Pursuit of European Stability and French Security, 1919–1933*. Chapel Hill: University of North Carolina Press, 1978.

Lenczowski, George. *The Middle East in World Affairs*. Ithaca, NY: Cornell University Press, 1952.

Leuchtenburg, William E. *The Perils of Prosperity, 1914–32*. Chicago: University of Chicago Press, 1970.

Levin, N. Gordon. *Woodrow Wilson and World Politics: America's Response to War and Revolution*. New York: Oxford University Press, 1968.

Lewis, Bernard. *The Emergence of Modern Turkey*. London: Oxford University Press, 1961.

Lingenfelter, Sherwood Galen. *Yap: Political Leadership and Cultural Change in an Island Society*. Honolulu: University of Hawaii Press, 1975.

Longrigg, Stephen H. *Oil in the Middle East: Its Discovery and Development*. London: Oxford University Press, 1968.

——. *Syria and Lebanon Under French Mandate*. London: Oxford University Press, 1958.

McDougall, Walter A. *France's Rhineland Diplomacy, 1914–1924: The Last Bid for a Balance of Power in Europe*. Princeton, NJ: Princeton University Press, 1978.

Marks, Sally. *The Illusion of Peace: International Relations in Europe, 1918–1933*. London: Macmillan, 1976.

May, Ernest R. *The World War and American Isolation, 1914–1917*. Chicago: Quadrangle, 1959.

Medlicott, W. N. *British Foreign Policy Since Versailles, 1919–1963*. London: Methuen, 1968.

Mikesell, Raymond F. *United States Economic Policy and International Relations*. New York: McGraw-Hill, 1952.

Mosley, Leonard. *Power Play: Oil in the Middle East*. New York: Random House, 1973.

Moulton, Harold G., and Pasvolsky, Leo. *War Debts and World Prosperity*. 2 vols. Port Washington, NY: Kennikat, 1971.

Murray, Robert K. *The Politics of Normalcy: Governmental Theory and Practice in the Harding–Coolidge Era.* New York: W. W. Norton, 1973.

Nearing, Scott, and Freeman, Joseph. *Dollar Diplomacy: A Study in American Imperialism.* New York: Monthly Review Press, 1966.

Nelson, Keith L. *Victors Divided: America and the Allies in Germany, 1918–1923.* Berkeley: University of California Press, 1975.

Neu, Charles E. *The Troubled Encounter: The United States and Japan.* New York: John Wiley, 1975.

Noggle, Burl. *Into the Twenties: The United States from Armistice to Normalcy.* Urbana: University of Illinois Press, 1974.

Notter, Harley. *The Origins of the Foreign Policy of Woodrow Wilson.* Baltimore: Johns Hopkins University Press, 1937.

Pamlényi, Ervin, ed. *A History of Hungary.* London: Collet's, 1975.

Parrini, Carl P. *Heir to Empire: United States Economic Diplomacy, 1916–1923.* Pittsburgh: University of Pittsburgh Press, 1969.

Paxson, Frederic L. *American Democracy and the World War.* Vol. 3, *Postwar Years: Normalcy, 1918–1923.* Berkeley: University of California Press, 1948.

Payne, Howard C., Callahan, Raymond, and Bennett, Edward M. *As the Storm Clouds Gathered: European Perceptions of American Foreign Policy in the 1930's.* Durham, NC: Moore, 1979.

Potter, Jim. *The American Economy Between the World Wars.* New York: John Wiley, 1974.

Sachar, Howard M. *The Emergence of the Middle East, 1914–1924.* New York: Alfred A. Knopf, 1969.

Safford, Jeffrey J. *Wilsonian Maritime Diplomacy, 1913–1921.* Brunswick, NJ: Rutgers University Press, 1978.

Schmidt, Royal J. *Versailles and the Ruhr: Seedbed of World War II.* The Hague: Martinus Mijoff, 1968.

Schuker, Stephen A. *The End of French Predominance in Europe: The Financial Crisis of 1924 and the Adoption of the Dawes Plan.* Chapel Hill: University of North Carolina Press, 1976.

Seton-Watson, Hugh. *Eastern Europe Between the Wars, 1918–1941.* London: Cambridge University Press, 1945.

Shwadran, Benjamin. *The Middle East, Oil, and the Great Powers.* New York: Frederick A. Praeger, 1955.

Simonds, Frank H. *American Foreign Policy in the Post-War Years.* Baltimore: Johns Hopkins University Press, 1935.

Smith, Daniel M. *Aftermath of War: Bainbridge Colby and Wilsonian Diplomacy, 1920–1921.* Philadelphia: American Philosophical Society, 1970.

Stone, Ralph. *The Irreconcilables: The Fight Against the League of Nations.* Lexington: University of Kentucky Press, 1970.

Stuart, Graham H. *The Department of State: A History of its Organization, Procedure, and Personnel.* New York: Macmillan, 1949.

Sullivan, Mark. *Our Times, 1900–1925*. Vol 6, *The Twenties*. New York: Charles Scribner's Sons, 1946.

Trask, Roger R. *The United States Response to Turkish Nationalism and Reform, 1914–1939*. Minneapolis: University of Minnesota Press, 1971.

Upthegrove, Campbell L. *Empire by Mandate: A History of the Relations of Great Britain with the Permanent Mandates Commission of the League of Nations*. New York: Bookman Associates, 1954.

Vinson, John Chalmers. *The Parchment Peace: The United States and the Washington Conference, 1921–1922*. Athens: University of Georgia Press, 1955.

———. *William E. Borah and the Outlawry of War*. Athens: University of Georgia Press, 1957.

Walder, David. *The Chanak Crisis*. London: Macmillan, 1969.

Wilkins, Mira. *The Maturing of Multinational Enterprise: American Business Abroad from 1914–1970*. Cambridge, MA: Harvard University Press, 1974.

Williams, Benjamin H. *American Diplomacy: Policies and Practice*. New York: McGraw-Hill, 1936.

———. *Economic Foreign Policy of the United States*. New York: McGraw-Hill, 1929.

Williams, William Appleman, ed. *From Colony to Empire: Essays in the History of American Foreign Relations*. New York: John Wiley, 1972.

———. *The Tragedy of American Diplomacy*. Cleveland: World Press, 1959.

Wilson, Joan Hoff. *American Business and Foreign Policy, 1920–1933*. Lexington: University of Kentucky Press, 1971.

Wright, Quincy. *Mandates Under the League of Nations*. Chicago: University of Chicago Press, 1930.

Yamato, Ichihasi. *The Washington Conference and After: A Historical Survey*. Stanford, CA: Stanford University Press, 1928.

ARTICLES IN BOOKS AND JOURNALS, PAMPHLETS, NEWSPAPERS, AND PERIODICALS

"After the Ruhr Invasion—What?" *Literary Digest*, 20 January 1923, pp. 7–8.

The American Committee for the Independence of Armenia. "The Lausanne Treaty and Kemalist Turkey." New York: n.p., n.d.

"Britain, America, Japan, and Yap." *The Nation*, 4 May 1921, p. 664.

Buell, Raymond L. "Oil Interests in the Fight for Mosul." *Current History*, March 1923, pp. 933–35.

Chester, Colby M. "Turkey Reinterpreted." *Current History*, September 1922, pp. 939–47.

Costigliola, Frank. "The United States and the Reconstruction of Germany in the 1920's." *Business History Review* 50 (Winter 1976): 477–502.

Daniel, Robert L. "The Armenian Question and American Turkish Relations, 1914–1927." *Mississippi Valley Historical Review* 46 (June 1959): 252–75.

Davis, Norman H. "American Foreign Policy: A Democratic View." Foreign Affairs 3 (September 1924): 22–24.

———. "Comments Upon the Conference on the Limitation of Armaments and Far Eastern Questions." New York: Council on Foreign Relations, 1922.

"The Emergence of Yap." *Current Opinion*, April 1921, pp. 443–47.

Falkus, M. D. "The German Business Cycle in the 1920's." *Economic History Review* 27, 2nd ser. (1975): 451–65.

Grew, Joseph C. "The Press Conference of Lausanne, 1922–1923." *Department of State Bulletin*, 26 September 1955, pp. 498–506.

Hyde, Charles C. "Charles Evans Hughes." *The American Secretaries of State and Their Diplomacy.* Ed. Samuel Flagg Bemis. Vol. 10. New York: Pageant, 1958.

Lamont, Thomas W. "Three Examples of International Cooperation." *Atlantic Monthly*, September 1923, pp. 537–46.

Leffler, Melvyn. "The Origins of Republican War Debt Policy, 1921–1923: A Case Study in the Applicability of the Open Door Interpretation." *Journal of American History* 59 (December 1972): 585–601.

"New Bill of American Rights." *Outlook*, 4 May 1921, pp. 11–12.

New York Times for 1920–1927.

Nish, I. H. "Japan and the Ending of the Anglo–Japanese Alliance." *Studies in International History.* Ed. K. Bourne and D. C. Watt. Hamden, CT: Archon, 1967, pp. 369–84.

"Principle of Yap." *New Republic*, 4 May 1921, pp. 279–80.

"Putting World Peace Up to America." *Literary Digest*, 13 January 1923, pp. 16–17.

Snyder, J. Richard. "William S. Culbertson and the Formation of Modern Commercial Policy, 1917–1925." *Kansas Historical Quarterly* 35 (Winter 1969): 397–410.

Spencer, Frank. "The United States and Germany in the Aftermath of War." *International Affairs* 43, part 4 (1967): 693–703.

Temin, Peter. "The Beginning of the Depression in Germany." *Economic History Review* 24, 2nd ser. (1971): 240–48.

"That Chester Concession." *Current Opinion*, June 1923, p. 66.

Thayer, Lucius Ellsworth. "The Capitulations of the Ottoman Empire and the Question of Their Abrogation As It Affects the United States." *Journal of International Law* 17 (April 1923): 207–33.

"Uncle Sam Demands a Front Seat." *Independent*, 23 April 1921, pp. 428–29.

Wimer, Kurt, and Wimer, Sarah. "The Harding Administration, the League of Nations and the Separate Peace Treaty." *The Review of Politics* 29 (January 1967): 13–24.
"Yap and Djombi." *Outlook*, 11 May 1921, pp. 45–46.

INDEX

A

Africa, 54, 57, 63, 66, 70–71, 179
Alexandris, Apostol, 94
Alien Property Custodian, 25, 28
Allen, Henry T., 125–26
Allied Supreme Council, 27, 74, 111, 180
American Bar Association, 142
American Board of Commissioners for Foreign Missions, 101
American Committee Opposed to the Lausanne Treaty, 101
American Expeditionary Force, 125–26
American Historical Association, 70, 124
American Philosophical Society, 100
American Protective Tariff League, 160
Anatolia, 74, 75, 76
Anglo-Japanese alliance, 60–62, 65, 67, 179
Argentina, 171
Armenia, 9–10, 73, 76, 84, 87, 101–02, 106, 179–80
Army War College (U.S.), 29
Ataturk, Kemal, 74–79, 82, 86, 90
Atlantic Monthly, 130
Australia, 64
Austria, 12, 14, 18, 19, 23, 34, 36, 38, 66, 98, 116
    international loan for, 127–30
    plight of, 29–30, 127–28
Austrian-American commercial treaty (1928), 154, 162, 170–73, 176, 181
Ayres, Leonard P., 135–36, 138

B

Baldwin, Stanley, 131
Balfour, Arthur, 65, 69, 121
Bánffy, Nicholas, 31–32
Bankers' Committee, 119–22, 130, 180
Barthou, Louis, 122, 132–33
Barton, James L., 101–04
Baruch, Bernard, 45
Beerits, Henry, 13n. 1
Belgium, 61, 70–71, 107–08, 117, 123, 125, 129, 136–37, 140, 144, 147, 163, 179
Bemis, Samuel Flagg, 4
Bethlen, Count, 169
Bismarck, Otto von, 163
Bliven, Bruce, 154
Blodgett, David T., 43
Borah, William E., 4, 5, 6, 16, 23, 35, 40, 102, 115, 146, 166
    as an economic internationalist, 178, 182–83
    opposes separate peace, 36–38, 43–52, 178
    opposes Yap Treaty, 66–69
    and Reparation Commission, 110, 126
    supports Knox resolution, 19
    supports Turkish-American treaty, 103–04
    as Wilson's moral successor, 41, 52, 178
Boyden, Roland W., 109, 111, 116, 118–24, 127–28, 139
Brandegee, Frank B., 16, 36, 38
Briand, Aristide, 108
Bristol, Mark L., 74–78, 82–83, 87–90, 101–02, 104–05

199